THE FORESTERS' SCRIBE

Members of the Newfoundland Forestry Companies, Craigvinean, Dunkeld, Scotland, 1917.
(Courtesy of The Rooms Provincial Archives Division, VA 55-5.1)

THE FORESTERS' SCRIBE

*Remembering the Newfoundland Forestry
Companies Through the First World War Letters of
Regimental Quartermaster Sergeant John A. Barrett*

URSULA A. KELLY

ISER Books

LIBRARY AND ARCHIVES CANADA CATALOGUING IN PUBLICATION

Title: The foresters' scribe : remembering the Newfoundland Forestry Companies through the First World War letters of Regimental Quartermaster Sergeant John A. Barrett / Ursula A. Kelly.

Names: Kelly, Ursula A. (Ursula Anne), 1956- author. | Container of (work): Barrett, John A., 1872-1955. Correspondence. Selections.

Series: Social and economic studies (St. John's, N.L.) ; no. 87.

Description: Series statement: Social and economic studies ; no. 87 | Includes bibliographical references and index.

Identifiers: Canadiana (print) 20200355082 | Canadiana (ebook) 20200355880 | ISBN 9781894725736 (softcover) | ISBN 9781894725842 (EPUB) | ISBN 9781894725859 (Kindle) | ISBN 9781894725866 (PDF)

Subjects: LCSH: Barrett, John A., 1872-1955—Correspondence. | LCSH: Great Britain. Army. Newfoundland Forestry Companies—History. | LCSH: World War, 1914-1918—Regimental histories—Great Britain. | LCSH: World War, 1914-1918—Personal narratives, Canadian. | LCSH: World War, 1914-1918—War work—Great Britain. | LCSH: World War, 1914-1918—War work—Newfoundland and Labrador. | LCSH: Lumbermen—Newfoundland and Labrador—Biography.

Classification: LCC D547.N55 K45 2020 | DDC 940.4/12718—dc23

Front cover images: Postcard portrait of Regimental Quartermaster Sergeant John A. Barrett by A.F. MacKenzie, Birnam, Scotland, 1918. (Courtesy of Archives and Special Collections, World War One Artifacts 09.01.004, Memorial University of Newfoundland). Newfoundland Forestry Companies shoulder badge. (Courtesy of Archives and Special Collections, World War One Artifacts 04.03.007, Memorial University of Newfoundland).

Back cover images: Newfoundland Regiment caribou pin. (Courtesy of Archives and Special Collections, World War One Artifacts 23.03.012, Memorial University of Newfoundland). Original letters of Regimental Quartermaster Sergeant John A. Barrett. (Courtesy of the Barrett family).

Copy editing: Sandy Newton

Cover design, page design and typesetting: Alison Carr

Published by ISER Books
Institute of Social and Economic Research
Memorial University of Newfoundland
PO Box 4200
St. John's, NL A1C 5S7
www.hss.mun.ca/iserbooks/

Printed in Canada
26 25 24 23 22 21 20   1 2 3 4 5 6 7 8

Funded by the Government of Canada | Canada

CONTENTS

LIST OF IMAGES

FOREWORD

Newfoundland and Labrador does not yet have a balanced historical overview of its participation in and contribution to the United Kingdom's effort in the First World War, an account that would be what St. John's journalist Sir Patrick T. McGrath (1928) called "a real record for all time of the part Newfoundland played, on sea and on land, abroad and at home, in the great struggle" (p. 2). In this regard, until the publication in 1964 of the government-commissioned history by Gerald W.L. Nicholson—*The Fighting Newfoundlander*—on the 50th anniversary of the start of the war, several previous efforts to produce a general account had fallen short. What had been completed and published generally concentrated on the gallant efforts of the Royal Newfoundland Regiment (RNR) and its heroic participation in the Battle of the Somme at Beaumont-Hamel on July 1, 1916. That tragedy, resulting in the near depletion of the Regiment's ranks, has received the most attention and understanding.

As historian James Candow (2016) recently observed in his review of The Rooms' major centenary commemoration of the war and postwar Newfoundland and Labrador, public memory is "dominated" by an emphasis on the Royal Newfoundland Regiment and Beaumont-Hamel. There has not been much commemoration for the thousands of other Newfoundland men and women who served in other branches of the country's military. There is much still to be known of all who served in the Newfoundland war effort—not only the soldiers of the Royal Newfoundland Regiment, but also the naval volunteers, merchant seamen, medical doctors, nurses, and airmen, as well as those who served directly in the armed forces of the UK, Canada, and the United States.

In *The Fighting Newfoundlander* (running to over 500 pages), Gerald Nicholson devoted nine pages, about 3,700 words, to one little-known aspect of the Newfoundland war effort, the Newfoundland Forestry Companies (NFC). Their service to King and Country has now been documented in Ursula Kelly's *The Foresters' Scribe*, which provides a welcome contribution to our understanding of another aspect of the Newfoundland war effort.

Newfoundland loggers in 1917 were needed to harvest forests in Scotland for the war, a safer alternative to the UK's dependence, now threatened by German submarines, on importing timber by sea from Norway, Finland, Sweden, Portugal, Canada, and the United States. Kelly provides a historical overview showing how the unit was established and the foresters were recruited, as well as detailed information on the controversies over commissions and other aspects of the NFC's formation. There is information on the recruits' transport to Scotland and life there, including their work and off-hours activities, their relationship to Canadian foresters, their ability to adapt their logging methods to meet local conditions, and their re-integration into civilian life in Newfoundland.

Kelly has published widely on the twentieth-century history of local loggers. Her latest effort is based on the published writings of Curling resident John A. Barrett, a journalist and forester who also served the Forestry Companies as their press correspondent, from its formation in April 1917 to the foresters' return to Newfoundland and the unit's disbandment in August 1919. Captain Leo Murphy did similar yeoman duty as a reporter for the Newfoundland Regiment. Kelly has compiled from the Newfoundland press Barrett's letters for the 1917–19 period, which describe the departure of the first foresters from Newfoundland to Scotland and their living and working conditions in Scotland. Kelly provides an analysis of the content of these letters as well as a biographical essay on Barrett, who—like several foresters—returned with a Scottish war bride.

Barrett's letters provided reassurances to those on the home front. On November 18, 1917, Barrett informed his Newfoundland readers that the foresters were well supplied with dried cod and that ten quintals had recently been received as "a free gift" from Bowring Brothers of Liverpool. "It is quite a treat," he wrote, "to have some of our own codfish served up to us once or twice a week, and it being such a palatable article, is much enjoyed in the mess." A month later, the foresters were visited at their work camps by Newfoundland Governor Sir William Davidson and Prime Minister Sir Edward Morris, who had gone first to France to visit the soldiers of the Newfoundland Regiment. The Governor informed the public on his return to Newfoundland that the "foresters have done their work thoroughly well." The Newfoundlanders had introduced a "number of improvements previously unknown in Scotland and looked upon as welcome novelties, and the output . . . was many times as great as the output would have been under normal conditions, if the work had been placed in the hands of local woodsmen."

Along with others ineligible for combat service, the Forestry Companies provided the opportunity for males over the age of 30 to participate directly in the war. Barrett was 43 when he enlisted, while John R. Martin, NFC #8232, of Manuels, for example, was 50 when he enlisted on June 9, 1917. (His son, Corporal Robert B. Martin, RNR #499, was a Blue Puttee.) More than 500 men served overseas in the NFC, with three deaths occurring in the line of service.

After the war, however, it was the exploits of the Royal Newfoundland Regiment that gained the most attention from government and public alike. Despite an apparent oversight from the Regiment's Padre, Father Thomas Nangle, foresters were included in the monument unveiled on July 1, 1924, at the National War Memorial in St. John's, but their contributions to the war effort have otherwise long been forgotten. *The Foresters' Scribe* is a major contribution in bringing the foresters back into the narrative of Newfoundland and Labrador's Great War history.

Melvin Baker, PhD
St. John's, NL

ACKNOWLEDGEMENTS

It was my great pleasure to meet and to consult with the family of John and Ena Barrett—their children Rose E. Barrett Gillam, David G. Barrett, and Arthur W.F. Barrett, and their grandchildren Helena Barrett MacLean and John Barrett. Together they deepened my understanding of Quartermaster Sergeant John A. Barrett and the postwar life of John and Ena. I thank each of them for graciously embracing this project and displaying consistent openness and generosity toward me.

I have been fortunate to meet and work with a large number of wonderful archivists and librarians during my research for this book. Jane Anderson, archivist at Blair Castle Archive, in Pitlochry, Perthshire, Scotland, fielded a steady stream of questions related to the area where the Newfoundland Forestry Companies worked. David Arbuthnott and Ruth Brown of Dunkeld Community Archive and Michael Haigh of Aberfeldy Museum, Perthshire, were also very helpful. I am thankful to the staff at The Rooms Provincial Archives, St. John's, in particular Melanie Tucker, Craig Tucker, Charles Young, and Larry Dohey, as well as to the staff at Library and Archives Canada, Ottawa. Kory Penney of the Maritime History Archive at Memorial University was also helpful. I have benefitted greatly from the expertise of Pauline Cox, archivist at the Memorial University of Newfoundland Folklore and Language Archive, throughout several other related projects. I also thank the staff of the Queen Elizabeth II Library of Memorial University, including those with Archives and Special Collections, the Digital Archives Initiative, and the Centre for Newfoundland Studies.

Many people in both Scotland and Newfoundland and Labrador answered questions or provided information, advice, or professional services to me. They include Major Michael Pretty, The Trail of the Caribou Research Group; Frank Gogos, Royal Newfoundland Regiment Museum, St. John's;

Sydney House, Forestry Commission Scotland; Norman Davidson, Forestry Memories, Scotland; Clive Ashton-Clements, Wee Country at War, Aberfeldy; David Mercer, Church Lads Brigade, St. John's; Daniel Devine, Grand Falls-Windsor Royal Canadian Legion #12 Museum; Dr. Ean Parsons, military and family historian, St. John's; Bryan Marsh, blogger, Paradise; Audrey Burke, Grand Falls-Windsor Heritage Society; Daphne Clarke, Trinity Historical Society; Neville Samson, Church of the Holy Martyrs, Port Union; Pat Angel, genealogist, St. John's; Myron R. King, Environmental Policy Institute, Grenfell Campus, Memorial University; and, Dr. Melvin Baker, prolific, generous, and respected historian of Newfoundland and Labrador.

I extend my thanks to the impressive team at ISER Books: Dr. Fiona Polack, a fabulous academic editor whose thoughtful suggestions strengthened my work; Alison Carr, the managing editor and designer, who listened carefully and patiently so as to create the elegant aesthetic of this book; and Randy Drover, book publicist and fine poet and conversationalist. I also thank the two anonymous reviewers who offered excellent suggestions, as well as enthusiasm and support for the book.

This book is the third project in as many years for which Sandy Newton was editor. It was my privilege and pleasure to collaborate again with such an exceptionally skilled and engaged editor. Sandy has an immense and positive impact on my experience of publishing and the quality of the finished product.

The Foresters' Scribe has been published with the help of a grant from the Federation for the Humanities and Social Sciences, through the Awards to Scholarly Publications Program, using funds provided by the Social Sciences and Humanities Research Council of Canada.

The expeditious writing of this book was enabled by a University Research Professorship. I sincerely appreciate the support of Memorial University and the Faculty of Education. I am especially thankful to Dr. Rhonda Joy, Associate Dean of Graduate Programs and Research, whose kindness and collegiality over the years have helped sustain me in my work. I also thank Dr. Karen Goodnough, Dean of Education, for her support. As well, I thank Cathy Madol and Helen Manning of the Finance and Administration Office of the Faculty of Education, who oversaw the research funds for this book and from whose diligence, integrity, and good will I benefit on a regular basis.

I warmly acknowledge my colleague and friend, ethnomusicologist Dr. Meghan Forsyth, School of Music, Memorial University, who was a collaborator on previous instalments of the "labour-of-love" series about the woods workers of Newfoundland and Labrador.

I am blessed with the friendship of Dr. Clar Doyle—scholar, educator, artist, playwright, theatre director, music aficionado, and more; truly, a man for all seasons.

I am thankful for the care and support of my siblings—Ed, Linda, Glenis, and Andrea—and a large cluster of nieces and nephews of whom I am immensely proud.

Finally, in all aspects of my life, I benefit immeasurably from the steadfast love and companionship of Patricia Singer.

ABBREVIATIONS

ANDCo – Anglo-Newfoundland Development Company

CEF – Canadian Expeditionary Force

CFC – Canadian Forestry Corps

FPU – Fishermen's Protective Union

GWVA – Great War Veterans' Association

NFC – Newfoundland Forestry Companies

NOFU – Newfoundland Overseas Forestry Unit

NPA – Newfoundland Patriotic Association

RFC – Royal Flying Corps

RNR – Royal Newfoundland Regiment

RQMS – Regimental Quartermaster Sergeant

UK – United Kingdom of Great Britain and Ireland (In 1927, "UK" became
an abbreviation for the United Kingdom of Great Britain and Northern
Ireland.)

VAD – Voluntary Aid Detachment

WFS – Women's Forestry Service

WPA – Women's Patriotic Association

I

INTRODUCTION

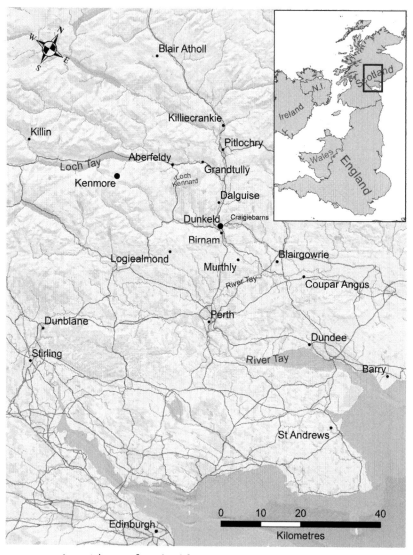

A partial map of Scotland featuring the area around Dunkeld
and Kenmore, Perthshire, where the NFC operated.
(Courtesy of Myron R. King, Environmental Policy Institute,
Grenfell Campus, Memorial University of Newfoundland)

S everal years ago, in 2012, I undertook a study of the songs and stories of woods workers in Newfoundland and Labrador. My purpose was to explore how those who had built our early lumbering and logging industries had documented and shared their experiences through such compositions. The first pulp and paper mill, which had opened at Grand Falls in 1909, closed in 2009, but there was limited popular evidence of the cultural impact of the century-old industry, as might be seen in professional song recordings and published accounts like those available in other locations where woods work was a central occupation. Through my research, I discovered a large, albeit fragile, body of related archival materials, specifically songs, recitations, poems, and oral histories, that demonstrated an extensive but largely overlooked creative production of woods workers in the early decades of the industry.

Similarly, despite its economic and cultural significance, few scholars have attended in any comprehensive manner to the history of the forestry sector of Newfoundland and Labrador.[1] Fewer still have studied its expressive culture, in particular, the legacy of songs and stories,[2] or attempted to

1 Historians Rainer Baehre (2011), James Hiller (1982, 1990), and Dufferin Sutherland (1991, 1992, 1995) are notable exceptions.
2 Folklorist John Ashton's study of the lumber-camp song tradition of Central Newfoundland is the exception. Ashton challenged the preconceptions of early collectors who ignored this sector and this aspect of its expressive culture. See Ashton (1986).

make this legacy accessible for public remembrance and revitalization. Several projects and publications later,[3] some of these gaps have been addressed, although there remain important stories to tell arising from this original research. One such project, the multimedia and interactive travelling exhibit *Songs and Stories of "The Forgotten Service"* (Kelly & Forsyth, 2018a), celebrated the Newfoundland[4] foresters who served in the United Kingdom (UK), mostly in Scotland, in both the First and Second World Wars. Descendants of the foresters with whom I spoke during the research for that project often commented, "What did they do in Scotland? What was life like for them while they were away?" The exhibit attempted to answer these questions, but it became clear during the research that there was far less known about the foresters of the Great War than those of the Second World War, whose story is better documented.[5] Upon their return from service, foresters of both wars, like other veterans, talked little about their overseas experiences. Family history pilgrimages to Scottish towns in search of answers are increasingly common—to Dunkeld and Kenmore, near the sites of First World War forester camps, and to places such as Ballater, Carrbridge, and Grantown, near some of the numerous Second World War camps. But there is very little material about the Newfoundland foresters available in Scottish archives, and about the foresters of the Great War, in particular.[6] This dearth of information intensified my desire to explore and

---

3   See, for example, Kelly (2014) and Kelly and Forsyth (2018a; 2018b).

4   Historically, "Newfoundland" was the official settler name of the geographic entity that included both the island of Newfoundland and the mainland of Labrador. In 2001, the province's official name was changed to "Newfoundland and Labrador." Usage throughout this book is in keeping with the official name in the period of time under discussion. At the time of the Great War, "Newfoundland" was not yet a part of Canada.

5   See Curran (1987) for an account of the Newfoundland Overseas Forestry Unit (NOFU) of the Second World War. See also Jeddore (2015) for a Mi'kmaw forester's account of service in the NOFU.

6   In her social history of Scottish forestry in the twentieth century, *Voices of the Forest*, Mairi Stewart (2016) included a photo of the camp at Craigvinean and a single sentence about the impressive log chute built there by the NFC.

to document their story more fully, both as part of the history of Newfoundland in the Great War and of early twentieth-century woods work in Newfoundland, generally.

There is now much written about the members and activities of the Royal Newfoundland Regiment (RNR) during the First World War.[7] A central focus of this material is the Battle of the Somme and the Regiment's role on July 1, 1916, at Beaumont-Hamel. The staggering losses for the Allied forces on that first day of the four-and-a-half-month battle—the highest death toll of any day of the war—included the near annihilation of the First Battalion of the Regiment.[8] The pall cast over Newfoundland by the magnitude of those losses, combined with the desperate efforts of politicians to reinvent immeasurable tragedy for political gain, shrouded all else. Historic attention to the Great War has, in ways, reproduced this myopia, resulting in an uneven account of Newfoundland's role within the conflict.

More recent scholarship, however, questions and reinterprets this role, thereby revitalizing an increasingly expansive account by adding nuanced analysis and highlighting other service contributions. For example, two books have focussed on the contributions of the Newfoundland Royal Naval Reserve (Hunter, 2009; Parsons & Parsons, 2009). Feminist historians have added important analyses of Newfoundland women in a variety of wartime roles, including in the Women's Patriotic Association (Duley, 2012) and the Voluntary Aid Detachment (Bishop-Stirling, 2012). As well, historian Sean Cadigan (2013) has developed a compelling and substantive critique of historic commemorative practices and the political consequences for Newfoundland of the contestation and manipulation of the memory and meaning of Beaumont-Hamel.

The Regiment's forestry unit, the Newfoundland Forestry Companies (NFC), however, has remained an underexamined wartime service whose

---

7   For a discussion of efforts to document Newfoundland's First World War history, see Baker and Neary (2012).

8   Of the 800 or so soldiers of the Regiment who fought at Beaumont-Hamel with the 29th British Division, more than 700 were killed, wounded, or missing in action (Baker, 2017).

story has been a mere historical sidebar to that of the combat battalions of the Regiment. *The Fighting Newfoundlander*, an official history of the Newfoundland Regiment by G.W. Nicholson, includes only a short essay devoted to the NFC. This partial chapter of a few pages in a 15-chapter, 600-page tome[9] was, until now, the most comprehensive account of the forestry unit. Despite this lack of substance, historians writing since Nicholson's 1964 publication have not redressed the short-shrift coverage, a slight most recently repeated in the marginal place of the unit's story in First World War centenary remembrance practices in Newfoundland and Labrador.

Today, more than a century since its formation, little is known of the Newfoundland Forestry Companies. There exists no thorough account of the unit that details its emergence, its work in Scotland, where the NFC was posted from mid-1917 until early 1919, and the importance of its contribution. In addition, there has been no analysis of what such an account might add to our understanding of the Great War. This introduction and my concluding essay, in which I reflect on the Newfoundland Forestry Companies and the Great War, address these gaps. They provide a context for reader engagement with the letters included in the middle section of this book, penned during the war by Regimental Quartermaster Sergeant (RQMS) John A. Barrett, NFC #8028, who wrote regularly from Scotland about the doings of the NFC. Barrett's letters—another example of the creative production of Newfoundland's forestry sector—also construct a foundation for a reconsideration of the historic significance of the wartime service of the NFC.

---

9   Nicholson (1962) made even shorter shrift of the large Canadian Forestry Corps (CFC) in his history of the Canadian Expeditionary Force (CEF), devoting only two pages to it.

URSULA A. KELLY

THE NEWFOUNDLAND FORESTRY COMPANIES, 1917–1919

On August 4, 1914, the United Kingdom declared war on Germany. A year later, with no end to the conflict in sight, a shortage of tonnage—ship cargo-carrying capacity—pressed on the government of the UK. The destructive impact of German U-boat warfare on vessel traffic compromised the government's ability to supply the nation in continued conflict, including meeting its timber needs. Timber was essential to the war effort and huge quantities[10] were required for a variety of purposes: to make pit props, the support beams used in coal mines (coal being a main energy source for the war); to construct and maintain trenches; to build barracks, duckboards, and fence posts; to make poles for communication lines and anti-landing structures; and to build bridges, railways, and ships.

The forest industry of the UK was small; since the time of the Napoleonic Wars, most of its supply of timber—more than 90 percent (Oosthoek, 2013)—was imported from the colonies, the Scandinavian countries, and Russia.[11] The importing of timber put a huge demand on tonnage and, by 1915, to create room for munitions, foods, and other wartime essentials, a large home supply of timber became necessary.[12] To address the problem, the government formed the Home-Grown Timber Committee under the Board of Agriculture—later the Timber Supply Department of the Board of Trade—which identified for harvest the forests and wooded estates of England and Scotland ("Newfoundland and the War," 1917).

There was a shortage of skilled woods workers—tree fellers, haulers, and sawyers—in the UK, as well. Most eligible men were on the front lines of war.

---

10 For an analysis of the provenance of the timber used at the Front, see Haneca, van Daalen, and Beeckman (2018).

11 In 1913, the UK imported 11,589,811 imperial tons (11,775,792 tonnes) of lumber; in 1917, it was reduced to 2,875,143. Home-grown timber production in 1913 was 900,000 tons; in 1917 it was three million (Great Britain War Office, 1922, p. 716).

12 For an overview of the problem, the solutions, and the impact of the timber crisis on forestry in Scotland after the war, see House (2017).

In early 1916, the government appealed to Canada, a major source of its timber imports, to establish a forestry battalion. The response was rapid and, by May, Canadian foresters and equipment were on the ground in the UK, producing timber for the war effort. Several battalions followed and, by late 1916, for more efficient administration, they were reorganized into companies under the Canadian Forestry Corps (CFC). By war's end, the CFC's total strength—including officers, support personnel, foreign nationals, and prisoners-of-war—exceeded 30,000, and its 101 companies were located in various parts of the United Kingdom and France (Bird & Davies, 1919; Nicholson, 1962).

As noted earlier, Newfoundland was not a part of Canada during the First World War.[13] Like Canada, it was a dominion—and it was the oldest colony of the British Empire. For hundreds of years, the settler economy of Newfoundland had centred on fishing, but in the second half of the nineteenth century a commercial lumbering industry emerged, based mainly on the harvesting and milling of white pine. By the 1890s, there were several large lumber mill operations in bays around the coastline, developed by entrepreneurs from Canada and Scotland (Thoms, 1967). By the early 1900s, white pine resources had waned, but the spruce and fir so well-suited to pulp and paper production had caught the attention of foreign investors. By 1909, the Anglo-Newfoundland Development Company (ANDCo), owned by English newspaper barons and brothers Alfred and Harold Harmsworth—Lord Northcliffe and Lord Rothermere, respectively—were operating an integrated mill at Grand Falls. As well, Albert E. Reed, an English papermaker, had established a large pulpwood enterprise at Bishop's Falls in 1911.[14]

At the onset of war, Newfoundland focused its first support efforts on recruitment for the Regiment, which had distinguished itself by late 1916 in both the Gallipoli Campaign and the Battle of the Somme. When the government of the UK indicated a need for foresters from the colonies, Newfoundland

---

13 Newfoundland became the tenth province of Canada in 1949.

14 For an account of the emergence of the pulp and paper industry in Newfoundland, see Hiller (1982). For an overview of the history of woods work in Newfoundland and Labrador, see Kelly and Forsyth (2018b).

leaders responded again. As they saw it, the emerging industrialization of the forestry sector of Newfoundland provided an available pool of professional woods workers who could help fulfil the wartime timber needs of the Empire. The Director of Timber Supply in London, Mayson M. Beeton, was the first president of the ANDCo and was keen to see a Newfoundland contribution to resolving the problem of timber supply for the war. Beeton (1917c) later called it "a fine opportunity for showing what the Newfoundlanders can do as woodsmen in comparison with the various other nationalities which are engaged on this work throughout the United Kingdom" (p. 2).

Volunteer recruitment to maintain the Regiment, however, had stretched the limits of Newfoundland's small and widely dispersed population. In outport communities, where most Newfoundlanders lived, life was organized around a family-based fishery. It was a household subsistence economy in which men held a central role on a year-round basis: fishing occupied the spring to fall months, along with the spring planting of vegetables and the fall harvesting. Hunting (caribou, birds, rabbits) was a fall-through-spring activity that included sealing at the front[15] during March. Gathering the family fuel supply of wood occupied winter months. Removing men from this cycle of production could have dire effects on a family's well-being.

As losses from fatalities and injuries began to steadily outnumber new recruits for the Regiment, the limits of volunteerism grew increasingly apparent to those organizing the war effort, and debates about conscription intensified. Away from the outports, in the mainport and seat of government in St. John's, there seemed to be limited understanding of the demands of outport life (Martin, 2009). The finger of blame for low recruitment numbers was regularly and unfairly pointed toward the men of the outports,[16] as well as the women some believed might be holding them back from their duty to serve. An entreaty by Governor Harris ("An Appeal," 1918) at the launch of

---

15   This "front" is the local term for where seals amass on ice floes in late winter and early spring off the coasts of northeastern Newfoundland and southern Labrador.

16   Despite a prevalent belief that outport residents were not doing their part, approximately 73 percent of those who joined the RNR and NFC during the war came from rural Newfoundland (Cadigan, 2009, p. 187).

the final recruitment campaign of April 1918, prior to the introduction of conscription later that spring, was addressed to all the people of Newfoundland "but especially to those of the outports" (p. 3).

Establishing the Unit: "Men We Must Have, and Tonnage; Nothing Else Matters"[17]

Despite known recruitment challenges, Prime Minister Morris (1917a) wrote to Governor Davidson in February 1917, while visiting the United Kingdom, to say that officials were "keen here in London to establish a battalion of Newfoundland foresters" (p. 2) to contribute to the work of Timber Supply, at that time a Department of the War Office. Morris thought it possible to send men for the early spring-to-fall period, to avoid a negative impact on the woods industries at home, which were operating largely on a fall-to-spring schedule. Davidson (1917a) responded quickly on March 25, writing to Walter Grieve, Secretary of the Newfoundland Patriotic Association (NPA)—which oversaw recruitment until August 1917—asserting: "No man deserves the claim to Manhood or the right to Citizenship who fails to answer to this summons" (p. 3).

In a telegram on April 2, Viscount Walter Long, Secretary of State for the Colonies, outlined the terms of the proposal developed in consultation with Beeton (Long, 1917). Beeton's understanding of the culture of the Newfoundland lumber woods was evident, especially so in Long's recommendation that "each Company should be composed of men, where possible, who had already worked together in the logging camps of Newfoundland in order to facilitate recruiting and to encourage esprit de corps" (Long, 1917, p. 7). The Companies would join foresters from Canada,[18] the United States,[19] Portugal, and Finland, as well as those from the UK, including over 1,600 members of

---

17   A line from Davidson (1917a).

18   For an early account of the Canadian Forestry Corps of the First World War, see Bird and Davies (1919).

19   For an account of the Twentieth Engineers, the American regiment of forestry engineers, see Simmons and Davies (1920).

the Women's Forestry Service (Great Britain War Office, 1922, p. 716), the so-called "lumberjills."

Long officially confirmed the need for a non-combat, uniformed military unit, organized into companies not battalions, and with all costs from enlistment to demobilization borne by the government of the UK. "Newfoundlanders will work under the control of their own officers," Long (1917, p. 6) stipulated, and under the general direction of the British War Office Timber Supply Department and its director, Mayson Beeton. The pay for foresters was on par with those for other services, with bonuses for men with specialized skills.[20] Provision for postwar pensions was also included. Wages were set out as per diem rates, which were included in Schedule 1 of "Regimental Rates–All Arms." Wages typically included regular daily pay and a per diem field allowance, and they increased with rank. For example, privates earned $1 per day plus a 10¢ field allowance, sergeant foremen and sawyers earned $1.65 per day, and captains earned $3 per day plus a 75¢ field allowance (Bennett, 1917).

Plans unfolded quickly. On April 4, 1917, Governor Davidson (1917a) issued a call to "lumber men and all skilled workers not eligible for service in the Regiment or the Royal Naval Reserve to serve as foresters in the United Kingdom" (p. 3). The NPA endorsed Long's proposal at a meeting on April 8 at which the name of the unit—the Newfoundland Forestry Companies—was also decided.[21] The NPA also agreed with Long that only those ineligible for the Regiment due to age or impairment would be considered (Davidson, 1917e). They followed the Canadians with this restriction, who had changed their target recruit pool when the fifth forestry battalion was requested; they sought, instead, men who were suitable for forestry work but did not meet the standards for combat services (Bird & Davies, 1919).

---

20 For the complete pay scale, see Bennett (1917).

21 Nevertheless, the NFC is commonly referred to as the Newfoundland Forestry Corps and, sometimes, the Newfoundland Forestry Battalion. In official correspondence, it was also called the First Newfoundland Regiment Forestry Companies—see, for example, "An Appeal to the People" (1917). As well as being historically correct, "Companies" is also technically correct within the British Army organization.

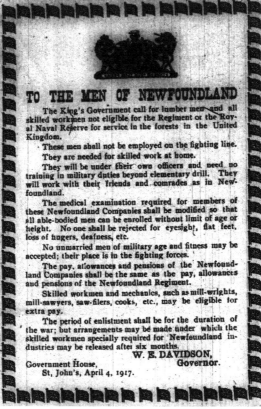

Governor Davidson's call to the men of Newfoundland.
(*The Western Star*, April 11, 1917, p. 3.)

At a follow-up meeting on April 16, the terms and official name for the unit were confirmed ("The Forestry Companies," 1917). In a telegram to Governor Davidson that same day, William Scott, manager of the ANDCo at Grand Falls, identified some of the tools of the trade required to equip the Companies for overseas work. His list included: 12 dozen 3½-foot crosscut saws; 6 dozen 6-foot lance-tooth saws; 600 double-bit axes; 200 single-bit axes; 1,200 double-bit axe handles; 400 single-bit axe handles; 200 peavie[22]

---

22 A long wooden stick with a two-ended hook—one end short and pointed and the other long and curved—that is used as a leverage tool in logging. It is also spelled peavey.

handles; and 40 sets of double-team harnesses (Scott, 1917). Governor Davidson (1917b) emphasized to Beeton the importance of the men having tools familiar to them and "not the English tools" (p. 1). Enlistment in the NFC for the duration began immediately, with provision for exceptions for those whose skills might be needed in industries at home.

On April 17, Eldon Sellars, a draper from St. John's, was the first to enlist in the newly formed unit. He was assigned service number 001, prefixed by the numeral 8 to denote the regular members of the NFC.[23] Sellars had two brothers with the Regiment and another brother with the Royal Flying Corps (RFC). Sellars was among the first draft of foresters to depart St. John's on May 19 aboard the SS *Florizel*. His brother Newman boarded the same ship in February 1918 to join the RFC—and died when the *Florizel* went aground in a blizzard near Cappahayden, Newfoundland. After the war ended, Eldon Sellars was also among the last few foresters to leave Kenmore, Scotland, the final site of NFC operations. He was demobilized at St. John's on June 29, 1919.

Commissions: "Newfoundlanders First, Where Capable and Available"?[24]

Secretary Long also included terms of organization and leadership—a proposed unit of five companies, each commanded by a Captain and two subalterns selected from a pool of Regiment officers who were no longer fit for combat on the Western Front. Non-commissioned officers, Long suggested, could be drawn from the pool of camp foremen with the ANDCo at Grand Falls and the Albert E. Reed and Company at Bishop's Falls (Long, 1917).

Several experienced lumberers wrote Governor Davidson to request commissions in the new unit. Davidson, in consultation with the Executive

---

23 Commissioned officers had service numbers beginning with a zero.

24 The editor of *The St. John's Daily Star*, H.M. Modsell, argued that this rule should apply to the assignment of commissions in the NFC ("Capable, Available," 1917, p. 1).

Committee of the NPA, decided on leadership for the NFC. But the process quickly became contentious when, in a secret memo to Prime Minister Edward Patrick Morris, copied to NPA Forestry Committee Chair Walter Grieve and J.A. Clift of the NPA Reserve Force Committee, Davidson named his choice of officers for A Company. When the NPA Joint Committee assigned the task to recommend and endorse commissions heard of the memo, at the May 9 meeting to discuss officer selection, several members walked out, forcing Davidson to explain his overstep and withdraw his recommendations (Davidson, 1917d).

The officers of the NFC were gazetted on May 15, 1917 ("Published by Authority," 1917). As Officer Commanding, the Forestry Committee and Davidson appointed Major Michael S. Sullivan, NFC #0–191, who had been an engineer with the Reid Newfoundland Company, an assistant manager with the ANDCo at Grand Falls, and an independent pulpwood agent in St. John's. Formerly of Placentia, Sullivan had represented Placentia and St. Mary's in the Liberal government of Sir Robert Bond from 1904 to 1909 (Bates, 1994). Beeton believed that Sullivan's familiarity with woods operations through his dealings with the ANDCo and his leadership experiences were both important assets for the NFC.

Acknowledging Sullivan's lack of military experience, Beeton (1917a) noted that there was "a small nucleus of officers and non-coms from the Newfoundland Regiment who are unfit for active service at the Front who will be able to fulfill the more purely military duties in connection with the organization and work of these Companies" (p. 1). The appointment as Adjutant of Captain Hector H.A. Ross, RNR #768, of St. John's, who had been injured in the Gallipoli Campaign, brought this military experience to the leadership of the unit. Ross, who was born in Toronto, was studying electrical engineering with the Reid Newfoundland Company when he enlisted with the Regiment, after which he quickly earned a commission ("New Lieutenants," 1915). Ross was attached to the NFC on May 18, 1917. The appointment of other Regiment soldiers would follow.

Other initial commissions were assigned to leaders in the woods industries, most of whom had arrived in Newfoundland at the turn of the century to take advantage of lumbering and logging opportunities. All had extensive knowledge of, and experience in, woods operations.

Major William H. Baird, NFC #0–192, of Norris Arm, was commissioned as Captain in the newly formed NFC. Baird had immigrated to Newfoundland in 1900 from Maccan, Nova Scotia, to pursue lumbering operations in Central Newfoundland with the Exploits Lumber and Pulp Company. By 1905, he was operating a mill at Northern Arm. In 1907 he had a mill at Burnt Arm and, in 1909, one at Botwoodville, where he was also Justice of the Peace ("Entries," 1907–11). At the time of his enlistment, he had been the Manager of the Carbonear-based Saunders, Howell and Company logging and milling branch at Norris Arm for several years.

Captain Hugh W. Cole, NFC #0–170, of Badger Brook, was from Farnham, Surrey, England. He had come to Newfoundland in 1905 to work with the ANDCo, where his cousin served as Secretary to Lord Northcliffe at Grand Falls. In 1908, Cole was the ANDCo lead on the great "Reindeer Trek" led by Mi'kmaw guide Mathieu (Mattie) Mitchell of Norris Point, which delivered Lapland reindeer overland from St. Anthony to Millertown in late winter, where they would be used as experimental hauling animals.[25] Cole became Superintendent at Badger Brook in 1912, where he was dubbed "King Cole" or "King of Badger" (Thoms, 1975). He was also immortalized in "The Badger Drive," one of the earliest and most popular song compositions about the pulp and paper industry in Newfoundland (Kelly & Forsyth, 2018b, pp. 71–73).

Michael J. Gillis, NFC #8044 / #0–193, a lumberer from Highlands, Codroy Valley, and Guy W.N. Harvey, NFC #0–194, an English civil engineer with the ANDCo, were both commissioned as Second Lieutenants. William T. O'Rourke, NFC #0–195, a clerk from St. John's and former member of the Regiment, was assigned as Quartermaster, with an honorary rank of Lieutenant. Albert J. Noble, NFC #0–26, an accountant with the London office of the ANDCo, was a civilian appointed to the position of Liaison Officer between

---

25 Sir Wilfred Grenfell imported 250 reindeer in an experiment to meet the food needs of the people in northern Newfoundland. The ANDCo added 50 animals to Grenfell's order. There are several extant accounts of this journey; for a narrative by the foresters' scribe, see Barrett (1945).

Timber Supply and the Pay and Record Office, as requested by Beeton and at an unpaid and honorary rank of Lieutenant.

Captain Henry S. Crowe, NFC #0–25, of Millertown, joined the NFC in the summer of 1917. The nephew of timber baron Harry J. Crowe, he had immigrated to Newfoundland from Nova Scotia in 1905 to work with his uncle. He had operated his sales and shipping office in St. John's and worked at several of Harry Crowe's Newfoundland lumber operations. He later joined the ANDCo and became Woods Superintendent at Millertown in 1915 (Thoms, 1967). At the time of the formation of the NFC, Crowe had already served six months with the Canadian Forestry Corps in France. Mayson Beeton (1917c) requested Crowe's transfer based on the value of his experience at Millertown and suggested a lack of experienced Newfoundland-born personnel from which to draw to lead the NFC.

Crowe's transfer was controversial, particularly in the context of some public dissatisfaction with the lack of commissions for Newfoundland-born foresters that played out in the St. John's newspapers. *The St. John's Daily Star*, in particular, took issue with the lack of commissions for local foresters. In an editorial on May 16 ("Alas! The Poor Native!," 1917), the day following the announcement of commissions for the NFC, the editor of the *Daily Star* asserted:

> The man on the street now holds that wire-pulling, and not merit, is the decisive factor [in commission appointments for the NFC]. He is persuaded that family and business connections count overmuch in this connection. He thinks that the ordinary native will figure only when an appointment is not coveted by the influential stranger and the influential fellow countryman. (p. 1)

Beeton and Harry J. Crowe[26] had become well acquainted with each other through the formation of the ANDCo. Crowe had moved to Newfoundland

---

26 For a biography of Harry S. Crowe and his ventures in Newfoundland, see Baker (2005).

from Halifax in 1902 and purchased dozens of mills and timber leases in central Newfoundland to build his company, Newfoundland Timber Estates, which was incorporated in 1903. Seeing the potential of the plentiful softwood timber for paper-making, he had entered into negotiations with the Harmsworths who, in 1904, sent Mayson Beeton to Newfoundland to investigate the feasibility of a pulp and paper enterprise. The ANDCo subsequently acquired many of Crowe's holdings. Crowe had also been influential in attracting papermaker Albert E. Reed to Bishop's Falls (Thoms, 1967; Baker, 2005).

The younger Crowe's transfer and commission were spearheaded by Mayson Beeton himself. In a lengthy letter to Governor Davidson, dated June 22, 1917, which was later heavily redacted for distribution to Minister of Militia Bennett, Sullivan, and Grieve—and subsequently published in *The Evening Herald* (Beeton, 1917e)—Beeton (1917c) wrote candidly about his unflattering impression of Newfoundlanders, while revealing that he relied on Davidson to excuse the "slight irregularity of procedure" he had invoked to obtain Crowe from the CFC (p. 4). In a later letter to Governor Davidson dated August 18, Beeton (1917f) dismissed public concerns about commissions, stating, "one must consider efficiency and not place of birth as the true test of selection" (p. 1). Following strong lobbying by Beeton, which was accompanied by a threat to resign his position (Beeton, 1917d), Crowe's transfer was approved by the Forestry Committee in late July 1917 (Grieve, 1917).

At headquarters, District Officer Commanding Major Alexander Montgomerie, perhaps aware of the potential effect on esprit de corps, as well as public perception in Newfoundland, countered with a recommendation for promotion to Captain of Lieutenant David Thistle, NFC #0–181, of St. John's, formerly of the Crown Lands Office. Montgomerie (1917) noted in a memo to Minister Bennett that Thistle "would seem to rank on an equality" (p. 2) with the others. Thistle's son was manager of *The St. John's Daily Star*. The editor of *The Evening Herald*, Patrick T. McGrath, a friend of Beeton's, argued it was the disaffection of said manager that was the real impetus for the criticisms of commissions levied by the *Daily Star* ("Native Officers," 1917). Amidst the disagreements around Crowe and commissions, Sergeant Josiah R. Goodyear,

RNR #573 / #0–166, of Grand Falls, who transferred to the NFC in mid-July, was also approved for commission as Captain (Davidson, 1917g).

Still, the public wrangling continued. When Second Lieutenant Noel James, NFC #0–171, who was originally from England and married to Major Sullivan's sister-in-law, returned to St. John's on extended compassionate leave, the father of a Regiment soldier objected in a letter to *The Evening Advocate*. He questioned why James was allowed to remain in Newfoundland when soldiers "belonging to this Country" who had been wounded multiple times were returned to the theatre of war, and others with years of war service could not get leave at all ("Those Lieutenants," 1918, p. 6).

Recruitment: "An Absolute Failure"

The physical requirements for service in the NFC were amended from those of the Regiment. Minor impairments—such as flat feet, loss of digits, reduced vision or hearing, and inadequate weight and height—were no longer reasons for ineligibility to serve. The attestation files of the NFC include several recruits who wore a glass eye, experienced reduced hearing, or exhibited other features that would have rendered them unfit for combat service. Of the 778 who came forward for the NFC, 278 were rejected ("Report," 1920, p. 10), a rejection rate of almost 36 percent. The total rate of rejection for the Regiment, despite the relaxing of standards earlier in the war, was almost 47 percent (Martin, 2009, p. 70).

The average "apparent" age of the NFC members was 26 years. It was not uncommon, however, for recruits to adjust their age at attestation. The youngest recruit, Private Harry Stares, NFC #8265, of Port Blandford, declared he was 17, but he was only 14; the oldest, Lance Corporal Thomas F.J. Sullivan, NFC #8125, St. John's, stated he was 53, but he was actually 70. Boys the age of Stares often worked in the woods operations of Newfoundland by secretly adjusting their ages, as Stares had. Sullivan's age, however, was no secret. *The Evening Telegram* announced Sullivan as "the oldest man in khaki in the Newfoundland forces . . . physically a strong man and although having reached the allotted span of years is as active as many men fifty years his junior" ("70 year old," 1917, p. 2).

Enlistment ultimately reached 500, a number that included 484 foresters,[27] 14 officers, and two additional enlistments in the UK ("Report," 1920, p. 10).[28] Only four men who enlisted with the NFC later transferred to the RNR.[29] On the advice of the Canadian Forestry Corps, which had been reorganized into companies of approximately 170, the recruits were organized into three companies,[30] not five as initially planned. Despite three dozen or so transfers from the Regiment to the NFC, including a small number of Blue Puttees,[31] the unit came nowhere near reaching Beeton's hoped-for number of 1,500 (Beeton, 1917a).

---

27 There is a small discrepancy between the numbers documented by the Department of Militia in Newfoundland and those compiled by the Great Britain War Office (1922) in London, which listed a total of 479 foresters who went overseas.

28 These tallies did not include the men who transferred to the NFC from the RNR. Their names are listed in the Nominal Roll included in Appendix B. At least 4 percent of those who served with the NFC later also enlisted in the Newfoundland Overseas Forestry Unit, a Second World War civilian unit of approximately 3,600 foresters that was formed in 1939 to provide timber for the UK effort in that war. This percentage is conservative and could be as high as 12 percent. Given incomplete files from both wars and a plethora of identical names of enlistees in both units, it is difficult to ascertain exact numbers.

29 They were Private George Newell, NFC #8492, St. John's; Private Brian Potts, NFC #8093, Millertown; Private Dorman Rideout, NFC #8187, Pilley's Island; and Private Michael J. Walsh, NFC #8306, Unknown.

30 G.W.L. Nicholson (1964) stated that only two companies were formed. Information in forester attestation papers and the correspondence of Barrett and other foresters confirm that there were three.

31 The "Blue Puttees" was the home-grown name for the First Five Hundred of the Royal Newfoundland Regiment, the first draft who departed St. John's for the UK aboard the SS *Florizel* on October 3, 1914. They were so named for the nonstandard colour of their puttees, made of blue cloth because of the unavailability of the standard issue khaki at the time of enlistment. There is some variance in the quoted number of men in this first draft. Sharpe (1988) cites 536; 537 is the number used by Roberts (2014).

Despite the ANDCo projections of lower employment opportunities in all its sectors for the 1917–18 season, because of reduced production related to the shortage of tonnage available to export paper, officials felt the numbers from the outports were disappointing (Davidson, 1917e). Added to the labour needs of the family-based economy, which limited the number of available men, the fishery was also doing well, providing what was believed to be another disincentive to enlistment. In a letter to Minister Bennett in early May, Governor Davidson (1917c) frankly stated that, with the cuts to jobs with the ANDCo in the coming year, "the men thus free from local work would be fools not to join the Foresters under these circumstances. If they don't, and then call on the Government for subsistence next winter, they deserve to be in want." Elsewhere, Davidson (1917e) expressed his belief that "the men need time for reflection," and that Newfoundland's "champion woodsmen" would eventually embrace the benefits of service under what he saw as attractive terms (pp. 8–9).

But among Newfoundlanders, there was both less enthusiasm for the war and increasing suspicion of government motives following the losses at Beaumont-Hamel. In a letter to Beeton shortly after recruitment for the NFC began in May 1917, Governor Davidson recounted some of the local lore that surrounded enlisment. Some feared that the NFC was a Trojan horse and, once recruits arrived in Scotland, they would be transferred to the Regiment and redirected to the Front. There were also rumours tied to social divisions that prevailed at the time, particularly those related to religion. Some believed Prime Minister Morris, a Roman Catholic, was targeting Protestant denominations for recruitment and leaving Roman Catholics at home to ensure electoral support in an imminent election (Davidson, 1917f). Beeton (1917c) disdainfully replied:

> I thoroughly realize from my knowledge of men and affairs in Newfoundland the difficulties you are up against, especially now that, unfortunately, sectarian and political issues appear to have been raised in connection with the Forestry Corps. I note your analysis of the causes to which may be attributed the lack of recruits. In any other country it would be difficult to imagine how

such arguments could be seriously advanced, but apparently in Newfoundland no theory appears to be too wild to advance, once the spirit of sectarian politics is aroused. (pp. 2–3)

The Evening Herald ("Recruiting," 1918) presented in unequivocal terms its case against those men eligible for the NFC who failed to enlist, noting that men who enlisted could

> make about twice what they can make at home, while they take no risk whatever, except the unlikely one of being torpedoed on the way across. . . . Nevertheless, in spite of this, recruiting has collapsed. . . . One may ask, what are the reasons, and the only plausible ones that can be assigned are cowardice, indifference, and men being so well off otherwise that there is no compulsion on them to seek employment in this way. (p. 5)

The recruiters' frustration with the perceived indifference of the recruit pool could be seen in some of the correspondence to the Forestry Committee. A case in point was a telegram to Walter Grieve from Magistrate H.F. Fitzgerald of Grand Falls, following Fitzgerald's recruitment visit to Millertown in the spring of 1918. Fitzgerald (1918a) wrote:

> [We] went to Millertown Friday, taking Sergeant Goodyear and Private Rendall. Both returned wounded soldiers. [They] met there about thirty strapping men just paid off from the river drive. We talked and pleaded with them, urging enlistment in any branch but got no response. They apparently regarded all with stolid indifference and later left for their homes on the coast. In my opinion, 'tis high time some drastic measures were adopted to meet these conditions. (p. 1)

The men Fitzgerald described would likely have been at Millertown since the fall of the previous year, and would have participated in the fall cut, the winter haul-off, and the spring drive with only a short Christmas break at home, if that. Perhaps they were reluctant to entertain the prospect of yet another prolonged absence from home—or, in this case, one of indeterminate length—which would bring more hardship for their families. What the recruiters saw as "stolid indifference" may have been more akin to polite patience, as they readied for the trip home to take up the responsibilities that awaited them there.

Following two major recruitment drives for all service sectors, one in October 1917 and another in April 1918, the Newfoundland government invoked conscription on May 11, 1918. Small drafts of foresters continued to cross the Atlantic until the war ended, six months later—the final draft arrived at Kenmore in October 1918. Among the last drafts, only a few men were conscripts. As the forestry operations were ending in Scotland, Major Montgomerie (1919) wrote to Minister of Militia Bennett on January 4, describing recruitment for the NFC as "an absolute failure" and adding that "the people simply look upon this [forestry] work as a job and they would prefer to stay home where they can make more money [in the fishery]" (p. 34).

Enlistments: "A Motley Crowd"[32]

A large majority of the men who enlisted with the NFC were unmarried. Approximately two-thirds were of a Protestant faith—specifically, Church of England, Methodist, and Salvation Army; the remainder were Roman Catholic. Approximately one-third listed St. John's as a home address. The other two-thirds arrived for their training in St. John's by rail and coastal boat from all parts of the Island and Labrador. They were drawn from small communities—some of which no longer exist—in distant bays and peninsulas,[33] places where distinct identities were expressed through language and dialect, stories and songs, lineage and faith.

---

32   A term used by John Gallishaw (1916, p. 4) to describe recruits for the Regiment.
33   See Sharpe (1988, p. 43) for a breakdown by area.

For many, travel between St. John's and home communities, especially those in northern Newfoundland and Labrador, could involve a journey by dog sled to meet a coastal boat and/or train, and often involved overnighting in communities along the way. It was a particularly long, costly journey for the men of Labrador—and its intricacies and challenges were not necessarily appreciated at headquarters. Dr. Harry Paddon of the International Grenfell Association wrote to Chief Staff Officer Lieutenant Colonel Rendell on behalf of some Labrador soldiers who had not been fully reimbursed for their travel costs. Upon returning from overseas, these men had left by steamer from St. John's on November 24, 1918, and disembarked at Battle Harbour, Labrador, still some 300 miles from home. There they awaited dog teams to complete the journey, arriving home January 26, 1919—two months later! In this letter of 1922, Paddon called it a "tax on patriotism" (p. 1) to have to bear travel expenses and inconveniences oneself due to the short-sightedness of those in command.

There were several recruits to the Regiment from Indigenous communities of Labrador, but only two who joined the NFC. Robert G. Learning, NFC #8454, of Cartwright, a 34-year-old labourer, was married with four children and living in St. John's when he enlisted on December 14, 1917. Learning served for the duration. Joseph (Job) Michelin, RNC #637, a 19-year-old trapper from Grand Village,[34] was a student at Bishop's College in St. John's when he enlisted in the Regiment in 1914. Michelin was wounded at both Gallipoli and the Somme. Following a medical discharge in 1917, he became a recruiter. When the NFC was formed, he re-enlisted and embarked for Scotland with the fourth draft on December 11, 1917, where he served for the duration.

The cultural, linguistic, and geographic communities from which recruits came also included the Mi'kmaq and Francophones of the Island. Among them was 33-year-old Private Lawrence Mitchell, NFC #8373, a lumberer from Norris Point. Mitchell had accompanied his father, Mik'maw guide and prospector Mathieu Mitchell, on part of the 1908 Reindeer Trek and at that

---

34 Originally Mud Lake, Labrador. Mud Lake was renamed Grand Village by Albert Dickie of Stewiacke, Nova Scotia, who established the Grand River Pulp and Lumber Company there in the early 1900s.

time likely met Hugh Wilding Cole who would become an NFC officer. Private Julian Benoit, RNR #4224, a 26-year-old fisher from Ship's Cove, was one of several Francophones in the NFC. Benoit transferred from the Regiment to the NFC because he could neither read nor write English, the language of military instruction. His experience in lumbering, however, translated well in the NFC, in which he served for the duration.

As with the general population of Newfoundland, first-language skill levels in reading and writing varied among the men of the NFC.[35] Signing—the ability to sign one's name—is sometimes used to estimate literacy rates in historic contexts, with caveats.[36] A review of enlistment files shows that approximately 20 percent, or 1 in 5, of the foresters signed "X" as their attestation. Of those who signed "X," approximately 80 percent, or 4 of 5, listed a home address outside St. John's and off the Avalon Peninsula. It is not possible to know the actual literacy levels of the men of the NFC, but these figures correspond with the picture of a family-based subsistence economy that explains the limits of both literacy and voluntary recruitment: labour was needed to maintain the family economy and school attendance and war service reduced available labour.

Nor is it possible to know the extent of the challenges produced by limited literacy. Given the ongoing issues with allotments, allowances, expenses, pay, promotions, and pensions documented in the attestation files, however, it is reasonable to question the relationship of literacy—in this context, the extent to which one could both read *and* write—and self-advocacy for the men of the NFC. Attestation files suggest that many with higher literacy and education levels articulated their concerns regularly to headquarters. But any perceived drawbacks were often countered by a strength: the recruits were drawn from communities with a tradition of interdependence, and they were

---

35 While definitive rates are not available, literacy rates for this period in Newfoundland have been estimated to be lower than other jurisdictions (parts of Canada, for example). For a discussion of literacy rates in late-nineteenth-century Newfoundland, see Alexander (1980); for a rebuttal of Alexander, see Curtis (1990).

36 For a discussion of the limits of signing as a literacy measurement tool, see Curtis (1990).

used to relying on the skills of the collective, which compensated somewhat for individual challenges. Many files contain letters written or transcribed by others on behalf of a forester.

There were also strong familial links among the Companies, with at least six father/son sets and eight pairs of brothers, as well as men who were cousins and in-laws. Many had left large families of several dependents in order to serve overseas. In the face of illness, accident, death, and other difficulties, their absence often caused great hardship. For example, Sergeant John Hancock, NFC #8065, a lumbering foreman from Norris Arm and father of five, enlisted at age 40 along with his oldest son, Howard, NFC #8073, who was 18. In March 1918, while they were in Scotland, the family home at Norris Arm was destroyed by fire. The NFC organized a fund to restore the house and belongings, and contributions were published in St. John's newspapers throughout the spring of 1918.[37]

In some families, all eligible men and boys had enlisted in either the Naval Reserve or the Regiment, thereby reducing sources of subsistence at home; even with the separation allowance, the absence of men intensified the burden for women during the war. In rare cases, a request, sometimes mediated by a minister, doctor, or teacher, was made to return a forester in order to help an ill or bereaved parent. Ellen Howell of Northern Bay raised her nephews, the Hogan boys, from their early years, following their parents' sudden deaths. Two enlisted with the NFC—Gerald, the oldest at 21, and John, 17—and one with the Regiment. By the time Gerald and John enlisted in the NFC, Private Bernard Hogan, RNR #2252, was a prisoner-of-war. When Private Gerald Hogan, NFC #8111, was killed at Kenmore in August 1918, Ellen Howell (1918) wrote to Governor Harris to explain the toll his loss would take and to request that one of the two boys remaining overseas—Bernard or John—be sent home. Some of her words would have resonated across the country:

> I reared the boys well with a noble, heroic spirit as you will notice
> by their volunteering so young, before they were expected. They

---

37 See, for example, "Generous Donations" (1918) and "Hancock Benefit" (1918).

gave in their ages older than they were so as they would be accepted. I could have stayed them if I chose as they were obedient, but the Country's call was there. (pp. 2–3)

Governor Harris (1918), through his private secretary, replied to reassure Howell that he realized "how nobly your nephews have done their duty" (p. 1) and that he would inquire about Private Bernard Hogan. Hogan was repatriated from Germany in December 1918 and returned to Newfoundland in June 1919.

Skills, Training, and Fitness: "All Well and in the Pink of Health"[38]

Approximately half of the men who joined the NFC named lumbering or lumbering-related work—lumberer, woods worker, mill hand, or scaler, for example—as their occupation.[39] Those without lumbering or logging experience were trained at the Catholic Cadet Corps Armoury, St. John's. Large logs and other props were used to develop and test skills and progress was vetted by a Qualifications Committee. Some members of the public with extensive experience in woods camps, however, were not convinced of the effectiveness of such training. Lemuel Simmonds ("Forestry Battalion," 1917), an experienced woods operator, wrote to *The St. John's Daily Star* to express his "outrage" at the lack of experience of those being accepted for the NFC. He questioned "how many camp foremen would employ fifty clerks, office hands or typists from the city offices to work in a lumber camp" (p. 8).

Led in military training exercises by Sergeant-Instructor Benjamin Hussey,[40] all recruits were expected to learn only elementary drill procedures.

---

38 Private John R. Martin, NFC #8232, of Manuels, described the foresters thus in a letter from Scotland to a friend in Newfoundland ("Our Soldier Lads," 1917).

39 Not all files are available or complete, but the number of cases where occupation was unavailable is not large enough to change significantly this broad calculation.

40 He was later appointed Company Sergeant Major Benjamin Hussey, RNR #4325, St. John's. Hussey applied for a commission with the NFC upon its formation

Delays in dispatching the recruits could result in work hold-ups overseas, so there was little time for more advanced training. This minimal preparation may have contributed to some of the disciplinary issues that arose in camp. Conduct sheets reveal dozens of foresters with a long list of infractions that ranged from absence from roll call, overstaying pass, disobedience, insolence, drunkenness, and assault, to crimes that resulted in incarceration at Perth Prison, such as a breach of peace conviction that received a two-week sentence and a bigamy conviction for which a nine-month sentence was imposed.

In an appeal for recruits in the spring of 1917, then Lieutenant David Thistle (1917) wrote that the government of the UK requested Newfoundland lumbermen "because of their knowledge of the business and general fitness" (p. 33). Attestation files, however, record numerous cases where medical issues arose for foresters while overseas, raising questions about the general health of the unit. At the time, many communities in Newfoundland had no health services and poverty was common. There was a dearth of knowledge about basic disease prevention; vaccinations for illnesses that are taken for granted in the twenty-first century were non-existent.[41]

Early instances of medically discharged foresters drew attention to the need for stricter medical testing and for younger and more robust recruits. By March 1918, 29 foresters had been discharged, almost all for medical reasons (Timewell, 1918). Major Montgomerie (1918) flagged the problem in a letter to Adjutant Captain Ross: "One thing that has caused considerable trouble is the sending back of Forestry men on the medical certificate of the M.O.[42] especially as in some cases there did not appear to be any good <u>Medical</u> reason for their return" (pp. 1–2). But according to Corporal Henry Stewart, RNR #618, of Paisley, Scotland, who was a 26-year-old medical-room orderly with the NFC, many foresters were unable to maintain the pace and

---

but was refused on the basis of his essential service as trainer at the Regimental Depot at St. John's (Ayre, 1917).

41   For a historical discussion of health services in Newfoundland and Labrador, see Baker and Miller Pitt (1984).

42   Medical Officer.

physical demands of the work. Stewart (1917) commented on the "heavy" sick parade,[43] which was due, in his estimation, to "the men not being quite strong enough for the heavy work they attempt to do" (p. 2). In May 1918, on the eve of conscription in Newfoundland, the Legislative Council emphasized the need for strict medical testing for conscripts, citing unsatisfactory medical examinations and the case of the NFC—from which, it noted, "fully fifteen percent of those enlisted . . . have had to be discharged because they were not fit for service" (p. 3).

Along with minor illnesses were more serious and chronic conditions. Some men were diagnosed with heart conditions or developed respiratory illnesses, including influenza and pneumonia. There were cases of measles, mumps, and scabies, as well as syphilis and gonorrhea.[44] A small number of foresters later died of diseases diagnosed while in, or exacerbated by, service—including carcinoma, epilepsy, and pulmonary tuberculosis.[45] At demobilization, 109 foresters—or more than one in five men—were discharged as medically unfit ("Report," 1920, p. 10).

Work in Scotland was demanding and dangerous and the hilly terrain was a challenge to harvest. Work accidents resulted in two deaths,[46] and more serious injury or death was barely averted on some occasions. One such incident involved Private Charles Rideout, NFC #8087, of Moreton's Harbour, a teamster who was injured while descending Craigvinean with a load of iron. As recounted by witness Private Ephraim Hull, NFC #8191, of Springdale, the rear brake of the sled Rideout was driving broke, and the

---

43 "Parade" refers to the formal assembling of troops for inspection or marching.

44 A perusal of attestation files suggests that these sexually transmitted infections (STI) were common among the Regiment. According to Peter Neary (1998), by 1930, venereal disease (VD—"STI" is the current medical usage) was identified as a serious health problem in Newfoundland. Neary did not examine the problem in the context of the First World War. Cases of STI in the Canadian Expeditionary Force were estimated at over 15 percent, the highest of any force on the Western Front (Herring, 2014).

45 In this book I have limited my discussion to the fatalities that occurred while the NFC was in Scotland, of which there were three.

46 Sergeant Barrett includes accounts of each of these fatalities in his letters.

horses were unable to bear the full weight of the load on the decline. When Rideout's reins broke under the pressure of trying to control the horses, he jumped off the sled—but it, and a piece of iron, struck him, fracturing one of his arms and some ribs (Hull, 1923).

The attestation files, which cover the foresters' time in the unit, provide little evidence of accidents and injuries. Given the nature of early twentieth-century woods work, however, other incidents than the one in which Rideout was injured likely occurred. The NFC had a medical hut at all its locations, which is where foresters whose condition was not serious enough to require hospitalization beyond camp were treated.

Chutes and Scows, Salt Cod and Mayos

In the early days, as the NFC was being formed, the nature of its work in the United Kingdom was unclear. There was the possibility of cutting pit props in Wales or doing clean-up work throughout the country in small groups. In June 1917, Beeton confirmed the NFC's assignment would be felling and milling timber at Dunkeld, where approximately 1,200 acres (485 hectares) of forest were available, and at Kenmore, where there were approximately 800 acres (325 hectares) of harvestable forest (Beeton, 1917c). Anticipating the job ahead, he emphasized to Davidson the need for men with experience in building railways and scows—the flat-bottomed boats used to transport cargo that were a staple of Newfoundland woods operations (Beeton, 1917b). At each site, the NFC won the praise of officials and locals alike for their use of home-grown solutions to solve transportation problems that improved efficiencies, met the demand for wartime timber, and earned the NFC the moniker of "handymen of the Empire" ("The Responsibilities," 1919, p. 4).

At Dunkeld, the NFC faced the challenges of a steep mountain of forest: Craigvinean. Scottish authorities believed the work required a costly rail system for removing felled timber. The Canadian Forestry Corps had walked away from the job, deeming it too difficult (Woodford, 1930). But the Newfoundland officials, with the guidance of Captain William Baird, saw a solution: building a timber chute of the sort used in Newfoundland woods operations.[47] Touted as the longest in the world, the chute the NFC built was a lumbering marvel for those in the Scottish timber industry, as well as for locals. The use of horses and sleds also increased efficiencies. At Craigvinean, a railway siding was also built to expedite the loading and movement of lumber. Overall, the NFC provided inexpensive solutions to what were believed to be costly transportation problems ("Our Foresters," 1918).

At Drummond Hill, approximately a mile from Kenmore, where the Companies were fully relocated from Craigvinean by early summer 1918, the NFC also faced challenges. There, the timber source was nearby, although the hill was very steep, but efficient and economical transportation of timber was a problem. The initial plan was to transport timber down Loch Tay to Killin Station, but it would require costly upgrades to the existing railway (Maxwell, 1919). The use of scows, a cost-efficient transport solution drawn from woods practices in Newfoundland, could have added another aspect of Newfoundland logging operations to the workscape of Scotland. In the end, however, it was decided to transport harvested wood to the mills by horse and sled, where it was dressed, loaded onto trucks, and taken to the railway at Aberfeldy for shipment. Still, road transportation was also costly and trucks were in limited supply, which resulted in backlogs and delays, and extended overseas service months beyond Armistice.

Their inventive approach to challenges, characterized by a quick intelligence accented by broad-based skills—being "Jacks-of-all-trades"—was a source of pride for the foresters. Peter C. Mars (1924), a Scottish-born, Newfoundland-based poet, captured these traits in "The All-'Round Newfoundlander," an 18-verse poem from which these two verses are excerpted:

> As a logger, he's a princeling; he can drive a stream as well
> And, often, when he blasts the jam, he takes a chance on hell.

---

47 Barrett provided descriptions of the chute in his letters. Lance Corporal William J. Woodford, NFC #8211, St. John's, described the chute in an essay in *The Veteran* (Woodford, 1930).

He's a devil in white water when the logs go racing by
And he revels in the danger for he's not afraid to die.

To build a house from sill to roof, he needs no college pass
He's a handy man with axe and saw; there's no one in his class.
He saws his lumber, cuts his stone, and ofttimes bakes his brick
Where another would be daunted, he simply works the trick. (p. 53)

The foresters wore their accomplishments in Scotland as badges of honour, pinned firmly to their identity as Newfoundlanders, the King's subjects from "the Ancient Colony."

When pitted against the Canadians, with whom they were often confused in the Old Country, the desire to excel ran deep, as indicated in events such as sports day competitions between the NFC and the Canadian Forestry Corps. The common conflation of Newfoundland and Canada was a sore point for Newfoundlanders generally. Lieutenant Owen Steele, RNR #326 / #0–89, of St. John's, recalled that during the Regiment's first trip overseas in 1914 the *Princess Royal* was sighted and its crew greeted them with the Canadian anthem. The Newfoundlanders corrected with "Britannia Rules the Waves." Steele (Facey-Crowther, 2002) explained: "We are very particular here that we are not classed as Canadians . . . we are much prouder of our distinction as Newfoundlanders" (p. 30). Captain Sydney Frost, RNR #28 / #0–123, a Canadian from Yarmouth, Nova Scotia, who had been working in St. John's when the war began, also recounted this incident, additionally noting that, before launching into "Britannia Rules the Waves," the Newfoundlanders first responded with the "Ode to Newfoundland," which "conveyed nothing to [the crew]" (Roberts, 2014, p. 65). Frost added that "not being close enough to pick up the Newfoundland accent, doubtless the entire ship's company of the *Princess Royal* still took us for Canadians" (Roberts, 2014, p. 65). It is entirely likely, however, that, had the crew been able to hear, they might have noted the resemblance of the accents to those of their own West Country, as well as Ireland, from where so many of the Newfoundlanders' ancestors came and whose inflections could still be detected in their speech.

Private Francis T. Lind, RNR #541, of Little Bay, also bemoaned the regularity with which the Regiment's soldiers were mistaken for Canadians in both England and Scotland (Lind, 2001, p. 3, pp. 21–22). As Adjutant Captain Arthur Raley (1916) wrote to Captain Hugh A. Anderson of the Newfoundland Contingent of the Pay and Record Office, in his report about the Regiment at Gallipoli, "the common mistake of associating [the Regiment] with Canada is hard to get out of the public mind. It makes every true Newfoundlander rightly indignant to be confused with any country other than his own" (p. 3).

The proud distinction also extended to diet, especially the penchant for dried salt cod, which the Newfoundland foresters and the Regiment generally shared.[48] The strict implementation of rations in the United Kingdom during the War meant a meagre diet for foresters, who spent long hours at physically demanding work. In Scotland, the foresters supplemented their rations with local fish and game—deer, salmon, birds—as they did at home. Merchants on both sides of the Atlantic who had connections to the fish trade also donated regular supplies of dried cod. In a letter of thanks to the donors, written by the Minister of Militia on behalf of Major Sullivan, Bennett noted the importance of such donations, because "the difficulty of getting food on the other side, especially fish, is daily increasing" ("Fish Donations," 1918, p. 4).

Another staple—tobacco—was also in short supply. Tobacco in the UK and Europe was expensive and its taste unpopular with the Newfoundlanders. In both the Regiment and the NFC, the Mayo brand cut plug tobacco was preferred for chewing or smoking. Private Francis Lind noted the shortage of good tobacco in one of his regular letters to *The Daily News* in St. John's. A tobacco drive followed that resulted in an approximately 1,700-pound (770-kilogram) shipment to the Regiment at Stobs Camp, Scotland, which earned Lind the nickname "Mayo." Other drives and shipments of "May-O-Linds"

---

48   The Fish and Brewis Fund was one of several developed by the Women's Patriotic Association. Its purpose was to supply the Regiment with the so-called "national dish" (Davidson, 1917e, p. 13), which is a combination of cooked salt fish and hard tack (hard bread), served with drawn butter or small pieces of fried fatback pork called "scrunchions."

followed. Quartermaster Sergeant John A. Barrett also mentioned Mayo tobacco in his letters, noting at one point, "If a person is seen here with a stick of Mayos he is envied beyond measure, and the owner of it has to guard well his treasure." As with the Regiment, regular supplies of tobacco were shipped to Scotland from St. John's for the NFC, throughout its time overseas. As late as fall of 1918, as the war was ending, approximately 1,000 pounds (450 kilograms) of tobacco—half Mayo and 250 pounds (115 kilograms) each of British Colonial Dark and Light—were shipped to Kenmore (Bennett, 1918).[49]

WARTIME CORRESPONDENCE AND THE LETTERS OF QUARTERMASTER SERGEANT JOHN A. BARRETT

Writing letters was the primary way those overseas communicated with home, though postcards and telegrams were also used. Letters maintained ties during long, stressful, and grievous separations, boosted morale for everyone overseas and especially those at the Front, and provided friends and family at home with some reassurance, along with a small, partial glimpse of the realities of wartime service. As Martha Hanna (2014) points out, generally broader literacy rates at the beginning of the twentieth century enabled the flourishing of written correspondence by soldiers and civilians during the war. In Newfoundland, increased (although still limited) literacy among the population, regular mail service, and the existence of numerous newspapers—in both the capital of St. John's and other places such as Harbour Grace, Twillingate, and Bay of Islands—meant that letters were more readily and easily crafted, delivered, and shared at home and on the Front.

---

49 J.O. Hawvermale, an American and manager of the Imperial Tobacco Company (Newfoundland) Limited, was well known for his generous donations of tobacco to both the Regiment and the Forestry Companies.

In his letter of October 29, 1917, then Quartermaster Corporal John A. Barrett commented on the letter-writing activity at the NFC camp at Dunkeld. Describing the newly constructed recreation hut, he wrote:

> It was intended to have a room in it set apart for a library and to be used by our men as a place where they could go and transact their correspondence. Such a room is very necessary, as the men find it rather difficult to write letters in the huts, which are not very brilliantly lighted at night.

While most letters home were written to individuals and families, in many cases, as letters in this book demonstrate, they were shared with local newspapers, which gave them a wider audience.

Like their counterparts worldwide,[50] historians of First World War Newfoundland show an increased interest in wartime memoirs and letters that deliver a sense of the experiences of those who left home to serve. In the past two decades, several memoirs and collections of letters have been published: the memoirs of Sydney Frost (Roberts, 2014), Howard Morry (Morry, 2014), and Anthony J. Stacey (Stacey & Edwards Stacey, 2012) of the Newfoundland Regiment; and the letters of Francis Lind (2001), Owen Steele (Facey-Crowther, 2002), and Curtis Forsey (Riggs, 2007), also of the Regiment, and of Frances Cluett (Rompkey & Riggs, 2006) of the Voluntary Aid Detachment. All were published as important primary sources of the wartime experiences of Newfoundlanders and Labradorians. As Facey-Crowther (2003) points out, diaries and letters such as these serve a two-fold purpose: "to bear personal witness and . . . to document for future reference" (p. 33).

In this latter respect, especially, another series of locally written wartime letters, those of RQMS John A. Barrett of the Newfoundland Forestry Companies, is important, yet they have been largely ignored by historians. I first read some of Barrett's letters while researching Songs and Stories of "The

---

50   For an annotated account of Canadian letters and memoirs, see Tennyson (2013). For an international overview of war letters, see Jolly (2001).

Forgotten Service" and was surprised by the detail they provided about the unit, which had not translated into any comprehensive account of the NFC's activities. Coupled with the paucity of available historical accounts and information (alongside what was sometimes misinformation) about the NFC, the lack of attention to Barrett's letters struck me as a significant oversight. It is the purpose of this book to present Barrett's letters, which, while largely written as official correspondence, are nonetheless a complement to these other collections of Newfoundland letters from the First World War. In so doing, I also hope to tell the story of the NFC in a more substantive manner, one that encourages a re-examination, appreciation, and remembrance of its contributions and that prompts a rethinking of the dominant narrative of Newfoundland in The Great War.

Introduction to Barrett's Letters

Along with the many other duties in the Quartermaster's Office, in 1917 Timber Supply assigned to Corporal Barrett the responsibilities of press correspondent. A professional journalist, Barrett had worked in the Newfoundland newspaper industry for decades prior to enlisting with the NFC. While there may have been many official reasons for his regular letters home—to encourage enlistment was one of the most important—Barrett outlined his own intent to his readers in an early letter on July 28, 1917, written only a few weeks after the first draft of foresters arrived in Scotland: "[H]ere I am again writing you on behalf of the Company,[51] so that their relatives and friends in dear old Terra Nova may have the pleasure of hearing from us all at one time." To these friends and relatives—his readers—he was "your scribe," and the foresters were "our boys."

Despite Barrett's intention to inform those at home, because of low literacy rates and limited access to newspapers in isolated and less populated areas of Newfoundland, many relatives and friends were unable to glean information

---

51 At this point, there was only one company of the NFC in Scotland.

about the overseas lives of their loved ones by reading them in print when they first appeared. As well, Barrett's original letters[52] were addressed to *The Evening Herald*, a St. John's-based newspaper whose editor, P.T. McGrath, was a member of the Forestry Companies Organization Committee, suggesting that the arrangement to publish them was between Timber Supply and that newspaper. Given the friendship between McGrath and Mayson Beeton, this arrangement was likely. But if the letters were intended both to inform and to encourage recruitment, their availability to the largely St. John's-based readership of the *Herald* limited their reach.

Many of Barrett's letters, however, were eventually also published elsewhere, including in *The Western Star*. That paper was based in Curling and Barrett's brother Andrew was its editor. In addition, *The Western Star* published several apparently personal letters sent from John to Andrew Barrett. Over the duration of Barrett's service, 32 letters were published in *The Evening Herald* and 30 in *The Western Star*; 25 of these are duplicates. There are 37 letters reproduced in this volume, and they are drawn from both sources.

The Western Star began to print the same letters as *The Evening Herald* in September 1917, by which time *The Herald* had already published eight and *The Western Star* only two (which were, in all likelihood, personal letters from John Barrett to his brother). Much of the content of these two early *Western Star* letters is similar to that of the first letter published by the *Herald*. Because the two early letters to *The Western Star* were published first and offer more detail—for example, about the NFC's departure from St. John's and the voyage to Halifax—they are included here in lieu of the first letter to *The Evening Herald*. Seven of Barrett's "official" letters (published in *The Evening Herald*) follow, and the remaining 28 are Barrett's letters (official and personal) as they appeared in *The Western Star*.

A few of Barrett's letters—those detailing what may have been considered more widely appealing and newsworthy events (the visit of Governor

---

52   There are 32 originals extant; they were written at Dunkeld between July 9, 1917, and April 21, 1918. All were typed on 8- by 13-inch foolscap. They are part of the private collection of the Barrett family.

Davidson, lumber sport competitions with the Canadians, etc.)—were also published by *The Twillingate Sun*, *The Evening Advocate*, and *The Evening Telegram*. Typically, Barrett's letters were published in Newfoundland three to four weeks after they were written in Scotland. They range in length from approximately 300 to 1,300 words, with an average length of 800 words. Of the total number of published letters, 27 were written during the period between the NFC's departure from St. John's in May 1917 and the end of that year.

Beginning in spring of 1918, Barrett's letters became less frequent. After the NFC's move to Kenmore in late spring of 1918, he wrote only four until the disbandment of the unit in 1919. This period was a busy time for the Companies—the logistics of the move, the complexities of operations at Kenmore, and a general shortage of officers (both Quartermaster Lieutenant O'Rourke and Lieutenant James were on compassionate leave) increased Barrett's duties in the Quartermaster's office. His correspondence tasks were clearly difficult to maintain. As well, a fire at the *Herald* building in late 1918 resulted in suspension of publishing until spring 1919. Barrett's last two letters, possibly personal letters to his brother, were published in *The Western Star* (the second to last letter was also published in *The Evening Advocate*).

A salutation was not always included in the published versions of Barrett's letters. When it was, it was "Dear Sir" or "Sir" (with one exception[53]), indicating the formal nature of the correspondence. In his closure, which was consistently included in the official letters, there was no reference to his rank.[54] The more formal closure did not appear in the first two and final four letters, again suggesting that they were personal correspondence to Andrew Barrett.

---

53 The letter of August 23, 1918, begins with the salutation "Dear Brother." In the published version, it also had no signature. First published in *The Western Star*, it was likely a personal letter to Andrew Barrett. Upon publication in *The Evening Herald*, it was accompanied by a notation indicating it was copied from *The Western Star* to satisfy the interest of *Herald* readers in its contents.

54 They were signed: "Yours respectfully, J.A. Barrett, Newfoundland Forestry Companies."

The majority of Barrett's letters, however, were not written as private correspondence. They were open and public letters directed not to an individual or a family but to a broad collective—Newfoundlanders (initially the residents of St. John's, where the *Herald* was distributed)—and published as official accounts or reports[55] of the NFC. They did not require, nor did they receive, a response. Liz Stanley (2004) elaborates on this kind of letter:

> [O]pen letters are usually didactic, written by someone with a high status if not a pre-eminent position in relation to a particular community, with the community collective being addressed. Open letters trade on values and meanings shared in common; but although having communicative purpose, they are not directly responded to because they are pronouncements to be read but not to be answered by writing back. (p. 207)

In his letters, Barrett assumed, or perhaps hoped to achieve, points of view that would be shared by his reading audience and, as an extension of himself, by the Forestry Companies. The common ground covered many themes, but most especially a love of the homeland, loyalty to the Empire, high regard for the Regiment and Naval Reserve, the importance of the contributions of the NFC, and the responsibility of all who were able to contribute to war service to do so. Barrett's personal voice and a sometimes chatty and humorous tone were effective means to establish a sense of shared purpose and concern with the home audience.

All wartime correspondence was censored, but open letters written in an official capacity were both more purposeful and more limited in what they revealed. Barrett's letters were crafted within the command structure of the NFC and were vetted accordingly. Despite these limitations, the letters offer a sketch of the activities of the Companies and, in so doing, provide a

---

55 At first, the *Herald* used a headline that indicated the order of the report in the sequence—"Fourth Report," "Fifth Report," etc. This practice was discontinued after the "Eleventh Report" and replaced by a version of "With Our Foresters."

glimpse of service life in Scotland. When complemented by information gleaned from attestation files and other documents of the period, a fuller picture of the unit emerges than has been previously available or recorded.

Scope and Content

Barrett's letters reiterate the unique mission of the small unit of which he was a part. For him, this non-combat mission was both an opportunity for service—to contribute meaningfully to the war effort—and for personal growth. Only a few months after deployment, on September 15, 1917, Barrett wrote about the foresters: "Although not being on the firing line or anywhere near it, yet they are soldiers in every sense of the word. . . . And there is hardly a man who will not return after the war bigger than when he left home." Barrett represented their time in Scotland as a learning opportunity that would also benefit Newfoundland when the foresters returned. Displaying equal measures of affection and respect for his home country, "dear old Terra Nova," and his host country, Barrett saw, from forestry and farming to education and industry, the potential to learn and to adapt what was discovered for the benefit of the homeland.[56]

Overall, Barrett's letters are studied, sometimes eloquent, accounts that provided Newfoundland audiences with a carefully crafted and enticing picture of the NFC. On June 26, 1917, he wrote: "Military discipline is being maintained, and the boys are adapting themselves to it with the aptness noted of Newfoundlanders." Barrett described in detail the work and accomplishments of the Companies, along with the warm reception provided to the foresters by the Scottish people, which included an interest in the NFC's unique approaches to harvesting and milling of timber. On December 2,

---

56   For example, an editorial in *The Western Star* published shortly after Barrett's return (and possibly written by Barrett himself) was clearly influenced by his knowledge of Scotland. It presented an argument for a forestry policy for Newfoundland such as the one adopted in Scotland in 1919 to advance conservation and afforestation after the war ("A Forestry Policy," 1919).

1917, he proudly announced to readers: "The visitors see the great trimmed logs sliding down the chute to the milldam, and watch them being hauled up the jack-ladder[57] into the mill. They keenly follow the process of operations until the huge stick is converted into the required sizes of lumber and taken out on rollers to be carted to the piles in the yard. The newness of it all thrills them, and they extend congratulations for the work we are performing."

The letters also provide a cultural snapshot or "pen picture" of Scotland, an approach Margaretta Jolly (2001) points out was common in wartime letters and that deflected from the more difficult aspects of service. Barrett's letters are a travelogue of landscapes, landmarks, and local weather, an account of sites visited and history learned. They are a small compendium of local culture, language, and lore. Along with the day-to-day workings of the Companies, readers are given a little of Scotland itself. Barrett regularly included poems, songs, and short excerpts of articles, to share with his readers at home the cultural tenor of the times in the United Kingdom, along with examples of how the Scottish exalted the Ancient Colony in story and song. From Barrett's letters it is also possible to gather a sense of how enamoured with their new home many of the foresters were.

These ingredients—a beautiful country, welcoming people, and smitten foresters—along with work as meaningful service, all so carefully presented by Barrett, were intended not only to inform and console those at home but also to aid recruitment efforts there. Captain Hugh A. Anderson (1918b) of the Newfoundland Contingent of the Pay and Record Office in London wrote about the need for more men to the editor of *The Evening Herald*, following a convalescence trip to Kenmore with the NFC:

> There is an urgent and growing need for more [foresters] and it must be the duty of every Newfoundlander who is, for some reason, unfit to fight, to enlist at once under Major Sullivan's banner

---

57 A ladder or belt operated by a chain system and used to transported timber from pond to sawmill.

and help in the vital work. . . . A more interesting and healthy life could not be found, beside which the lucky forester would be given a trip for nothing to a part of the world which in peace times many an American paid hundreds of dollars to see. (p. 3)

Anderson's observations are, again, a reminder of purposeful crafting of war correspondence. In a personal note to editor McGrath, attached to the letter, Anderson wrote (1918a):

On several occasions, the Foresters have extended their hospitality to members of the Pay and Record Office in London who have been run down and wanted a change. They are doing great work in Scotland, and if you can help them by the publication of the enclosed, they (and I) will be grateful. (p. 1)

Along with a cultural snapshot, Barrett offered readers a glimpse of changes in the UK that were prompted by war and that also resonated at home. For example, several times in his writing, Barrett provided observations on the wartime contributions of women, both to the well-being of the foresters and soldiers and to the overall war effort. Shortly after his arrival in Scotland, on June 16, 1917, Barrett wrote about what he had seen from the train window as the NFC travelled from Ayr to Dunkeld: "Owing to the scarcity of men, many women were to be seen working on farms, in factories, and at other vocations, all filling positions that before the war were occupied by men. And success is attending their noble efforts." Later, on September 15, 1917, he turned their work into a lesson to the men at home who had not enlisted: "The women of the Empire have set a good example to our men, by donning khaki and overalls and engaging in work they were at one time looked upon as being incapable of performing. And they are doing it very creditably." His letters gesture to the significance of women's war work and the opportunities it provided to women, which would ultimately contribute to and enhance the struggle for emancipation long after the war.

For the lumberer, Barrett's letters offer familiar references to woods work, but in the context of a military operation. For the lay reader, the letters are an introduction to adaptive lumbering during wartime. They captured the impressive scale, intricacy, and efficiency of the operations developed by the NFC—from harvesting and transporting to milling and shipping. But they also make clear that wartime service in Scotland was not only about work. They offer reading audiences details and delights of life in another context. Barrett shared the novelty of "aeroplanes" and "bikes," and the pleasures of morale-boosting concerts and sports competitions, not to mention budding romances. Today, through their balanced account of camp work and cultural interchange between the Newfoundlanders and the Scots, set against the ever-present backdrop of the sacrifices and struggles of those on the battle-grounds of the Front, the letters provide a glimpse of life on the Scottish homefront in the early twentieth century.

Barrett sometimes resorted to humour to capture and enliven otherwise more mundane moments and accounts. In early September 1917, describing his efforts to adjust to European plug tobacco, something to which many of the foresters could relate, he hyperbolized:

> Being an inveterate smoker, I have been spending some little time with "My Lady Nicotine" before starting to write this; and very vexatious have my efforts been. The kind of plug tobacco generally sold here is of such a nature that it cakes very hard in the pipe, requiring little less than a cord of matches to keep it lighted, and a mustard plaster on the neck to assist in drawing the smoke through the stem of my dudeen.

In another instance, on October 22, 1917, he wryly described the daily battle to conquer the forests of Craigvinean Hill:

> There was a cessation of hostilities between our men and the trees from Oct. 8th to 18th, to enable our forces to remove the dead "bodies," which in their thousands strewed the hillsides.

But now they have again renewed the engagement. Every day the battle rages long and furious, and at eventide the Camp is astir with tales of the thousands of giants slain with axes and saws.

In a similar vein, in his letter of December 29, 1917, he described Christmas dinner away from home: "Turkey was readily overthrown and as quickly divested of its supports by the hearty lads of Newfoundland."

The Official and the Personal

In both his official and personal letters, Barrett's perspective is clear, and clearly shaped by his varied experiences prior to enlistment and his position as a non-commissioned officer. While Barrett's tone differs somewhat in his official and personal writings, being unsurprisingly more casual and intimate in the personal letters, he consistently offers a palatable and reassuring view of the NFC as a professional military unit, marked by equal measures of discipline, order, honour, and productivity—a unit of which Newfoundlanders could be proud. As is common in wartime letters (Jolly, 2001), Barrett's correspondence focusses on the positive and avoids the controversial. Where problems existed—and the attestation files indicate that there were problems—they are either downplayed or unnamed. While some omissions may be explained by official parameters placed on content, undoubtedly Barrett's personal tact and sense of diplomacy also shaped content.

This point is reinforced by reference to a personal letter Barrett wrote on Christmas Eve, 1917, to his brother Doyle in Saskatchewan, which was submitted by Doyle Barrett to *The Twillingate Sun* for publication ("Spare Our Blushes," 1918).[58] As with the personal letters to Andrew Barrett, included here, that were published in *The Western Star*, many of the topics

---

58 With the exception of the sections quoted here, this letter duplicates content from other published letters and is, therefore, not included in this volume.

about which Barrett wrote to Doyle—official visits, wartime work of women, rations, concerts, European tobacco—are similar to those that appeared in his official letters. Details, too, are similar, although often rendered in a more casual style. As would be expected, the personal letters contain many more specific references to people—the Ballams, Reverend Allen, etc.— and life in the Bay of Islands area. In his letter to Doyle, for example, Barrett ("Spare Our Blushes," 1918) mentioned their brothers George and Gilbert, both of whom had immigrated to Sydney, Nova Scotia, and subsequently enrolled in the Canadian forces when the war began. The reference offers some hint of how the Newfoundland foresters experienced their camps and how they may have differed from the camps of the Canadian Forestry Corps:

> I hear from George[59] and Gilbert[60] quite frequently. Gilbert was up to see me for a couple of days before he went to France, and I was delighted to see him. He was looking fine. I don't think George likes the conditions of things in the Camp where he is; there does not appear to be the same treatment accorded the men he is among as our men get, and our men think their lot pretty severe, although they can get a pass any night or weekend they want one. (p. 2)

Where the attestation papers reveal the constraints of camp life, by recording infractions related to resisting them, Barrett's official letters reveal no such discord—this information could have discouraged enlistment. It was not until he penned his recap, written in 1952 (see Appendix C), that Barrett mentions the "clink"—the NFC prison hut—although he also noted that it was rarely used.

---

59 Private George W. Barrett, CFC #2330408, Sydney, Nova Scotia, Canada. George enlisted with the Nova Scotia Forestry Depot and served in France and Belgium with the CFC.

60 Sergeant Gilbert P. Barrett, CEF #715476, Sydney, Nova Scotia, Canada. Gilbert enlisted with the 106th Battalion, Canadian Expeditionary Force.

The frankness often reserved for personal correspondence was also evident in Barrett's discussion of the Christmas season, his first in Scotland, in the letter to Doyle ("Spare Our Blushes," 1918):

> I spent my Christmas in the southern part of Scotland, and it was a "green" one, somewhat different from what I had been accustomed. Yet, I spent a very enjoyable one with friends. . . . Will you credit it that on Christmas Day I saw farmers at work sowing wheat, harrowing, and ploughing their land? It did not look very winterlike here. Christmas Day is never observed by Scotchmen in this country, although in England it is the day. The principal day in Scotland is New Year's Day, "when brither Scots foregather"[61] and taste the barley brew. (pp. 1–2)

Barrett's approach to the NFC fatalities while in Scotland—Privates Taylor, Hogan, and Wyatt—also highlights differences between the official and personal letters. His elaborate account of the death and funeral of Private Taylor, the first fatality, was in an official letter; it emphasizes the solemnity of the military service, reiterates the character of Private Taylor, and includes sympathies to his parents and family. His account of Private Hogan's death and funeral, rendered in a personal letter, offers far fewer details and points of emphasis. Details of the disappearance and subsequent drowning of Private Wyatt in late 1918, after Armistice, and the recovery and interment of his body in spring 1919, are not mentioned in any of Barrett's correspondence.

---

61 "When brither Scots foregather" is a line from the song "A Wee Deoch-an'-Doris," written and composed by Gerald Grafton and Harry Lauder.

Enforcing the Official Line

In several instances in Barrett's official letters, content was reshaped or re-moved,[62] likely at the request of a higher-ranking officer; letters published in newspapers contain the revised content. A glaring example involved Barrett's comments on commissions and separation allowances, sore points among the soldiers and the Newfoundland public. In his original letter of November 18, 1917, Barrett wrote the following about an upcoming round of promotions:

> A report is being circulated to the effect that Lieutenant Cole and Lieutenant Crowe are about to be promoted to the rank of Captain, and CSM James is to receive a Second Lieutenancy. Their commissions will likely be issued before this appears in type. This reminds me of a statement made in the Recruiting Notices at home last spring, to the effect that we would be officered by Newfoundlanders. Should the above-mentioned appointments come into effect, we will have five Englishmen as officers. Not with any spirit of prejudice do I say it; but there are native-born Newfoundlanders who are in every respect as well qualified as those of any other country to direct the affairs of the Forestry Companies. (p. 1)

In the same letter, perhaps fearing the effects of these and other inequities on esprit de corps or recruitment possibilities, Barrett added:

> When men of other countries are appointed over the heads of Newfoundlanders in this unit; and when by the granting of Separation Allowances to married men, who are working side-by-side with the single men, there is small wonder for the lack of enthusiasm for enlistment on the part of young single men at home.

---

62 The originals are marked to indicate where content is edited or replaced with rewritten content.

Respecting the Separation Allowance, it may be all very well for
the married man; but if the authorities expect to get good results
from the single men and a continuation of enlistments from this
class, there is need of some radical changes being made. (p. 1)

The revised and published version (see page 150) was considerably less
pointed, with editorializing reduced to a minimum. On the matter of the
commissions, the revised letter reads:

A report is being circulated to the effect that Lieutenant Cole and
Lieutenant Crowe are about to be promoted to the rank of Captain;
and Command Sergeant Major James[63] is to receive a 2nd Lieutenancy. Their promotions will likely be issued before this appears
in print. The men have had practical experience in the work at
which they are engaged, and during the time we have been here,
both Lieutenants Cole and Crowe have very efficiently performed
the work allotted them. To them all are extended the congratulations of the Companies.

The issue of disparities in the effects of the granting of separation allowance[64] to married members was thus modified:

Now that the Separation Allowance is being granted to married
men and those with an aged father or mother dependent on them
for support, there should be no reasonable excuse for anyone
withholding from enlisting for the Forestry Companies, and we
look for a goodly increase in our numbers pretty soon.

---

63 Command Sergeant Major Noel G. James, RNR #3486 / #0–171, St. John's.
64 The separation allowance was a portion of a soldier's salary plus additional gov-
    ernment funds; it was paid to a dependent whose income was negatively affect-
    ed by his absence. Minister of Militia Bennett announced the allowance in the
    fall recruitment campaign of 1917 ("An Appeal to the People," 1917).

With the exception of letters that appeared in *The Evening Herald*, Barrett's letters were published with few editorial changes. Sometimes poems he had included were omitted, perhaps for space considerations; in other instances, excerpts only were used, for a more pointed presentation of the material. It is possible that, on at least one occasion, editors may have feared the omitted content would have offended some sensibilities. Barrett opened his letter of March 2, 1918, with a short comic rhyme about the busyness of work, but that was omitted in the published versions in both *The Evening Herald* and *The Twillingate Sun*. The rhyme read: "Last week my work was so congested / And things to write of were not newsy / So down my pen was laid and rested / From scribbling things sober or boozy." In the context of temperance movements and prohibition, editors likely considered it wiser to omit the rhyme.

Generally, *Herald* editor Patrick McGrath took a more hands-on approach to Barrett's writing, regularly deleting or modifying phrases and sentences, re-ordering paragraphs, and, in some cases, editorializing and updating information. For example, when Barrett wrote about plans by Dunkeld locals who were of "the fair sex" to host a social for the foresters, McGrath added an update, likely also intended to encourage enlistment: "It is to be hoped that another Company shall have arrived by that time and be participants of the honours."

· · ·

Studying Barrett's letters gave me an opportunity to revisit the formation and service of this small non-combat unit of the Newfoundland Regiment and, through his descriptions of the NFC's work in Scotland, to feel some connection to the men who chose to serve during the war in the only capacity for which they were eligible. The letters were also an opportunity to reconsider the importance of the contribution of the NFC in the larger context of the First World War, during which combat strength was a crucial but not the sole part of the battle. In an age of wood, timber supply played no small part, leading UK Prime Minister David Lloyd George to remark in 1919, as the new Forestry Commission was formed, that the country "came closer to losing the war through lack of timber than want of food" (House, 1917, p. 2).

Without Barrett's letters, there would be no first-hand account of the NFC available to those of us who continue to inquire about its overseas operations. Despite the limitations inherent in any official letters about war and wartime work, for forester families and others—historians, educators, genealogists, and the general public—Barrett's letters bring insight and meaning to the work of the NFC and provide some answers to questions about work and life during those war years in Scotland. They are a useful account of this small but important unit of the Newfoundland Regiment, whose members, like those of other wartime services, also "did their bit" for the Newfoundland contribution to the Allied war effort.

JOHN A. BARRETT: A SHORT BIOGRAPHY[65]

On April 20, 1917, aged 43 and unmarried, John Archelaus Barrett enlisted with the Newfoundland Forestry Companies at St. John's. Barrett was assigned the rank of Corporal and departed for Scotland with the first draft of foresters less than a month later, on May 17. He remained with the NFC for the duration. In the fall of 1917, Barrett refused promotion to Quartermaster Sergeant of B Company in order to remain in his initial assignment with A Company atop Craigvinean ("Spare Our Blushes," 1918). On February 11, 1919, at Kenmore, Barrett was promoted to Regimental Quartermaster Sergeant. After he departed Kenmore in early June of 1919, he was assigned to the Pay and Record Office in London. Barrett was demobilized at St. John's on August 4, 1919.

During the NFC's time in Scotland, Barrett performed many jobs—quartermaster, storekeeper, ration corporal, and orderly. He was also assigned the job of press correspondent by Timber Supply in London. In this latter role, over the approximately two years the NFC operated in Scotland,

---

65   This biography was gleaned from numerous sources, including the family genealogy (D.G. Barrett, 1989) and conversations with family members.

Barrett wrote letters to Newfoundland newspapers to apprise readers of the work of its foresters overseas.

Barrett's assignment as the foresters' official scribe was most apt. He was born in Freshwater, Carbonear, in 1872, but in 1880 his parents moved to his mother's home of Twillingate, just as Jabez P. Thompson, formerly of *The Harbour Grace Standard* newspaper, was establishing *The Twillingate Sun*. At the age of 12, Barrett became a printer's devil with the *Sun*, where he worked until 1894. By then well-versed in the newspaper business, he moved to Trinity to become editor of *The Trinity Record* ("Some Early Recollections," 1950).

In late 1899, Barrett moved to Birchy Cove (soon to be renamed Curling[66]) to become a member of the founding staff, with editor Walter S. March, of *The Western Star*. The newspaper was published in Birchy Cove, which was at the time the hub of the Bay of Islands. In 1904, following the departure of March, Barrett became editor, a position he held until 1908, when *The Western Star* was sold. His brother Andrew became managing editor in 1911[67] ("Some Early Recollections," 1950). For a short time before the war, John Barrett also worked at the York Harbour Copper Mine.

In 1920, John Barrett and Ena Constance Culbard were married at Dunkeld, Scotland. Their wedding was announced in both the *Dundee Advertiser* and *The Western Star* ("Culbard–Barrett Marriage," 1920). Soon thereafter, they sailed for Newfoundland and settled in Curling. They named the family cabin on the shores of Deer Lake "Kenmore," the Scottish town where the couple had spent their honeymoon.

Ena Constance Barrett was a published poet, and she continued to write and publish after her move to Curling. Her poetry demonstrated a deep love and appreciation for her adopted home and earned her the unofficial moniker of "Newfoundland's poet laureate" ("Ena Constance Barrett," 2018).

After the war, Barrett held various positions, including serving for many years as the first manager of the Board of Liquor Control. He became a Justice

---

66   Birchy Cove, Bay of Islands, was renamed Curling in 1904 to honour Reverend James John Curling, an Anglican priest who served in the area from 1873 to 1888.

67   Andrew L. Barrett was editor of *The Western Star* from 1912 to 1941.

Regimental Quartermaster Sergeant John Archelaus Barrett and
Ena Constance Culbard on their wedding day, June 17, 1920, Dunkeld.
(Courtesy of the Barrett family)

of the Peace, a notary public, and a Commissioner of the Supreme Court of
Newfoundland. He was devout, patriotic, and civic-minded. He attended
closely to community affairs in Curling, often writing letters to *The Western
Star* to promote ideas for growth and development in the Bay of Islands. He
was a member, and eventually president, of the local Board of Trade. He was
also an avid fly fisher and outdoor enthusiast and was accomplished at cricket
and billiards.

Barrett made one attempt to enter politics. In 1928, he sought the Liberal
nomination in Humber District, along with a young Joseph R. Smallwood.
When then Liberal Prime Minister Sir Richard Squires decided to run in the
district where earlier in the decade he had "put the hum on the Humber,"[68]

---

68 Squires had used this campaign slogan in the 1923 election. It referred to a plan
    to build a second pulp and paper mill on the Humber River at Corner Brook,
    which at the time was a small lumber village. The second mill, initially operated
    by the Newfoundland Power and Paper Company, opened in Corner Brook in
    1925. The history of the Corner Brook mill is recounted in the song "Hum on the
    Humber," composed by Brendan Mitchell (Kelly & Forsyth, 2018b, pp. 267–70).

Barrett secured the Tory nomination instead. He lost to Squires in the general election (Smallwood, 1973).

In 1927, Barrett presented a proposal to the Great War Veterans' Association (GWVA) for a war memorial for Bay of Islands. As Honorary Secretary of the Citizens' War Memorial Committee, he ensured the fulfilment of the goal; the memorial was unveiled on July 3, 1932 ("An Outstanding Figure," 1932). For years, the light atop the memorial was operated from a switch at the Barrett home: it was turned on at dusk and off at dawn. The family also maintained the grounds of the memorial.

A writer, historian, and public intellectual, Barrett documented in photographs and essays the emerging stories of his beloved communities and the country of Newfoundland. After the Great War, Barrett continued to write and to publish. His column, "Reminiscent of Bygone Days" published in *The Western Star* between 1945 and 1949, provides an invaluable account of the early history of Bay of Islands. Barrett was well known in the area for his local knowledge and insight. Charles R. Fay, the Cambridge economic historian who met Barrett on his travels around Newfoundland in 1952, called him "Curling's Grand Old Man" (Fay, 1956, p. 213).

John and Ena Barrett had four children: John, Arthur, David, and Rose. Their oldest, Royal Canadian Air Force Pilot Officer John H. Barrett, was killed in 1942: aged 20, he died when the passenger ferry SS *Caribou*, crossing from North Sydney, Nova Scotia, to Port-aux-Basques, Newfoundland, was torpedoed and sunk by a German U-boat. Second son Arthur, a career broadcaster and retired Flight Lieutenant of the Royal Canadian Air Force Bomber Command, died at St. John's in 2019, at the age of 95. David Barrett lives in Welland, Ontario, and Rose Barrett Gillam lives in Mount Pearl, Newfoundland and Labrador.

John A. Barrett died in Curling on July 10, 1955, at the age of 83. Ena C. Barrett died at Grand Falls in 1967.

2

THE LETTERS OF REGIMENTAL QUARTERMASTER SERGEANT JOHN A. BARRETT JUNE 1917 TO JANUARY 1919

Regimental Quartermaster Corporal (later Sergeant)
John A. Barrett by A.F. MacKenzie, Birnam, Scotland, 1918.
(Courtesy of Archives and Special Collections, World War One
Artifacts 09.01.004, Memorial University of Newfoundland)

In compiling and presenting the letters of Sergeant Barrett, my intent was to create a narrative of the day-to-day doings of the Newfoundland Forestry Companies—a resource that would provide readers, albeit partially, with both a chronology and a detailed account that had the letters at their centre. But not all pertinent information was available through the letters, nor would some of what was included in them necessarily be self-evident to most readers more than a century later. I addressed both of these issues in the organization and editing of the letters.

John Barrett's letters were not always published in the order in which they were written (and, as has been noted, the same letter was sometimes printed on different dates in more than one paper). They are presented here in that sequence, however, along with the headline and subtitle under which they appeared in the newspaper version reproduced. Newspaper publication venues and dates are included with each letter.

With the exception of minor editing—such as correction of misspellings and inaccuracies, some of which may have occurred in typesetting—the letters are presented as published, with common writing practices of the time maintained. For example, capitalization and gendered usages have been retained. Information that a reader might require for greater comprehension is provided in footnotes or, if a longer account is warranted, following the letter in which its reference arises or near the date on which the information fits chronologically. Where available, I have provided sources for the additional material—poems, songs, excerpts—that Barrett included in his letters. It is possible that Barrett himself penned some of the short unattributed rhymes; the authors of other unattributed items could not be traced.

As indicated earlier, few letters were written during the time the NFC was posted at Kenmore. The narrative gaps created by a dearth of accounts from this later period are partially filled in a general account of the NFC that Barrett wrote in 1952, in which he provides additional information about the time at Kenmore in particular. This account, published in *The Western Star*, is included in Appendix C in an abridged form and with minor editing applied, as in the letters.

I have also attempted to address omissions and gaps through the use of other documentation. Where appropriate, I have inserted additional material to complement Barrett's content, to provide useful context, and to enhance the picture of life with the Companies that he relayed. This material includes excerpts from the handful of available letters and published reminiscences from other foresters, and letters to editors and other items in newspapers in both Scotland and Newfoundland. Based on my research—a review of attestation files, primary documents, and secondary materials—I have created my own accounts of some key events. These include, for example, the wreck of the SS *Florizel* while Major Michael Sullivan was aboard and the third fatality of the NFC, neither of which is mentioned in the letters. Given the dearth of documentation about the NFC,[1] in my coverage of the unit I attempted to provide as much detail and context as possible—in both the opening and concluding essays and in subsequent shorter pieces included in the letters section.

---

1   There are also few accounts of other wartime forestry services of both the First and Second World War. See Caplan (1983) for an interview with Thomas Gillard of Southern Arm, Newfoundland, who enlisted with the CFC in the First World War. See Curran (1987) for an account of the Newfoundland Overseas Forestry Unit of the Second World War. See also Jeddore (2015) for an individual forester's account of service in the NOFU. For an account of a CFC forester's experiences in Scotland in the Second World War, see a compilation of the letters of Pat Hennessy of 15 Company (Jarratt, 2016).

In some instances, I have also created brief individual snapshots of foresters who exemplify an aspect of the story of the NFC. Unless otherwise indicated, information provided about individual foresters was gleaned from attestation files. Barrett refers several times in his letters to photographs taken of the Companies at work, but there are very few still in existence. I have included some of the handful available that were taken at NFC sites in Scotland, hitherto unpublished, including several taken by Barrett himself. A timeline based on Barrett's correspondence and other official documents is also included, to clarify key events related to the NFC from its formation to disbandment. An updated NFC member list is included (Appendix B). Individual foresters referenced by Barrett are identified on first mention only by service number and hometown, according to the details recorded at attestation. I corrected names where misspelling at attestation could be confirmed through other sources.

CORPORAL J.A. BARRETT WRITES
INTERESTING LETTER FROM AYR, SCOTLAND[2]

June 12, 1917

At 4 o'clock the morning of May 19th, we were awakened by the man on night duty, and were reminded of the parade at 5 o'clock. There was very little time for those living far from the Armoury[3] to make the necessary preparations.

After roll call and other preliminaries, the stalwart lads of the Newfoundland Regiment and Forestry Companies to the number of about 300, marched to the ship[4] for embarkation. Although the hour was an early one, yet hundreds of the citizens of the Capital turned out to bid the boys "God speed." Steamboat and factory whistles shrilled the air, and as the troop ship moved slowly out the harbour, the lads crowded on the forecastle deck, promenade deck, and other prominent places, cheering and returning the farewell salutes fondly tendered by the thousands lined along the piers, and upon several prominent houses. Many an eye was dimmed with tears over the parting; but in reply to the question "Are we downhearted?" the boys unhesitatingly answered, "No!" and they really meant it, too.

The King's[5] men were favoured with "King's weather," a light nor'-wester was blowing, there was a cloudless sky, and scarcely a swell on the ocean—just a pleasant motion. Being favoured by such conditions, the boys could not be other than gay. Major Carty,[6] well and favourably known to the people of the

---

2   *The Western Star*, July 18, 1917, p. 2.
3   At the time, the Church Lads Brigade Armoury was the headquarters of the Regiment.
4   The SS *Florizel*.
5   The British monarch of the day, George V.
6   Lieutenant-Colonel George T. Carty, RNR #0–6, St. George's.

West Coast, was in charge of the troops, and he was untiring in his efforts to see that they were properly looked after.

On the way to Halifax, we enjoyed ourselves at various games, music, singing and dancing, and we were favoured with considerable talent in our company. A sweepstake was arranged, and a prize given to the person guessing nearest to the time of arrival at Halifax. This honour was awarded to Lieutenant Cole of the Newfoundland Forestry Companies.

Halifax was sighted at an early hour on Monday 21st, and as we drew in near McNab's Island, a large ocean liner, with over 800 wounded Canadian soldiers, passed quite close to us. Immediately upon arrival, we disembarked, and proceeded to The Armouries, which massive building was to be our headquarters whilst in Halifax.

On Tuesday night, death visited the ranks, and Private F. Smart,[7] of Alexander Bay, Bonavista Bay, was called away. He was a young man of 18 years, and bore an exemplary character. His death was due to uraemic poisoning, and his illness lasted only a few hours. His funeral took place the following day, and he was buried with full military honours.

Our stay at Halifax lasted several days, but a great deal of the time was occupied at squad drill. A number of the boys, having friends and relatives in this city, were given leave to visit them, and spent a jolly time sight-seeing.

Since leaving Newfoundland I have seen some interesting sights. The journey occupied two weeks, and the crossing to England was made in quite a large ship.[8] Of course, we had lots

---

7   Private Frank Smart, RNR #3578, of Alexander Bay, died of heart failure caused by uremic poisoning on May 22, 1917. His remains are interred at Fort Massey Cemetery, Halifax, Grave E77.

8   The White Star liner RMS *Olympic*, sister ship of the RMS *Titanic*, departed Halifax June 2, 1917, with more than six thousand troops.

of company, as there were several thousand troops on board. The weather was delightful and water smooth, which enabled us to have squad drill and route marches every day. American de-stroyers met us at sea and escorted us to port. Landfall[9] was made early Saturday morning, and a great deal of excitement prevailed, as all knew we were fast drawing out of the danger zone. It was quite a relief to all. A great many people visited the dock during the day, and some thirty thousand crossed in the ferry[10] to see the troops.

It was a charming drive through the country here. Quaint houses, picturesque scenes and well cultivated fields were every-where visible. Through every section of the country, scenes of thrift presented themselves. It was quite a change from riding on the trains at home, for, as we seemed to fly over the road, there was scarcely a jar or jolt of the train.[11]

A large crowd had gathered at the station[12] to welcome us, and accompanied us along the route to our quarters. All the boys seem to be enjoying themselves, and like this land of Robert Burns[13] extremely well. Vegetation is much advanced, and flo-rists have their grounds well laid out and all in bloom with such a variety of gay colours as can only be seen in bonnie Scotland. I often think of late Reverend John Allan[14] and how he used to

---

9   Liverpool, June 9, 1917.

10   Ferries crossed the Mersey River to and from ports on the Liverpool side.

11   The Newfoundland Railway, the narrow-gauge "Reid's Express" as it was known locally (it was built by the Reid Newfoundland Company), was notorious for its rough ride. An unknown logger described the train ride in his song "Reid's Express": "You'll think you're in some liner out in some heavy gale" (Kelly & Forsyth, 2018b, p. 79).

12   Ayr Railway Station.

13   Robert (Rabbie) Burns was born at Alloway, a suburb of Ayr that is now home to the Robert Burns Birthplace Museum. Burns was known as the Bard of Ayrshire and is widely regarded as Scotland's national poet.

14   Reverend John Munn Allan, a Presbyterian minister, served in Bay of Islands

praise the beauties of Scotland, and rave over the climate, its people, and charms.

About fifteen minutes' walk from the camp is a lovely sandy strand, an ideal bathing station, opening on to the Irish Sea, and many people daily congregate there.

Yesterday we saw for the first time an aeroplane.[15] It flew over us for a while and swooped down quite near to the ground.

I saw Sam Ballam.[16] He is here, getting along splendidly. George[17] left here half an hour after our arrival. He is a Lance-Corporal.

We will likely be here a while before going to our scene of operation. It is quite warm here, in fact, it was sweltering hot these two days. This evening, it is raining, with quite an electrical storm attending it. I was down to the strand and got caught in it.

We are quartered in camps here,[18] and it is a life that I am very conversant with. I am writing this with an upturned plate for a desk. It is not dark until after eleven o'clock, and some of the boys have not yet got accustomed to retiring in daylight.

Messrs. Cole and Harvey, late of the A.N.D. Company, Grand Falls, are with us as 1st and 2nd Lieutenants, respectively. Mr. Baird, of Norris Arm, is our Captain, and Mr. Beeton, also well-known at Grand Falls, is our Officer Commanding.[19] He inspected us to-day, and congratulated all upon their appearance and the

from 1902 to 1914. Allan studied Theology in Edinburgh and was the first New-foundlander to become a Presbyterian minister (Moncrieff, 1966).

15 The powered aeroplane (airplane) was still a novelty in 1917. American brothers Orville and Wilbur Wright conducted the first flight in 1903. Winged aircraft were first used in battle in 1911; their use became widespread in the First World War (MacIsaac, 2016).

16 Private Samuel Ballam, RNR #1440, Curling.

17 Lance Corporal George Ballam, RNR #3031, Curling. George Ballam was killed six months later during the Battle of Cambrai.

18 The Regimental Depot was at the Ayr Racecourse, built in 1907.

19 Major Sullivan did not arrive to Dunkeld until August, with the second draft.

stand they had taken, and trusted that many more in the Ancient Colony would soon enlist with the Forestry Companies and assist the Mother Land in the work set apart for us. Thousands from other British Colonies and the United States are being enrolled, and Newfoundland, with all her sturdy woodsmen, should not be behind other overseas Dominions.

Ayr, Ayrshire, Scotland

The first draft of the Newfoundland Forestry Companies was welcomed at Ayr, Scotland, by Mayson M. Beeton (front row, centre, in civilian dress) of the UK Timber Supply Department, June 12, 1917.
(Courtesy of the Barrett family)

Goodbye, Dear Mother

Melville Colbourne, NFC #8150, a lumberer of Purcell's Harbour, Twillingate Island, was 19 and the oldest of five siblings when he travelled to St. John's in May 1917 to enlist in the Newfoundland Regiment. Like many, he did not meet the physical standards for the Regiment and so, determined to serve, he enlisted in the newly formed NFC. On May 18, 1917, on the eve of the voyage to Halifax with the first draft, he penned a short letter to his mother, Lavinia (Windsor) Colbourne. Published on June 6 in *The Twillingate Sun*, Colbourne's note ("A Pathetic Letter," 1917) suggests how little many of the enlistees knew about where they were going or for how long.

> Dear Mother,
>
> We are going across tomorrow in the *Florizel* to Halifax, but I don't know where from that. We are going to England for the summer to cut wood. There are two hundred of us from the Regiment and one hundred from the Forestry Battalion.
>
> I tried twice for the Army and I had to go the second time to the Forestry doctor before I could pass. I shall have to be vaccinated.
>
> I am sending 60 cents a day home to you and I hope to get more pay shortly as I hope to be promoted to Corporal and do time-keeping.
>
> Don't worry about me, dear mother; I am trying to do my bit for King and Country. I could not be satisfied to stay home when I think of the other fellows who are gone out to fight for me.
>
> Good bye, dear mother,
> From your son, Melville (p. 2)

At dusk in Newfoundland, on the eve of Colbourne's departure from Halifax aboard the RMS *Olympic*, his father, John, was one of four crew who ran into trouble on the return trip from their fishing grounds in Notre Dame Bay. Their skiff, laden with herring, was swamped and all four men were drowned. Melville Colbourne served in the NFC for the duration and, as he had hoped, attained the rank of Corporal and was able to assign an allotment of 70 cents per day to his mother. He was demobilized at St. John's on April 11, 1919.

WHERE OUR FORESTRY COMPANY WILL OPERATE[20]
Highlands of Scotland Described by Corporal J.A. Barrett

June 26, 1917

I last wrote you from the pretty little town of Ayr, where we were quartered with the Newfoundland Regiment for a fortnight. On June 25th, we bid "au revoir" to our acquaintances there and joined train for here. We passed through quite a number of fine towns, the principal of which was Glasgow, where we had a tarry of over two hours; but being confined to the station we had no chance of seeing much of interest.

The scenery along the route was pretty and varied—one minute we were rushing through towns where numerous factory chimneys rose skyward, and then we would round the side of a mountain, getting a magnificent view of a valley with its well-kept and fertile farms and numerous cottages and farm houses dotted here and there. On every hand the scenes depicted thrift and industry. Owing to the scarcity of men, many women were to be seen working on farms, in factories, and at other vocations, all filling positions that before the war were occupied by men. And success is attending their noble efforts.

We reached Dunkeld Station early in the afternoon of 25th ult.[21] After attending to the necessary preliminaries, we started on a tramp nearly four miles to the place of encampment. It was a warm day, thus making the journey very trying. We took along some camps, cooking outfit, and other supplies, and by night we were comfortably set up on Craigvinean, a mountain overlooking Dunkeld, to the eastward. Since then our Company has been kept busy, some packing in supplies, some repairing roads, and

---

20 *The Western Star*, August 1, 1917, p. 4.

21 "Ult.," Latin for "ultimo," means "the previous month" and was likely an editorial addition to the letter, given its publication date.

others attending to various duties about camp. This week we shall be getting a quantity of lumber hauled up here, when the construction of houses will be undertaken, and conditions made more comfortable for the men.

The property upon which we are to operate is a section of the estate of the Duke of Atholl.[22] There is a goodly supply of fine timber on it, mostly larch and tamarack, and is very accessible. In the course of a few weeks, we hope to have everything in full swing here. Military discipline is being maintained, and the boys are adapting themselves to it with the aptness noted of Newfoundlanders.

The beautiful River Tay winds through the valley at the foot of the mountain, and the Highland Railway skirts its banks. Trains pass here at the rate of about two an hour. Looking down on the coaches from our Camp they appear about the size of baby carriages. About fifteen miles distant to the eastward is the pretty town of Coupar Angus, the home of the late Sir Robert Gillespie Reid.[23] It is a beautiful country, and the scenery is delightful. Up here on the mountain we can get a glimpse of some of the wild grandeur and beauty of the Highlands of Scotland. It is altogether different from the southern part of the country, and the peaks and mountains very forcibly reminding us of certain sections of Newfoundland.

There is considerable game hereabouts, there being an abundance of pheasants, ptarmigan, rabbits, hares, and deer. There are three species of the latter—red, roe and fallow deer— to hunt for which one has to have a license. Nearly every evening

22 James George Stewart-Murray became the eighth Duke of Atholl in 1917.

23 Reid was the builder of the Reid Newfoundland Railway. Completed in 1898, the main line was 548 miles (882 kilometres) long, running between St. John's and Port-aux-Basques. Additional branch lines extended the length to 906 miles (1,458 kilometres), making it the longest narrow-gauge railway in the world (Cuff, 2001).

some of them can be seen quite near the Camp. Of course, you know Newfoundlanders would not think of breaking the game laws of this country, any more than they would those of their own country.

The prices of most foodstuffs and certain luxuries are almost prohibitive over here. As an instance, tobacco costs about 30 cents an ounce. And then we have to "put that in your pipes and smoke it." Owing to war rations and high prices ruling, our boys do not stand to save much clear of their allotments.

Dunkeld, Perthshire, Scotland

• • •

"We Will Do Anything"

The large-scale entry of women into the workforce of the UK and into new jobs created by the demands of war or existing ones vacated by men who volunteered for military service, as observed by Barrett, was not lost on the women of Newfoundland. In the spring of 1917, as the NFC was being established, Governor Davidson issued an appeal to the men of Newfoundland to consider enlistment. Aware of the central role that women played in the successful recruitment of the country's men, Davidson (1917a) implored mothers and wives "to let their men go—nay, to urge them to go as becomes their manhood. Do not let your men have to endure the reproach of having been tried as True Men and found wanting" (p. 5).

One response to this appeal, signed by "Young Lady Willing To Do War Work" of Carbonear and published in The Daily News, suggested the political passion and pluck of at least some of the women of the colony. She ("Act the Man," 1917) wrote, in part:

If the Governor's appeal, which has appeared in all the papers of late, has not taken the required effect upon the young men of the community, it has upon the young women. . . . Now that [the men] have shown the Empire, the country, and the town that they don't want to go, we do; and if we cannot go, we'll do something to let them [and] that is my reason for writing. Look around the country and see how many positions the young men occupy, which we might—telegraph offices, banks, and many other positions that we young women would gladly fill, and fill with credit, if the young men will only go and do their bit. The women of England have been given this chance, and what job is there they cannot fill? Not one. Now, then, why not give the young women here a chance. . . . [W]hat can we do? We will do anything; we will go and form this Forestry Battalion, if the Governor wishes, to help win this war. If we young women of Carbonear had a chance, Sir, we would be first instead of the last as far as recruiting goes. (p. 7)

The effect of the war on the socio-economic lives of women in Newfoundland was not on par with the UK. In St. John's, approximately 30 percent of men (almost 1,400) who were between the ages of 18 and 32 in the 1911 census later enlisted in the Regiment (Sharpe, 1988), leaving labour gaps across the city. While some women entered non-traditional work during the war—for example, in a fledgling munitions factory in St. John's—the increased numbers of women in the wartime workforce occurred in what were considered more traditional women's jobs, including textiles, clerical, and retail work (Forestell, 1989). As Terry Bishop-Stirling (2015) noted, despite the immense contribution of the women of Newfoundland to the war effort, the First World War did not seriously challenge traditional gender roles in Newfoundland.

FROM OUR FORESTERS NOW IN SCOTLAND[24]

July 16, 1917

Dear Sir,

Despite predictions made at home respecting the ultimate destination and occupation of the Newfoundland Forestry Companies, many of them have been erroneously made. In my last letters to you I gave a brief account of our trip to Scotland, and my impressions of the country. The more I see of it, the stronger my impressions grow respecting its beauties, its productiveness, and of the need of more male workers in the various avenues of labour; because "While our manhood are a-fighting / And have had to leave our shores," thousands of the women of every station in life of Britain have shown their grit and courage by casting aside their wonted ease and leisure and apparel and are now clad in overalls, filling the places of the men who have been called to where the cannons loudly roar.

The climatic conditions in this country are very conducive to health, for since our arrival it has been beautifully fine, and warm, and dry, making working conditions for the Company very favourable. Not once has there been occasion for donning slicker coats. First when we came here, daylight lasted pretty well right through the 24-hours, and it seemed strange to most of us to be retiring while it was still daylight. But now we are getting accustomed to it; and each night, soon after turning in, sleep, "nature's sweet restorer," comes to us quite readily.

Since coming here an enormous amount of work has been performed. Nearly 30 railroad cars of supplies, lumber, etc., have been transported from the station; a large barn for the horses and forage, quartermaster's store and orderly room, a commodious

---

24   *The Evening Herald*, August 18, 1917, p. 2.

cook house and mess house have been erected, and living quarters for the officers and men are now in course of construction. By the end of this week we expect to move into them. A pipe line has been laid from a newly constructed dam to the various buildings from which a supply of good water for all purposes is assured. Up to the present all cooking has been done in the open air, and the men fed under canvas. But this method will be changed when we get into new quarters.

The timber in this section of the country is of fairly good growth, and consists principally of larch, horse chestnut, beech and elm. In felling these trees they will be cut close to the ground, thus avoiding any wastage of timber, such as is noticeable on many of the devasted hillsides and woodlands of Terra Nova. This is necessary for economic and other reasons. The men are very anxious for the time to come when they can get out and slay these giants of the forest. The logs will then be taken on wheels to the mill where they will be sawn into various requisites of the trade.

The lovers of hunting and fishing can find all the sport they desire hereabouts. An abundance of large and small game is to be found quite near our camp; and the kindly salmon and speckled trout are disturbing the waters of the River Tay, awaiting the cast of an angler's fly. If Messrs. Winter, Bartlett, Herder and other disciples of Isaac Walton[25] were here, their angling efforts would surely be attended with good results.

---

25 Walton was an English author known for *The Compleat Angler*, published in 1653. His so-called "disciples" were Newfoundlanders known to Barrett, possibly from the newspaper industry. At the time, H.A. Winter was the editor of *The Evening Telegram*; W.J. Herder was the publisher. Lemuel Bartlett began *The Daily Journal* in 1924, a short-lived publication with ties to Fishermen's Protective Union founder and politician William F. Coaker and A.E. Hickman, Newfoundland's shortest-serving Prime Minister, in whose business Bartlett worked.

Yesterday being Sunday, we paraded to church for Divine Service, and were favoured with a well-prepared discourse by the Rector of Dunkeld Cathedral. It was the first time since our arrival that the people of Dunkeld had the pleasure of seeing us on dress parade, and they commented very favourably upon our appearance, and the manner in which our men conduct themselves in the evenings when off duty.

In Newfoundland you speak of the "wee Scotch lassies"; but they are "no' so wee at a' " as your imagination may lead you to think. Many of them are buxom, blooming, fair ones, and are already becoming greatly attached to some of our lads. Don't be surprised if some of our confirmed bachelors join the Benedicts[26] before they return to the Homeland.

A great many tourists annually visit the Highlands of Scotland, a number of them staying off in this vicinity. The holiday season in many parts of Great Britain is now on, and numerous visitors can daily be seen cycling and motoring over the country roads of this neighbourhood. The roads are in excellent condition for such and cyclists do not think much of riding twenty and thirty miles to town and returning the same day. Some of our younger men have learned to ride this "bike,"[27] and are fast becoming great favourites with many lady cyclists.

Preparations are being made by a number of the fair sex for a sociable on behalf of our Company, and a pleasant time is predicted for all of us. It is to be hoped that another Company shall have arrived by that time and be participants of the honours.

---

26 A Benedict is a newly married man who had long been a bachelor. The name is a reference to Benedick, a character in Shakespeare's *Much Ado About Nothing* who, despite his professed dislike of marriage, eventually weds.

27 The bicycle debuted in Newfoundland and Canada in the late 1860s. The rudimentary nature of the road system in Newfoundland limited its use as a mode of travel to the St. John's area. See Sandland (1983).

The best of unity and fellowship exist in our ranks, and altogether the men are getting along splendidly, being well-fed and well-looked after by the officers in charge of them.

Dunkeld, Perthshire, Scotland

Three NFC members at Craigvinean, Dunkeld, ca. 1917.
(Courtesy of the Dunkeld Community Archive)

THIRD REPORT OF FORESTERS IN SCOTLAND[28]

July 22, 1917

Dear Sir,

It was a great disappointment to us when we learned this week that "B" Company would not likely be leaving for here before another month. This disappointment is made all the keener by the fact that we have been labouring hard to get furnished accommodations ready for them by the end of the month. However, they will be given an ovation whenever they arrive; and we hope that by that time their number will be supplemented by another one or two Companies.

During the past week or ten days, a great many visitors from Glasgow, Dundee, and other places, have been touring this section of the country. Yesterday's trains took thousands of holiday-seekers out of Dundee, many of whom have come North to spend their vacation. Dunkeld and the surrounding country towns are getting quite a few of them. In peace times, this town used to be overcrowded when the annual holiday season came around.

On Thursday a Cycle Corps[29] of 150 men reached Dunkeld. They were bivouacking throughout the country. Upon reaching here there was a downpour of rain, so Hotel Atholl was commandeered, and the men all had a comfortable shake-down for the night.

Private K. Pittman,[30] who was landed at Liverpool suffering from pneumonia, came to Camp three days ago. He is loud in praising the kind treatment accorded him by doctors, nurses,

---

28 *The Evening Herald,* August 23, 1917, p. 4.
29 The Army Cyclists Corps, a series of voluntary cyclist battalions.
30 Private Kenneth Pittman, NFC #8036, St. John's.

and visitors. Corporal J. Boone[31] and Private F. Meaney,[32] who were left behind at Ayr, have both been discharged from Hospital, and resumed duty with us.

Private Martin Collins,[33] who spent so many years with various wood-working concerns at St. John's, as saw-filer, is continuing the same occupation with us, and when on parade, he is able to stand up against it with most of the younger men. J. Griffin,[34] the shoe-repairer, will soon be established, as a repairing outfit has been ordered for him. Mattie Glynn[35] and Ed O'Brien,[36] of St. John's, and J.A. Campbell of Port au Port, are the principal members of the transports, and what they don't know about horses is meagre. Sergeants Hancock,[37] Lane,[38] Granville,[39] and Pike,[40] who had been engaged at lumbering in and about Grand Falls, Botwood, Badger, and other places in Newfoundland, are the lumbering foremen of the four sections of our Company. They know how to handle men, being alive to their requirements, and are treating them in a right and proper manner.

During the long evenings after duty, the men amuse themselves at various games, such as running, leap frog, high jumping, tug-of-war, etc. Boxing gloves have been ordered and we expect to have in the course of a few days several "Jack Johnsons"[41] in the ring.

---

31   Private James D. Boone, NFC #8063, Glovertown.

32   Private Frank Meaney, NFC #8038, Brigus.

33   Private Martin J. Collins, NFC #8055, St. John's.

34   Private John M. Griffin, NFC #8040, St. John's.

35   Private Matthew Glynn, NFC #8052, St. John's.

36   Private Edward O'Brien, NFC #8107, St. John's.

37   Sergeant John Hancock, NFC #8065, Norris Arm.

38   Sergeant Enos Lane, NFC #8115, Millertown.

39   Sergeant John H. Granville, NFC #8121, Millertown.

40   Sergeant Robert Pike, NFC #8066, Lewisporte.

41   Johnson was the American boxer and world heavyweight champion from 1908 to 1915; his nickname was the "Galveston Giant."

The number of visitors coming to see us is on the increase. They all express admiration for the work we are doing, and compliment the men upon their excellent behaviour.

Dunkeld, Perthshire, Scotland

An NFC member on horseback,
Craigvinean, Dunkeld, ca. 1917.
(Courtesy of the Dunkeld Community Archive)

FOURTH REPORT[42]

July 28, 1917

Dear Sir,

The week has passed rather pleasantly, with just enough work doing to keep us from getting rusty and here I am again writing you on behalf of the Company, so that their relatives and friends in dear old Terra Nova may have the pleasure of hearing from us all at one time.

What seems to gladden the hearts of all as much as anything else is to receive a letter from home. So far very few letters have been received from Newfoundland. Daily the boys flock to the office anxiously expecting letters from their wives, sweethearts, and friends. If they do not write home very often, there is not much excuse for those at home not writing oftener.

Several visitors were at Camp this week. Among them were Lieutenant A.J. Noble and wife, of London. They were highly pleased with the work we have performed.

A photographer, representing a Cinematograph Company, was here yesterday, and took several views of the boys as they were parading to work, armed with such implements as saws, peavies, axes, etc. You may yet see this picture on exhibition at St. Patrick's, or other amusement halls in the Colony.

Private E. Humby,[43] who was in Hospital at Ayr, suffering from measles, has returned to duty. Private Jacob Gillingham[44] and Private John Walsh,[45] who were in Hospital at Perth, I am pleased to report as convalescent.

---

42 *The Evening Herald*, August 25, 1917, p. 2.
43 Private Edward Humby, NFC #8084, St. Leonard's (now St. Lunaire-Griquet).
44 Private John Jacob Gillingham, NFC #8060, Bishop's Falls.
45 Private John F. Walsh, NFC #8072, St. John's.

A Cycle Corps of over 200 men billeted at Dunkeld yesterday, having cycled from St. Andrew's. They left again this morning for Blair Atholl.

Lieutenant Goodyear received a pair of boxing gloves this week, with which the boys have been amusing themselves; and many fistic bouts have taken place. Although some have had their noses pretty freely punched, yet they keep on trying for the championship. Corbett, Willard, Jack Johnson,[46] nor any other pugilist ever witnessed anything to equal these encounters.

Yesterday was a "Red Letter Day" for our Company. It was the beginning of log cutting operations. We had been ready for awhile, awaiting permission to use the axe upon these giant trees. This being granted, some fifteen of the lads, under Sergeant Lane, went at it with a will. The sound of the axe and saw cutting trees, and the sledges in driving the iron wedges, awakened the stillness of the woodland, and every now and again, a tall, shapely spruce or larch would come crashing to the ground. These sticks run from sixty to sixty-five feet in length, and measure on an average of about seventeen inches at the butt and five inches at the top. After being felled they are cut up into various lengths, some trees making five and six logs. By this evening one hundred and eighty-five logs had been cut down, and many of them "browed"[47] by the roadside; not a bad showing for two days. On Monday there will be more men in the woods, and a good output is expected the coming week.

The construction of a tramway from the timber belt to a point near the railroad is contemplated; in fact, a supply of rails for that purpose has already arrived. We haven't a Cobb[48] or a

---

46 Along with Johnson, James J. (Jim) Corbett and Jess Willard were also American professional boxing champions of the era.

47 To stack timber for measurement.

48 Alexander Cobb, of Perthshire, Scotland, was a roadmaster with the Reid Newfoundland Railway.

Steele[49] in our Company, but we have men who can construct this tram line in proper shape and give it the proper elevation on the curves.

After a very small rain shower last evening, the eastern sky was illuminated by a beautiful rainbow. The varied hues portrayed by it were the admiration of all who saw the rainbow. Looking out upon Craigiebarns from Craigvinean with the afterglow of a setting sun illuminating the heavens, this beautiful panoramic view could only be excelled by the charming sunset witnessed from the heights of Bay of Islands.

Many of the visitors to Dunkeld lately were young women who are employed in Munition Factories and other departments of the public service. To many their sacrifices may appear trifling; but they are all doing a noble work, and doing it ungrudgingly, for they realise that the enemy will only be beaten by everybody doing their "bit," without counting the cost.

> Well, well, dear girl, it doesn't really matter!
> Your uniform your secret's guarding true.
> The fact remains—'mid war, and woe, and clatter—
> You've done your "bit," so here's good luck to you!

Dunkeld, Perthshire, Scotland

---

49 David Steele of Fifeshire, Scotland, was also a roadmaster with the Reid Newfoundland Railway. He was hired by the ANDCo to oversee the 1908 building of the 35-kilometre rail line from the port of Botwood to the ANDCo mill at Grand Falls.

August 4, 1917

Dear Sir,

This week the Company moved out from under canvas, and we are all now into the huts built since we came here. The stoves for these are daily expected; but so far we have been exceedingly fortunate in not needing them for any purpose, except for cooking, as the weather has been delightfully fine and warm.

The bunkhouses for the men are quite roomy, being 30 x 20 feet, and the Sergeants' quarters 20 x 16 feet. The Officers' dwelling is 40 x 30, and the Quartermaster's store is 20 x 20. A cookhouse, with dining rooms for Sergeants and other ranks, furnishing ample space for two Companies, is 60 x 30. We have fairly comfortable accommodations, and everything is going along splendidly with us.

We often wonder how recruiting for the Forestry Companies is progressing at home, and if the young and middle-aged men fully realize the urgent need for more men, and still more men for this work. If they do there should be by this time enlistments enough for several companies. Hurry up, boys, or you may live to regret it; and remember, that you will be treated in a right and proper manner when you reach this country.

Today we had the portable saw mill operating under our control for the first time. Another mill, of greater capacity, has arrived and will be erected about half a mile from our quarters; so that when we get those two operating full time there should be a pretty good output of material. Since starting log-cutting on the 27th ult., enough trees have been felled to make 1,955 logs. Some of these trees are of such a size that one and two hours are sometimes occupied trimming the limbs therefrom. It is all

50   *The Evening Herald*, August 27, 1917, p. 4.

good timber that is here, and there is no growth of small woods to be found among it to engage extra time in clearing it away.

We are hoping to soon have a supply of good salt codfish sent up from London which Mr. Beeton has arranged for. The next thing the men would be wishing for would be a good supply of hard bread, with which to make that favourite dish called "brooze."[51]

Deer stalking (or what we call the hunting season in Newfoundland) begins on Monday, 6th inst.,[52] and we are expecting to see a number of sportsmen shooting in this vicinity. If so, we hope they may be successful in getting many trophies of the hunt, and maybe they will grace our larder with some venison—not that there is any scarcity of meat with us, but that venison at this season would be welcomed as a great luxury.

Matthew Anderson, Ayrshire policeman, has sent out the following verses, being constrained to write them after seeing, for the first time, our boys on parade:

THE FORESTERS FROM NEWFOUNDLAND
Matthew Anderson

I gazed today on a glorious sight
Which gave my heart such a pure delight
And raised my soul to a new height
The Foresters from Newfoundland.

Oh, it was a sight to enthuse and inspire
A friendship tested in smile and fire
An heroic link of our great Empire
All the way from Newfoundland.

---

51 Brewis, as in fish and brewis.
52 Barrett often uses this abbreviation for the word "instant," meaning "of this month."

Every kind of a hero was there
The tall, the short, the dark, the fair
While the glorious spirit to do and dare
Lit up those eyes from Newfoundland.

I've often read of that splendid Corps
But I never gazed on the lads before
Who heard the call on that far-off shore
And came to our help from Newfoundland.

And I thought of their mothers so far away
Praying for these young heroes today
That no evil spirit would lead astray
Their dear young lads from Newfoundland.

Token of friendship we love and revere
Emblem of Empire that's strong and sincere
Onward to victory with God ever near
I pray for the lads from Newfoundland.

A band of the Lancashire Hussars[53] entertained the town folk this evening at Cathedral Square. There was quite a large gathering present, who testified by hearty applause their appreciation of the musical renditions.

Dunkeld, Perthshire, Scotland

---

53 The Lancashire Hussars Yeomanry was a unit of the British Army.

The Newfoundlanders and the Scots

As Anderson's poem suggests, the people of Scotland greatly appreciated the service of both the Newfoundland Regiment and the Newfoundland Forestry Companies. Ties between the Scots and the Newfoundlanders strengthened throughout the war. An unidentified Regiment soldier described the mutual affection at the heart of this relationship as it occurred at Ayr ("Scotland and the Newfoundlanders," 1925):

Of all the associations formed in Scotland those with the Auld Toon of Ayr were the closest and most extensive. This was only natural in view of the long period which the [Regiment] depot remained at Ayr. During that time the Newfoundlanders came to regard the town and the neighbouring one of Prestwick as their homes, and the townsfolk on the other hand grew to know the boys individually and as a unit so well that it was said the Regiment shared with the Royal Scots Fusiliers the hearts of the people. No one who happened to witness the departure of a draft of Newfoundlanders for the Front would doubt that there was the pathos and humour about it that is only seen when the home town bids farewell. . . . The surging crowds; the trickling stream of khaki; the shouts and tears and singing; the manful attempts of the bandsmen to make themselves heard, and above all, our singing, for we were always noted for our buoyancy! Finally the last man presses himself through the turnstiles and soon the troop train is pulling out to the air of "Auld Lang Syne," and the roar of the fare welling crowd. Good Old Ayr, we shall never forget you!

It was a saying in the Regiment that every Newfoundlander had a home in Ayr and I can well believe it. . . . It was remarkable indeed the extent of the interest shown by these kind hearted people. One family I knew had kept in more or less close touch with seventy of the boys and not only made them heartily welcome when they were in training or on leave but sent many of them parcels while they were in hospital or in France. That was the spirit of the people towards us, and is it any wonder that we sing their praises? (p. 28)

SIXTH REPORT OF NEWFOUNDLAND
FORESTRY CORPS[54]

August 19, 1917

Dear Sir,

Since my last writing you there has been no cessation in our work. Log cutting, "browing," teaming[55] to mill, sawing, road repairing, hut erection and mill construction have been going on apace with the men working 10 hours a day every day of the week. This is being done so that ample accommodations may be provided for the men of the draft shortly expected to arrive.

During the past two days Sergeant Lane, with a small bunch of men, has almost completed two huts, each 30 x 20 feet. Another two are yet to be erected, making six in all. These do not include the other buildings I mentioned in my letter of August 4th. Then there is to be a recreation and other necessary buildings, as well as huts at the foot of the hill where the new mill is to be erected. Stoves are installed in all the huts and cook houses. Two tons of straw and also some mattress cases arrived a couple of days ago, and beds are being provided for everybody. So you will see from this that everything is being done for the comfort of the men.

Logging operations are being carried on so near the huts that the men come in to dinner every day, and can enjoy their roasts, vegetables and puddings much better than they would a dry lunch out in the bush. A large shipment of Newfoundland dried codfish came up from London last week, a very welcome gift from the Director of the Anglo-Newfoundland Development Company, which Mr. Beeton secured for us. It was quite a change to get something palatable and substantial in the fish line. This

54 *The Evening Herald*, September 14, 1917, p. 5.
55 The transportation of logs by a team of horses and sled; the driver was called a "teamster."

fish was packed by Job Brothers of St. John's whose name is a guarantee for a first-class fishery product.

In the course of a week or two it is hoped to have the new mill installed, and in running order, in the building now being erected at the foot of the hill. Then a tramline will be laid from the timber belt to a point above the mill, and a chute built from its southern terminus to the foot of the hill. These will be used for conveying logs from the woods to the mill, at a point near the railway track.

Last evening I went over the moors to one of the highest mountain peaks near our Camp. It was a hard climb; yet I was well repaid by the magnificent view obtained therefrom. It was my first time being on this peak although I had been near it before. The view was simply gorgeous. Looking away to the westward could be seen the towering peaks of several high mountains, some of them looking like huge sugar-loafs, and rearing to a height of over 3,000 feet above the sea level. Then there were the broad moors intervening with here and there the lochs of Skiach, Scoly, Kennard, Craige, Grandtully, and others. To the north was also another fine picture, stretching away and beyond the Pass of Killiecrankie, where the famous battle of 1689 was fought.[56] To the eastward I could look out and beyond Blairgowrie to the coast of bonnie Dundee, over thirty miles distant. In that direction were to be seen numerous lochs, and a number of towns and villages; but the country is not as mountainous as it is in other directions. Looking towards the south, the country again becomes more broken and rugged looking and a great many high peaks are visible, especially toward Logiealmond.

Gazing down upon the placid waters of the River Tay and the numerous Lochs, then upon the green fields, the hillsides purpleclad with heather, and those distance lofty peaks, it was a scene to

---

56   The Battle of Killiecrankie was fought by Jabobite and Williamite forces on July 27, 1689, during Scotland's First Jacobite Uprising.

captivate any lover of nature; and I am sure no artist could do justice to its beauties. Besides seeing numerous wild birds, such as moor hens, ptarmigan, pheasant, etc., I came across quite a few deer, being quite close to one doe and its fawn. This sight brought back to memory the days when I used to hunt caribou in Newfoundland. Whilst I was on the mountain, a train went south; and as it followed pretty closely the windings of the River Tay it looked like a huge snake threading its way through the Vale of Atholl.

Dunkeld, Perthshire, Scotland

SEVENTH REPORT OF NEWFOUNDLAND
FORESTRY COMPANIES[57]

August 26, 1917

Dear Sir,

It was an agreeable surprise we had on the morning of Thursday, 23rd inst., when a draft of Foresters arrived at an early hour. We had just finished breakfast, and were preparing for the day's work when word was received that those men had arrived at the Railway Station and were on their way up to camp. Some little excitement prevailed, as men hustled hither and thither finalizing the necessary preparations for the receipt of the draft. Upon their arrival they were issued with plates, mugs, knives, forks, and spoons, after which they retired to the cookhouse, where they were served with a hearty meal. After then ensued a busy time, as blankets and other necessary bedding were issued and the finishing touches given the bunkhouses.

Those of "A" Company were very solicitous from the new arrivals respecting their relatives and friends at home. But don't feel surprised when I tell you that the first enquiries of some were respecting tobacco. If a person is seen here with a stick of Mayos he is envied beyond measure, and the owner of it has to guard well his treasure.

It was hoped that Captain O'Grady[58] would be coming with the last Draft. We all have the kindest regard for him, and shall be forever grateful to him for his painstaking efforts when conducting our drill.

---

57 *The Evening Herald*, September 15, 1917, p. 4.
58 Captain James J. O'Grady, RNR #0–143, St. John's. O'Grady was attached to the NFC as Adjutant temporarily, only until May 26, 1917. Captain H.H.A Ross began his duties as Adjutant on May 20, 1917.

Major Sullivan is our O.C., with Captain Ross as Adjutant. Lieutenant O'Rourke is Quartermaster. Lieutenant M. Gillis will have charge of one of the mill gangs. These officers came with the draft, and the men all speak in the highest terms of the treatment received at their hands while on the trip from Newfoundland.

Logging operations are being continued as vigorously as ever, and from now on there will be something doing in Craigvinean woods. Already the hillsides are strewn with logs, awaiting transportation to the road. In the felling of this timber all the trees are notched with an axe by a special man in each gang, who works under the supervision of the sergeants. These men plan which way the trees may fall; the notcher always consults with his sergeant. Great care is taken in every instance to see that the axe cuttings are not too deep or broad, thereby avoiding the spoiling of any of the merchantable timber.

The cutting down of all this timber is going to change the appearance of the country about here, because at present this section is looked upon as the prettiest part of the whole of Scotland; the cutting down of those parts of the forest which are ripe for the axe will have the effect of exposing numerous brown, barren hills, and the game which now shelter on them will be driven further afield.

A trolley track has been laid from the little mill opposite the huts to a point on the hillside where the chute is to be built. The new mill at the foot of the hill is being rushed to completion. It is hoped to have it in running order by the 10th of September.

The weather of late has been working overtime treating us to an overabundance of "Scotch mist," as the folk hereabout term the rain we are getting. It couldn't possibly be wetter if it were "cats and dogs" instead of "Scotch mist." Of course, this weather has a tendency to dampen the cook's ardour for outdoor cooking. Speaking about cooks reminds me that two of our men are being sent to the School of Cookery, Edinburgh, to take a technical course.

All the boys are well and beginning to like this place very much. Once they get acquainted with the country folk as well as those of the town, they will like the place much better.

Dunkeld, Perthshire, Scotland

NFC foresters at the lumberyard,
Craigvinean, Dunkeld, 1917.
(Courtesy of the Dunkeld Community Archive)

EIGHTH REPORT FROM FORESTRY COMPANIES[59]

September 2, 1917

Sir,

Being an inveterate smoker, I have been spending some little time with "My Lady Nicotine" before starting to write this; and very vexatious have my efforts been. The kind of plug tobacco generally sold here is of such a nature that it cakes very hard in the pipe, requiring little less than a cord of matches to keep it lighted, and a mustard plaster on the neck to assist in drawing the smoke through the stem of my dudeen.

When the last draft of the Foresters came I managed to get from one of the number a few sticks of Mayos. It was really a treat; and then, the price of it was within my reach. When the boys get a present of tobacco from their friends at home, it is greatly prized, and looked upon as a great luxury. So my word to those having sons or husbands over here is to send them an occasional plug of their favourite weed.

Quite a few visitors have been to camp the past week. Amongst them were Captain McLennan and Lieutenant Gordon, of the Canadian Forestry Corps; Major Paterson,[60] who came over with the last draft; Colonel Middleton, of the Scottish Command; Major Timewell,[61] of the London Pay and Record Office; and several other prominent military and civil gentlemen.

On Saturday, 1st inst., there was a garden fete and sale at Stanley, about 12 miles distant. It was under the auspices of the Red Cross Society; and so well was it patronized that the sum of about three thousand dollars was realized. Some of our officers and

---

59 *The Evening Herald*, September 25, 1917, p. 5.

60 Major Lamont Paterson, RNR #0–7, St. John's. Paterson was the Senior Medical Officer and Deputy Director of Medical Services.

61 Henry A. Timewell, NFC #0–180, Chief Paymaster and Officer in Charge of Records, St. John's and London, England.

several of the men were present upon invitation. There were various sporting events, the program including chopping and sawing contests and tug-of-war for the Scots, Canadians, and Newfoundlanders. In the tug-of-war, our boys beat the Scots, but in the final contest, the Canadians were the victors by a very narrow margin. The wood chopping contest was keenly competed, our boys winning both the first and second prizes over the Canadians, but we lost to them on the sawing contest. Sergeant Ball[62] (of Ours[63]) exhibited great skill in cutting a 16-inch log in one minute and 56 seconds, beating all others by a wide margin. Our boys thoroughly enjoyed the outing and are looking forward to another trip to Stanley the latter part of this month, when there will be a log-rolling competition between the Canadian and Newfoundland Forestry Companies.

During the week a free gift of over sixty cases of Newfoundland dried codfish was received from the A.N.D. Company; also several sacks of potatoes. There has latterly been an increase in our field rations, so much so that our men are receiving an abundance of good food and are enabled to pursue their daily work without danger of their stomachs not being properly fortified.

There are a few of our men in hospital, suffering from minor ailments, but none of them of a serious nature. We now have an Improvised Haversack[64] and hope to have, in a day or two, a masseur or doctor's orderly stationed at the Camp. Then most of the minor ailments of the men will be treated on the spot.

The new tramline had its baptism on the 1st, inst., when the first load of timber was taken over it. Lieutenant Cole felt highly

---

62   Sergeant Andrew F. Ball, NFC #8230, Northern Arm.

63   A proud reference to those from Newfoundland who served in various First World War overseas capacities—the Regiment, Navy, Mariners, and Foresters, in particular.

64   A small bag used to carry work necessities, including supplies for treating minor injuries.

pleased at this work being performed without any difficulty being experienced. Pretty soon the trolleys will be running all day long conveying the logs from the timber belt to the chute, which will connect with the new mill. This reminds me that the building for this mill is about completed, and the machinery is being installed as quickly as possible.

A number of buildings for accommodating over one hundred men, a cookhouse and dining room, and officers' quarters are to be erected near the saw mill, and it is probable one whole company will be stationed there, whilst another will remain at its present quarters. All our men will then be comfortably housed, well fed, and properly looked after by the competent staff of officers in charge of them. I understand that the Quartermaster has requisitioned for a number of sectional huts, one of which is shortly to arrive. These huts will furnish splendid accommodation for the men and could be easily transferred to any other section of the country to which we may go.

Whilst the various buildings are being erected and other improvements taking place, the loggers are assiduously performing their duties felling the giants of the forest, and laying bare the hillsides of Craigvinean, letting the sunlight into nooks and crannies that have been hidden for ages. A few days of wet weather hampered operations slightly; but a change seems to have taken place, and our men are doing good work again.

The days are shortening, and the evenings close in much earlier than they did a month ago; consequently, lamps have to be lighted before roll call, and the men do not have as much time as they used to. Those who do not go to town can sit here and enjoy the scenic beauties of the country and revel in the picturesqueness of it all.

Here foxgloves, draped in pinkish robes
Rise up like sentinels;

And campion red, rears up its head
Above the shy blue-bells.
The ragged robin trembling waves
Beside the singing rills;
And honeysuckle scents the air
Around the "Burning Hills."[65]

We received a very fine gramophone and a variety of splendid records; also various games such as checkers, dominoes,
chess, cards, etc., and the men have no excuse for not being able
to find means of amusing themselves in the long evenings.

Dunkeld, Perthshire, Scotland

Stacked lumber at the foot of Craigiebarns, 1917.
(Courtesy of The Rooms Provincial Archives Division, A 103-95)

---

65 A reference to controlled burning of heather to increase pasture, or "muirburn"
(Wallace, 1903).

OUR WOODSMEN IN SCOTLAND[66]
Doings of the Forestry Companies —
Another Letter from Corporal Barrett

September 9, 1917

Dear Sir,

The glorious weather conditions of late have wrought a great change in our operations, and the boys have discarded the oil-skins which they wore for a few days. When it rains up here, every-thing is made very uncomfortable, owing to the soft spongy nature of the soil. But after a few hours of sunshine, the mud hardens so that you would imagine it had never rained.

Lieutenant S. Goodyear,[67] of the 1st Newfoundland Regi-ment, came from Barry, on Thursday, to visit his brother, Lieu-tenant H.K. Goodyear,[68] who is stationed with us.

We were paid a visit on Friday by Mr. M.M. Beeton and Sir John Stirling Maxwell.[69] After dinner, we were paraded, and were addressed by Mr. Beeton, who, on behalf of the English Govern-ment, extended a hearty welcome to the men of the second Draft of Foresters. He spoke very encouragingly to them, pointing out the great and urgent necessity of men for carrying on such work as we are doing. Although conditions are somewhat different from those under which the men worked in Newfoundland, yet he was pleased to find that we had so readily adapted ourselves to them; and congratulated the first Draft upon the great amount of work already performed. He hoped and believed that

---

66   *The Western Star*, September 26, 1917, p. 2. Also published in *The Evening Herald*, October 8, 1917.
67   Lieutenant Stanley Charles Goodyear, RNR #334 / #0–40, Grand Falls.
68   Lieutenant Harold Kenneth Goodyear, RNR #1193 / #0–74, Grand Falls, was wounded at Beaumont-Hamel. He was transferred to the NFC on June 11, 1917.
69   Sir John Stirling Maxwell, 10th Baronet; Chair of Forestry Commission Scotland, 1929–32.

the operations of the Newfoundland Companies would compare favourably with those of any other Forestry unit working in this country. Mr. Beeton is ever alive to the requirements of our men, and knowing them as he does from his experiences at Grand Falls, he is rendering every assistance possible.

Sir John Stirling Maxwell, who is well known all over the United Kingdom as one of the best authorities on lumbering and forestry pursuits, is taking a very keen interest in our operations. He also addressed us, and in the course of his remarks he paid a high tribute to the men who had come from Newfoundland to assist the Mother Country in her present need. He spoke in glowing terms of the deeds of valour of our Regiment in the field, and said it was the most famous Regiment associated with the most famous Battalion. As regards the Forestry Companies, Sir John said that by our improved methods we stood a good chance to demonstrate to both the English and Scotch lumbermen the most expedient manner in which to conduct lumbering operations.

After the addresses, we were lined up in various positions for the photographer, who had been engaged for the occasion. Some day you may see our physiogs[70] appearing in some Scottish magazine, because the journals on this side of the water like to get hold of anything pertaining to Newfoundland or Newfoundlanders.

On Saturday, the men quit at half-past eleven o'clock, it being the occasion of an unexpected pleasure. In the afternoon, a delightful concert, arranged by her Grace the Duchess of Atholl,[71] was given in the Town Hall, at Dunkeld, to which our men paraded. The Duchess of Atholl, who was accorded a very warm reception, contributed several pianaforte solos, and also played the accompaniments during the evening. The singers were Miss

---

70 Physiognomies.

71 Katharine Marjory Stewart-Murray, 8th Duchess of Atholl.

Lockwood, Sergeant Hayward,[72] and Mr. Alfred Heather, who sang with much success, and were heartily encored. Several cello solos were tastefully rendered by Private Charles Hambourg, of the Army Service Corps, while Mr. Selwyn Driver was particularly good in "pianorations."

Major Sullivan thanked the Duchess of Atholl for the great treat she had provided for us; and called for three cheers for her Grace and those who had so ably assisted her in entertaining us, which was accorded with right good will.

Her Grace, in acknowledging the appreciation, said she was well aware of the pressing need of instituting some sort of amusement for our men, who come so far to do their bit for the Empire, and who were now located amongst comparative strangers. She expressed great pleasure at being able to meet us, and hoped to be able to afford several such entertainments during our stay here.

After the musical part of the entertainment was over, refreshments were served to all the men. For this gift, we are indebted to Mr. Beeton.

In my next letter, I will try and give you a further descriptive account of this section of bonnie Scotland together with an account of some of its natural history.

Dunkeld, Perthshire, Scotland

• • •

The Goodyears of Ladle Cove

Stanley and Kenneth Goodyear were two of seven Goodyear siblings, six of whom served during the First World War. When the two brothers met at Dunkeld on September 6, 1917, as noted by Barrett, it had been almost a year

---

72   Private John C.M. Hayward, NFC #8470, Grand Falls.

since their youngest brother, Raymond, RNR #2156, had been killed in action at Gueudecourt, France. Their brother Josiah (Joe) was commissioned to the NFC in July 1917, after recovering from wounds received while fighting in France in November 1916. He would finally depart Newfoundland for Scotland months later, on December 11, 1917. Brother Hedley, who had been working as a schoolteacher in Toronto before the war, was in France with the Canadian Infantry in 1917. By 1918, both Stanley and Hedley would also have died in service. Sister Daisy (known as Kate), a nurse, worked with the Canadian Voluntary Aid Detachment during her professional training at St. Luke's Hospital in Ottawa; she would be enroute overseas when the Armistice was signed. Another brother, Roland, remained at home to work in the family business with his parents throughout the war.

The siblings, like their parents Josiah and Louisa Wellon Goodyear, were respected leaders in their communities. The Goodyears owned family businesses in Grand Falls, including first the Grand Falls Stables and later J. Goodyear and Sons, but their roots were in Ladle Cove, near Musgrave Harbour, Bonavista Bay. In 1908, they had moved away from the coast and inland to the newly built company town of Grand Falls. The Anglo-Newfoundland Development Company mill opened there the following year and the harvesting and processing of its timber, as well as spin-off industries, offered business opportunities for many, including the relocated Goodyears.

When Ken and Joe Goodyear were transferred to the NFC, they brought with them considerable experience in woods work, which included handling horses, along with demonstrated leadership. In a letter to Chief Justice William Horwood about his visit to the Regiment in France in December 1917, Governor Davidson (1918b) recorded these observations, which referenced the Goodyears' reputation and specifically that of Josiah Goodyear:

> Colonel Hadow[73] was bewailing the loss of Josiah Goodyear, who was the best transport officer that ever lived. You know the story

---

73   Lieutenant-Colonel Arthur L. Hadow, Officer Commanding, 1st Battalion, Royal Newfoundland Regiment.

of his transfer as Sergeant Major to the fighting ranks after young Ray's death, and the wonderful way in which he coolly saved his own life when the shell tore his leg. If there is any chance of getting him back from the Foresters the Regiment will be delighted, but I fear that his wound is a permanent disablement. (p. 32)

Captain Josiah Goodyear remained with the NFC as part of the command of operations.

In a letter to Major Rendell on October 30, 1917, Lieutenant Kenneth Goodyear of C Company requested a post at home in Newfoundland, citing the grief and loneliness of his parents.[74] At that point two of the Goodyear brothers—Ray and Stan—had been killed in action, Stan only weeks before, on October 10, 1917. Kenneth was likely the last of his family to see him alive, during their visit at Dunkeld. Hedley was killed in action on August 22, 1918.[75]

---

74   Others also wrote to request his return, including Magistrate H.G. Fitzgerald of Grand Falls (Fitzgerald, 1918b). Lieutenant Goodyear was repatriated and retired from the NFC on January 21, 1919.

75   The story of the Goodyear family was published by David Macfarlane, a grandson of Captain Josiah R. Goodyear. See Macfarlane (1991).

FORESTRY COMPANIES CUT OVER
MILLION FEET TIMBER IN ADDITION
TO CONSTRUCTION WORK[76]
Strong Appeal for More Recruits

September 15, 1917

Dear Sir,

Despite all predictions made a year ago as to the probable termination of the war, the end seems to be a long way off yet. One reason for this may be attributed to the holding back from Military service of thousands of men who should long ago have been wearing khaki. While the nation's very existence has been threatened, numbers of young men have manifested an indifference towards the real condition of things by withholding their enlistment. If, owing to disqualification, they cannot serve their King on the firing line, there are many avenues of employment through which they may show their zeal and patriotism. In this respect the women of the Empire have set a good example to our men, by donning khaki and overalls and engaging in work they were at one time looked upon as being incapable of performing. And they are doing it very creditably.

It must be admitted that Newfoundland has done nobly in furnishing so many stalwart young men for both Army and Navy. Many more would have enlisted but for various exemptions, and through obstacles placed in the way by their relatives and friends. Yet I am at a loss to conceive how it is that more of our young men have not signified their willingness to join the Forestry Companies, because there are thousands at home who are qualified for such a service who should be over here with us. There is a glorious work for all to do; and no man can show his patriotism in a more demonstrative manner than by a practical application.

---

76 *The Western Star*, October 10, 1917, p. 1.

In the work the Newfoundland Forestry Companies are per-forming, there is room for many more. We want all the young men available. When I say young men, I mean good, strong, healthy fellows—men who are accustomed to woods work, and are capable of standing up against the rigours of such a life. You well know that lumbering operations, in order to be carried on to a successful issue, require men of good physique. Of such a type, there are many in Newfoundland; and if the true condition of things and the urgent need of men could but be conveyed to them in the same light through which I view things, I really believe our numbers would be doubly increased within a short while.

I appeal to every married man and every young man quali-fied for service overseas, to thoughtfully consider the exigencies of the present moment; then, after carefully weighing them, go to the nearest Recruiting Station and enlist for this noble work. Don't let family ties keep you at home; because while absent from them your families will be comfortably provided for. Make supreme effort and join your comrades over here. You will re-ceive the best of treatment and kindest consideration at the hands of the officers, and be supplied with a free kit and equip-ment becoming your occupation.

All praise and honour is due those who have lately arrived here with us. Although not being on the firing line or anywhere near it, yet they are soldiers in every sense of the word. Each soldier is a MAN. And there is hardly a man who will not return after the war bigger than when he left home. It will not be for nothing that they have learned to endure hardship without mak-ing a song about it, that they have risked their lives for their country's sake. They are showing a strong determination to do what they can to help the Mother Country in her need. It must be borne in mind by all that our military and naval positions are sure to improve if we set our teeth and hold on. Therefore, it is the bounden duty of all of us to do what we can to help with the burden which must be borne if complete victory in the present struggle is to be obtained.

Work is still proceeding very favourably. Beside all the construction and transport operations, we have cut over one million feet of lumber. That is considered a very satisfactory showing, considering the comparatively small number of axe-men and sawyers employed up to the end of August.

The Duke of Atholl, upon whose estate we are operating, has very kindly promised to furnish us with rifle and ammunition, with which to shoot red deer. These animals roam wild over the hills quite near our quarters, as do also the roe and fallow deer. His Grace has also generously offered for our use one of the wooden buildings on the estate about two miles from Camp. This is to be removed and erected on the field near our new saw mill, and will be used as a Recreation Hall for our men.

Last Sunday a number of our men were, upon invitation, entertained at Birnam Institute,[77] where they were served with a tea, and later treated to some vocal and instrumental music. Her Grace the Duchess of Atholl and several other ladies are evincing a keen interest in the social welfare of the men of this unit; and I understand arrangements are being made for the furnishing of a series of entertainments and the supplying of free teas on certain evenings. Thus, you will learn that we are being very decently treated, in fact, perhaps a little better than we expected to be in these strenuous times.

Dunkeld, Perthshire, Scotland

---

77 The institute was a multipurpose community organization and venue in Birnam that was used during the war for soldier accommodations and entertainment.

A Skilled Class of Men

Barrett's emphasis on the desired criteria for recruits would have been appreciated by those in Newfoundland who understood the rigours and requirements of lumbering and logging. When recruitment for the NFC began, there was public concern about the appropriateness of the skill set of many of those enlisting. Whitbourne lumber-mill owner and operator Lemuel H. Simmonds ("Forestry Battalion," 1917) frankly expressed his concerns in a letter to *The St. John's Daily Star*:

> Dear Sir:
> All honour to every man or boy who is patriotic enough to offer his services in the great cause now presenting itself, whether this service be that of soldier, sailor, farmer, mechanic or lumberman.
>
> I read with much care and thought His Excellency's appeal to men to work in the woods of the Old Country and felt that if five or six hundred of our lumbermen enlisted in this battalion they would keep up the credit that our soldiers have won for themselves and their Island Home in the Mother Country during the past war.
>
> On reading *The News*[78] this morning, however, I was simply dumbfounded to find names of men and boys from offices and stores who are offering themselves and, more than that, are being accepted if they pass the medical examination.
>
> This, to my mind, Mr. Editor, is an outrage. It shows a gross lack of knowledge on the part of those in authority. A man for the lumber woods, if required for immediate work, must have a knowledge of the business, a knowledge that can only be gained by years of practical work in the woods. If it is the intention of the

78 *The Daily News*, a St. John's-based newspaper.

powers that be to train these lads and young men for this kind of work, then I can assure them from practical experience that it will take longer to do so than to train them for the army. If efficiency is essential in this movement why not put a competent man, who understands this business, in charge of the recruiting station and only accept those whom you would employ in a lumber camp at home? I think it would be worthwhile for the Committee to inquire how many men ever passed a medical examination before going in a lumber camp or how many camp foremen would employ fifty clerks, office hands or typists from the city offices to work in a lumber camp.

The same class of men that are wanted here are just the class wanted in England! If the intention is to give the boys a trip to England, then, of course, I misunderstand this appeal and England is not in need of help of this kind. If, on the other hand, England does want our lumbermen, I would make an earnest appeal to those in authority to be sane men, stop and think, and not let their hearts run away with their heads, or, in other words, do not try to put the proverbial square peg into a round hole.

L.H. Simmonds (p. 8)

INTERESTING LETTER FROM
CORPORAL J.A. BARRETT[79]

September 23, 1917

Dear Sir,

Yesterday afternoon was observed in Camp as a half-holiday, and there being a garden fete on at Murthly, about six miles distance, a number of our men went thither to participate in the sports. The event was under the auspices of the Red Cross, which proved a means of attracting quite a crowd from the surrounding towns. In the various contests in which our men took part, they were awarded first prizes for all, except the one for the leg cross-cutting, which honour went to the Canadians.

Madame Tempest,[80] Commandant, and Mrs. Recketts,[81] Matron, of V.A.D. Auxiliary Hospital, Dalguise,[82] paid us the honour of a visit on Friday. These ladies have been taking a marked interest in the physical welfare of our men, a number of whom have been treated for minor ailments at the above-named institution. This Hospital is in a charming location, being about a mile from Camp, and quite near the River Tay. The kindest treatment is accorded all patients, and everything possible is done for their comfort and speedy recovery.

Privates L. Hussey[83] (cook) and Martin Collins[84] (saw-filer), both of St. John's, have been recommended for discharge, and

---

79 *The Western Star*, October 17, 1917, p. 1. Also published in *The Evening Herald*, October 16, 1917.

80 Henrietta Frances May Tempest.

81 Susan Rotham Recketts, Sister-in-Charge.

82 Corporal Barrett provided more detail about the hospital in his letter of November 7, 1917.

83 Private William L. Hussey, NFC #8039, St. John's; Hussey was 45 when he enlisted in April 1917.

84 Private Collins was 59 when he enlisted in April 1917.

are to be sent home soon. They are both old men, and when they came here were not constitutionally fit for the work they were up against.

It is to be hoped that greater care may be exercised by the Recruiting Committees at home, and that in future only competent men should be taken in the Forestry Companies. In my last letter to you I tried to set this question very plainly before the public; therefore, I hope and trust that the healthy able-bodied men of Britain's most ancient Colony will rally to the colours and nobly take their stand alongside those of Canada and other Overseas Dominions.

Woodsmen are scarce in this country; in fact, there is scarcely a "fit" young man to be seen in any of the nearby towns, as they have all been drafted for the Front. So urgent is the need of labourers at home, that a command has been issued exempting Scottish woodsmen over 23 years of age from Active Service, they being required for work in the woods and at the various mills throughout the country. Therefore, for the sake of honour, King and Country, let the men of Newfoundland bestir themselves, and rise to the heights they should in the great forward movement and help to bring the war to a quick and satisfactory termination, not giving up hope and effort until their desires are realized. Remember that a tremendous responsibility rests upon us; but there is also a tremendous opportunity.

In some of the near-by farming districts as well as all over the country, there have been great efforts this year in agricultural purpose, and the keenest rivalry has been manifested amongst the farmers as to who would raise the best crops. To encourage his parishioners to grow large crops of potatoes, one clergyman offered prizes for the heaviest yield from one pound of seed. A professional gardener named Pigg won the competition, producing the extraordinary yield of 242½ lbs. from 1 lb. of seed. An amateur grew 126 lbs. One farmer has just turned up a handsome tuber weighing 20½ ounces from a phenomenal crop weighing from 4 lbs. 3 oz. to 5 lbs. 3 oz. to the stalk, and averaging 9 to 12 potatoes, excluding three or four small ones not counted in the eating number. I wonder what my old friend Sandy McDonald, in Bay of Islands, will think of this.

The gathering of the grain harvest is progressing with fair rapidity and the cutting is now nearing completion. On the whole it looks as if this year's wheat crop will be above the average. The difficulty of handling owing to weather conditions is aggravated by the scarcity of labour and the large acreage in grain this year; but most farmers report they are getting on as well as the weather conditions will allow.

Fortunately for us, our work has progressed so far without any men meeting with an accident of a serious nature. We have been supplied with certain medical stores, and our medical orderly dispenses these to men suffering from minor ailments; and of such cases there are always sure to be a certain number in a lumbering camp.

Construction work has been going on apace with logging operations, and this week another mill will be in working order. In order to get through with this work as soon as possible, another mill has been asked for, and is expected to arrive shortly.

Now that the season is changing to a little colder, I would remind the relatives and friends of our boys that in the course of another six or eight weeks they may be needing warm woolen socks and perhaps woolen mitts and other comforts. So, if you have an intention of supplying them with any of these articles, kindly have them sent forward before they are required.

An invitation has been tendered officers and men to visit
Dunkeld House, the residence of Lord Dudley,[85] and also the
grounds surrounding it. The acceptance of this invitation is set
for next week, when we expect to spend a pleasant afternoon
going over the beautiful grounds.

Dunkeld, Perthshire, Scotland

• • •

Patriotism and Pluck

Barrett's warnings about the demands of the work in Scotland and the
Companies' preference for young, strong, fit recruits, emphasized in his
letters of both September 15 and 23, did not detract from the enthusiasm of
those who, while older, nonetheless wished to serve. A letter from George
Best ("Splendid Spirit of Patriotism," 1917) of Trepassey to J.R. Bennett,
Minister of Militia, published in The St. John's Daily Star, captured this patriotic zeal:

> Dear Sir,
> Seeing your appeal in the paper for help to subdue this terrible
> war that is now raging, I feel it my duty to respond to the call. I have
> at present one young boy,[86] I can't call him a man, only in spirit
> and pluck. He is now somewhere in France or England where a
> few months ago he celebrated, as best he could, his seventeenth
> birthday.

85 Dunkeld House was the traditional home of the Dukes of Atholl; the current Dunkeld House was built by the 7th Duke of Atholl between 1899 and 1901. Lord Dudley was his brother-in-law (J. Anderson, personal communication, June 19, 2019).
86 Joubert B. Best, #2231X, Royal Naval Reserve.

Now, Sir, I voluntarily offer my services in this great fight. I know you won't take me for the Army or Navy, but there is a place in the Foresters I feel I can nobly fill. I have had an experience for the last thirty years, more or less, as foreman and manager of labour, more especially in the lumber business, and I have a confidence that I can adapt myself to most any kind of labour. All I ask for now is a chance to prove it, and I don't want to be denied of doing my bit.

I offer to take charge of the next contingent of Foresters that will leave for the other side, or any other lot that may leave in the near future.[87] Further, I am willing to go on a recruiting campaign, and help raise a contingent myself. Being so well-known around the Island, I may be able to influence some of the young men and older ones, too, to follow my example. . . .

Dear Sir, although I am living in my 58th year, I have a good healthy body and a real patriotic spirit and don't want to be denied the privilege either. This is no sham battle we are after. We have a foe to face, and a hard one at that. If this foe is to be conquered, it is time we realized it and got to work.

I am now at Trepassey where we have a splendid type of young men. And all that is wanting is the patriotic spirit infused in them. I have lived with these young men and I know them. Men with good morals and strictly religious and very lovingly attached to their parents.

Then there is the Peter's River, St. Vincent's and St. Mary's men, and lots of them, too. My opinion of these young men after living with them and knowing them is that there is not a better class to

---

87 Best requested a commission with the NFC, which was not granted.

be found in our Island home. I would like to see these men with the khaki suit on parading the streets of St. John's; then we would all have to admit that all the good men have not left Newfoundland yet, and wherever these men would chance to pitch, something would surely happen.

Now, Sir, I have explained to you my intentions. I know what I am talking about and don't want to be shut down. I will call at your office when I reach town.

In the fight,
George Best, HMC (p. 2)

Two days after his letter was published, on October 27, 1917, Private George Best, NFC #8402, aged 57, a carpenter and cooper originally from St. Anthony, enlisted with the NFC at St. John's. In the fall of 1918, at Kenmore, Scotland, Best was diagnosed with arteriosclerosis and deemed medically unfit for service. He was discharged at St. John's on December 17, 1918. He died of pulmonary tuberculosis in May 1920 at St. John's.

THE WORK OF THE FORESTRY COMPANIES[88]

In Tug-of-War Contest, Newfoundland Team
Win Championship of Eight Years

September 30, 1917

Dear Sir,

It is to be hoped that your readers will not draw the inference from my former letters that those who enlist with the Newfoundland Forestry Companies are going to have a continuous picnic, or that there is very little work for them to do. Those accustomed to lumbering operations who have enlisted with us know that the very name implies the nature of the work, and that it is no occupation for weaklings or uninitiated. The sturdy sons of Terra Nova who have become inured by their various vocations, are capable of withstanding all the hardships entailed by lumbering; and knowing what is expected of them, those lads now with us from the sea girt Isle have come over here with a whole-souled determination to do their share in lightening the burden of the Mother Country. And they are doing it, too; and that quite cheerily.

Every day we notice a change in the appearance of the hillside on the eastern portion of the Craigvinean. At 7 o'clock in the morning the men go forth to do execution, and if by the evening a gang of fourteen men fell fifteen or eighteen thousand feet of lumber, it is considered a good day's work. Of course, besides the felling of trees, there is a great deal of other work to be done, such as cross-cutting, browing, hauling to the mills, etc., after which follows the sawing and piling. There is sufficient work to keep everybody busy. The needs of the times demand it. Yet, no person is being overworked nor underfed, as is maintained by the healthy condition of the Camp.

---

88 *The Western Star*, October 31, 1917, p. 1. Also published in *The Evening Herald*, October 26, 1917.

Last Wednesday the little mill on the hill was closed, and the new mill took up its duties for the first time. Another saw mill is expected to arrive shortly. With this equipment running day and night, there should be a large output of lumber, necessitating the log trolleys being kept busy on the tramline conveying timber to the chute.

Some sixty men are at present employed in and about the new mill. Close by the mill have been erected good comfortable bunk-houses for the men, cook house and mess room, and canteen. Arrangements are being made for the installation of an electric light plant, which will mean quite a valuable addition to the outfit.

This afternoon (Sunday) the grounds surrounding Dunkeld House were opened to our men, and quite a few took advantage of the invitation, notwithstanding a walk of four miles. The scenery there is very picturesque, especially along the bank of the Tay. Beautiful trees, many of them foreign to us, adorn the ground, as do also numerous flowers, plants, and variegated shrubs.

Our men are looking forward with interest to the log-rolling and other contests which are to take place shortly at Stanley, where the Canadians are lumbering. In the last tug-of-war which our men contested, they were victors over a team that held the championship for eight years; naturally our lads would be feeling in high spirits, and hopeful of a continuance of good luck in sporting circles.

The other day I came across the following poem,[89] dedicated to the boys of the Newfoundland Regiment; and believing it would be of interest to your readers at home, I pass it on to you.

---

89 *The Western Star* published the poem separately on page 3 of its edition of October 17, 1917, along with a short introductory comment.

NEWFOUNDLAND[90]

P.E. Goldsmith[91]

(Newfoundland, the oldest British Colony, has given a large proportion of her manhood to the Great Cause, and out of her small population has suffered comparatively heavy losses. The Regiment has gained honour in France and Gallipoli, and the Newfoundland Royal Naval Reserve has played no small part at sea.)

There lies a Land in the West and North
Whither the bravest men went forth,
And daunted not by fog nor ice
They reached at last a Paradise.
Full two thousand miles it lay
Washed by a sea of English grey,
And they named it Newfoundland at sight;
It's rather the land of Heart's Delight.

Now after close five hundred years
You give us back with fearless eyes,
Dimm'd with glory but not with tears
The greatest gift that a Land can prize.
You give back all that there is to give,
The young who die so the Land may live,
Nor willed it otherwise.

---

90 The poem was written to celebrate Newfoundland Week in the United Kingdom. Barrett referred to these celebrations in his letter of October 7, 1917. The poem was originally included in the souvenir program for Newfoundland Week–A Concert, held at His Majesty's Theatre, London, on September 25, 1917. There are two versions of this poem, both of which were published in *The Veteran* in June 1925.

91 Philip Edward Goldsmith, Paymaster-Commander, Royal Navy.

Die? They were weary, God gave them rest.
Fall? They are raised for evermore.
Whether on Beaumont-Hamel's crest
Or "Caribou Hill" by the Turkish shore,
Never their glory can fade or fall
Who have won the greatest Cross of all;
Nor ever their country dies!

Ah! Men must know you to understand,
Have seen the cliffs of your rugged land,
Have seen the mist come rolling down
The hills that guard the glistening town,
Have seen the schooners creeping in,
And smelt the homely smell within
The fishing port asleep.
And in the rivers flowing free
Through the spruce woods to the sea
Have known the pools at break of day
Where silver-coated salmon play,
And seen the tangled river's brink
Where caribou come down to drink.
And beavers build and creep.

All this is shared by those who fell!
It is the Land they loved so well!
For many a soldier lying low
In some French village-battle glow,
Sees before his blood is spent
The sunset over Heart's Content.
Many a sailor lost at sea
Sweeping a mined-in channel free,
Sees his schooner far away.
And sunrise in Conception Bay.

Aye, though they died on distant shores
They died for This! It's doubly yours!
And there is Pride and Comfort too
To know what once they loved and knew.

There lies a Land in the West and North
Whither the bravest man went forth,
And daunted not by fog nor ice
They reached at last to a Paradise.
A Land to be won by those who durst,
No wonder the English choose it first,
And they named it Newfoundland at sight;
It's rather the Land of Heart's Delight.

Dunkeld, Perthshire, Scotland

• • •

Goldsmith's "Newfoundland"

Of the two versions of Goldsmith's poem, the better known is the one included in Barrett's letter. The version on the following page was likely the
original version, probably written before the Regiment battles at Gallipoli and
Beaumont-Hamel and the Newfoundland Week celebrations of September
1917. It offers a more intimate portrait of the poet's relationship to the Colony.[92]
It has also been published as "The Land of Heart's Delight."

---

92 Goldsmith served in the Mediterranean and likely spent time in Newfoundland
during his naval career. He would have also encountered Newfoundland sailors
who joined the Royal Naval Reserve prior to and during the First World War
("Paymaster-Commander Goldsmith," 1935).

NEWFOUNDLAND
P.E. Goldsmith

There lies a land in the West and North
Whither the bravest men went forth,
And daunted not by fog nor ice
They came at last to a Paradise.
Full two thousand miles it lay
Washed by a sea of English grey;
And they called it Newfoundland at sight,
It's rather the land of Heart's Delight.

I have seen the Mediterranean's blue
Lazily lapping the southern shores,
And groves where the orange blossoms grow,
And the cypress shading cathedral doors.
I have seen the moon in the desert place
Flooding the pyramid's stony face,
And crowned by the Banks of the sacred Nile,
Pharaohs, carved in an ancient style;
All I have loved and known.

But on moonlight nights, in the land I love,
I have slept with the stars and trees above,
By a big log fire that sputters and creaks,
And a river that sobs itself to sleep,
And perhaps with frightened eyes that blink
The timid deer comes down to drink;
These I have loved and known.
I have seen sweet places in foreign lands,
Gardens tended by cunning hands,
Houses old as the hills in fame,

Bearing the weight of a noble name;
All I have seen and known.

But Nature gardens the land I choose,
And gives her names such as lovers use;
Fortune Bay—was the fortune Love?
Conception—borrowed from Heaven above;
Breakheart Point—what a world of woe—
A maiden watching her lover go.
Heart's Content—here they came at last,
When the toil and grief of their life was past;
These I have loved and known.

There lies a land in the West and North
Whither the bravest men went forth,
And daunted not by fog nor ice
They came at last to a Paradise.
A land to be won by the men who durst,
No wonder the British chose it first,
And they called it Newfoundland at sight,
It's rather the land of Heart's Delight.

WHAT WAS BARREN MOUNTAIN SIDE
CENTURY AGO SUPPLIES GREAT BRITAIN'S
SHIPBUILDING MATERIAL TODAY[93]
And Newfoundlanders Are Preparing It

October 7, 1917

Dear Sir,

The day before yesterday we were very forcibly reminded of the approaching winter, for in the early morning as we looked away to the north we could see the loftier peaks capped with snow. It is all too true that the beautiful summer has passed, and now the autumn is upon us. But really this morning the surrounding hilltops present a very wintery appearance, as snow has been falling for several hours. Of course, this snow will not remain very long. I have been told that last winter was the severest felt here for years; but even then, there was not more than two feet of snow and the thermometer did not go down to zero. Should it not be any worse than that the coming winter, I am sure we can have no room to complain of the climate.

You have probably heard of the presentation by several of the leading firms of Sheffield,[94] of an aeroplane to Newfoundland. This presentation took place on the 29th September,[95] and was witnessed by a gathering of nearly 100,000 persons. Major Sullivan was present as the representative of the Forestry Companies, and the Regiment was represented by Lieutenant-Colonel

---

93 *The Western Star*, November 7, 1917, p. 4. Also published in *The Evening Herald*, November 2, 1917.

94 Sheffield, Yorkshire, England.

95 This presentation occurred during Newfoundland Week, a series of events devised to celebrate the 420th anniversary of what is believed to have been the arrival in Newfoundland of John Cabot, an Italian explorer commissioned by Henry VII, and the colony's contribution to the war effort. For an account of the gift aircraft and the presentation, see Warr (2015).

Whitaker.[96] The Newfoundland Regimental Band was in attendance, and played to the delight of the immense crowd. The
aeroplane, which is christened "Sheffield," has been presented
to Newfoundland as a unit of the Imperial Fleet, and it is expected to render a good account of itself. Preparations are now being
made at Nottingham for the presentation of an aeroplane to New
Zealand on the twenty-fifth of this month.

Whilst down to England last week, Major Sullivan visited
Liverpool, where, with others, he was banqueted by the Lord
Mayor. During his stay at Liverpool he secured from Mr. Henry
Bowring[97] the promise of 25 quintals of dried codfish for our
men. A further promise of 25 quintals was also made by Mr. S.
Job. So, you see, we stand a good chance of keeping our larder
fairly well supplied with the staple product of Newfoundland.

Our men have today been issued with cardigan jackets and a
suit of new underwear. But they will soon be needing woolen
mitts; and as the home-knit mitts of Newfoundland are about the
best and most serviceable for winter weather, I would suggest
that the relatives and friends of our men make a special effort to
send each man at least one pair of good home-knit mitts.

A correspondent of the London "Times" recently visited our
Camp and saw for himself the manner in which our work is being carried on. So impressed was he with these operations that
he sent a lengthy account to the "Thunderer,"[98] and as it makes

---

96 Lieutenant Colonel C.W. Whitaker commanded the Second Battalion of the Regiment from August 1915 until late January 1918.

97 Henry Bowring was a member of the Bowring merchant family of Exeter, Devon,
which traded in NL as Bowring Brothers.

98 This was a nickname for the London newspaper *The Times*. The paper is referenced in a verse of "The Badger Drive," a song composed in 1912 by John Val-
entine Devine of Kings Cove, Newfoundland, to celebrate the river drivers in the
country's new pulp and paper industry: "I tell you today home in London, *The
Times* it is read by each man / But little they think of the fellows that drove the

interesting reading, I herewith subjoin some extracts there-from:[99]

The great forests of Scotland, utilized during the last two generations as shooting preserves, have suddenly become an enormously valuable asset. Timber must be had in vast quantities for a hundred war purposes. We cannot import it. We must now perforce rely on the resources of our own island. Scotland is supplying more than its share. Men from the ends of the Empire are in the north today, clearing the hills, felling and dispatching their giant trees with the expedition of a Western lumber camp. Most of them are not Westerners, however, but Easterners, men from Quebec, Ontario, New Brunswick and Nova Scotia, together with hundreds of picked Newfoundland lumbermen, wearing khaki and serving under military discipline.

. . . This is a Newfoundland Camp on the Atholl estate. A few days ago, the Duchess of Atholl, after entertaining a party of woodmen guests, confessed that while she was glad to see them, and hoped to see more of them, her heart was heavy at the disappearance of her beloved woods. One can understand her grief. Up here on Craigvinean, the Craig of Goats, as it is rightly called, 800 ft. above the sea level, one gazes around upon what was one of the most beautiful wooded scenes in Scotland. In the immediate neighbourhood are grouped a succession of fallen giants—great, noble timber.

---

wood on Mary Ann / For paper is made out of pulpwood and many more things you may know /And long may our men live to drive it upon Pamehoc and Tom Joe" (Kelly & Forsyth, 2018b, pp. 71–73).

99 The entire article was reprinted in *The Evening Herald* ("A Lumber Camp," 1917). Several foresters also attached the article to letters home. See, for example, "Foresters Are Making Good" (1917).

Some distance below a lumber camp can be seen. Along the steep middle ridge of the hillside runs a temporary mountain railway built with lightning speed to the point where the great chute falls vertically, down which the thousands of great felled trunks—often more than half a ton in weight—go thundering to the mill below. This mill has been completed in an incredibly short time and the whole place has an air of hustling resolution. Planted down here, one might imagine that you were in Newfoundland. In truth Newfoundland has transferred its ways to the heart of Perthshire.

At first the Scotsmen were inclined to feel sore at the unconventional methods of the new comers, and various big challenges were exchanged. The cutting down of trees is a solemn affair and ought to be done with a certain stateliness. It ought above all to be done sparingly, and with a certain nicety according to estate traditions. That is the old British idea. But here are men doing it wholesale, leaving nothing behind.

The men now at work number about 300, to be increased very shortly, it is hoped, with fresh drafts coming along to about 1000. There are boys in their mid-teens here, too young to go to France to fight, but determined to do something to help win the war. On Sunday afternoons one sees the men of the Forestry Companies making friends with the country folk in every village around, looking in every way smart, good soldiers. And when their battalion marches into Dunkeld, it is difficult to believe that these same well-set ranks are made up of backwoodsmen who have volunteered their service from the freest life in the world—this life of the woods. They have received a warm Scots welcome from all—from Duke to cottager. The country around the Craig of Goats is as wildly beautiful as any Scotland has to show. The trees are magnificent. The lumber has been well cared for. The trees run straight and true and high. The axemen talk of some of the timber lovingly, as a connoisseur would talk of fine wine. There was one spruce tree whose main trunk was over 100 feet long. It was 29 inches in diameter at the stump, and 15 in. in diameter 53 ft. high. They got 97 feet of timber out of it.

It is over a hundred years since the Duke of Atholl resolved to plant the waste lands of his estate with spruce and larch trees. Over fifteen thousand acres, mainly of barren mountain side, was planted with 27,431,600 trees. Great destruction was wrought amongst these by storms, and thousands of trees were blown done. But sufficient were deeply rooted so as to withstand the storms of time, and today the demands of Great Britain for shipbuilding material are largely supplied from woods. But at the same time while we are cutting down great stretches of the most beautiful countryside, large numbers of Scots women[100] have been at work planting new districts afresh, for Scottish landowners are beginning to realize that under the conditions likely to prevail in the world for some time to come, their forests will be a great source of national wealth.

Dunkeld, Perthshire, Scotland

---

100 The Women's Forestry Service (WFS), formed in 1917, was a division of the Women's Land Army. The Women's Land Army participated in farming, foraging, and forestry during the First World War. For an account of their contribution, see Scott (1917). The Duke of Atholl sponsored a group of the WFS who were housed at Dunkeld. Friendships between its members and the men of the NFC were likely. On July 6, 1918, the NFC participated in the recovery of the bodies of three WFS members who had drowned in the River Tay ("Tragedy of the Tay," 1918).

Patriotic Concerts

Barrett mentioned visits to the Companies by photographers and cinema-tographers in several letters. Pictures of the work of the NFC were featured at events in Scotland and Newfoundland. On April 25, 1918, "The Newfound-landers at Dunkeld" premiered at The King's Cinema in Perth to a full house; subsequent viewings drew equally large crowds, causing the reviewer with the *Perthshire Advertiser* ("The King's Cinema," 1918) to proclaim:

> Wonderful things can take place at our own doors as well as abroad. This is one of them. To see the Newfoundland lumber-men in the forests of Atholl in winter bringing large trees to the ground with lightning rapidity, and then getting them to the world's largest chute, is indeed well-nigh marvellous. (p. 4)

Pictures of the NFC were also featured at recruitment events and patriotic concerts held in all parts of Newfoundland. Patriotic concerts were a staple of the Homefront wartime effort and were advertised and reviewed regularly in local newspapers. Patriotic concerts were both demonstrations of and inspira-tion for support for those serving overseas. As well as a way for those at home to "do their bit," these concerts helped uphold the spirits of those whose loved ones were serving. And they were largely organized and executed by women, from the teachers in small coastal schools to the wives of merchants, most of whom were members of the Women's Patriotic Association.[101]

Concerts were also a major form of fundraising throughout Newfoundland. Proceeds were usually dedicated to one of a variety of war-related funds. Ven-ues—from schools and community halls to casinos and auditoriums—were offered free of charge. Local bands, performers, and community leaders filled

---

101 It is estimated that the WPA had over 200 branches and more than 15,000 mem-bers throughout the country, including a branch at Battle Harbour, Labrador, and that it raised over $500,000 (Duley, 2012). After the war, this unified network of women from all sectors of the country played a crucial role in securing the vote for women in Newfoundland, achieved in 1925 (Bishop-Stirling, 2015).

the programs that usually included speeches, messages, songs, instrumentals, recitations, and theatrics that blended patriotism, poignancy, reverence, and humour. Songs such as the English "Keep the Home Fires Burning," the Canadian "Good Luck to the Boys of the Allies," and the American "Set Aside Your Tears 'Til the Boys Come Marching Home" were accompanied by homespun recitations such as "Our W.P.A.," readings of local letters from the trenches, and playful skits. When available, film and photo screenings of "Ours" overseas were also featured. Meals and dances sometimes followed concerts. Some local businesses closed their doors to encourage patrons to purchase concert offerings. On at least one occasion, a patriotic concert was also the site of an anti-conscription protest ("Sedition," 1918).

Grand Patriotic Concert,
BRITISH HALL, Tuesday, Nov. 6th, at 8 15 p.m.

At this concert the latest moving pictures of the Newfoundland Regiment and Forestry Companies will be shown.

Official moving pictures of the presentation of an aeroplane by the citizens of Sheffield to Newfoundland will be shown for the first time.

In addition to this, a programme of vocal and band music has been arranged, and some of our most prominent speakers have consented to deliver addresses.

ADMISSION FREE.

An advertisement for a patriotic concert.
(*The Evening Telegram*, November 3, 1917, p. 10)

PEN PICTURE OF PERTHSHIRE[102]
Scene of Operations of Newfoundland Forestry Companies

October 15, 1917

Dear Sir,

When so many eyes in Newfoundland are turned towards Scotland and the doings of the Forestry Companies, perhaps a few casual observations respecting the general characteristics and natural conditions of this section may be of interest to your readers. Most of what I here write came under my own notice, while for other information I have sought it from reliable sources. Without any attempt at prolongation, I shall be as brief as possible.

Situated as it is in the very heart of Scotland, its position has made Perthshire (the county in which we are located) the scene of some of the most important and stirring events in Scottish history, and almost every part of it is connected in some way with the past history of the country. The shire is divided into two distinct regions—the Highlands and the Lowlands. It is in the Highland region that we are operating. Here among the "Burning Hills" are stretches of open moorland, surrounded by sections heavily wooded with larch (juniper), Scots fir, elm, beech, etc. The Lowland region on the other hand is noted for its fertility; yet it is said that only about one-fifth of the entire area is cultivated. Scattered here and there over the country are numerous villages and towns, the houses of which are unusually well built of solid stone and lime roofed with flagstones or slates. The common fuel is coal brought by railroad from the south. Many and varied are the mountains, some of them rising to an elevation of about 3,000 feet, while many of the peaks exceed this altitude.

---

102 *The Western Star*, November 14, 1917, p 1. Also published in *The Evening Herald*, November 17, 1917.

The most beautiful and fertile valley in the whole county is that of Strathmore, which can be seen from the mountain near our Camp. Its greatest breadth is fourteen miles, dotted over which may be seen numerous villages, towns, and mansions.

The deer forests of this country are six in number, containing 94,750 acres. They contain large numbers of red deer, roe deer, and fallow deer. According to one of the sporting magazines, the rental of these deer forests yields as high as £75,000 a year. There are also said to be over 400 grouse moors, which are unsurpassed and yield excellent sport. The higher mountains afford an occasional resting place for the golden and white-tailed eagle, and the falcon is known to nest in the shire. Great numbers of sportsmen are annually attracted to the Highlands in pursuit of deer and game birds. The capercailzie,[103] a species of which was introduced into Newfoundland some years ago by Sir Robert Bond,[104] is very abundant here; and as we have been given permission to hunt any of the game, it is not infrequent to see the outer walls of some of our tents decorated with a string of fine birds.

The temperature is remarkably constant everywhere throughout the county, averaging 47 Fahrenheit for the year. The coldest month is January (26.50 Fahrenheit) and the hottest July (59 Fahrenheit). On the whole the climate may be described as mild and salubrious. Of course, in the more northerly and westerly parts, where the ground reaches a high elevation, the nature of the country makes it cold; but these sections are also dry and healthy, as they are screened from the northern blasts by the high mountain ridges.

---

103 Capercailzie (or Capercaillie) is a large wood grouse.

104 Robert Bond was the last Premier of Newfoundland (1900 to 1907) and its first Prime Minister (once Newfoundland was given Dominion status), from 1907 to 1909. At The Grange, Bond's home in Whitbourne, he introduced several ornamental tree species and, in 1907, 23 capercailzies from Copenhagen, most of which disappeared (Millais, 1907, p. 264).

Large deposits of peat are to be met with in Perthshire. Up until recent years, peat was the principal fuel in the Highlands. But the increased facilities for the transit of coal from the south have led to the gradual diminution of its use.

The Tay, which is the largest and most magnificent river in Scotland, rises at an altitude of 3,000 feet above sea level. This river sweeps majestically through the country passing within a short distance of our Camp. The valley of the Tay, which every day we look out upon, is a continued scene of unsurpassed beauty and loveliness. Lofty mountains rise on either side, their sloping sides being richly wooded. In the Highlands of Scotland in earlier days the main valleys would be the first to attract the population, and for this reason the valley of the Tay, which contains by far the largest amount of alluvial and arable land, is the most extensively cultivated.

Salmon fishing is practiced very extensively on the River Tay and its varied tributaries. Fish weighing up to 35 pounds is by no means uncommon. In fact, it seems to be an exception to find any fish under 18 or 20 pounds. The salmon fisheries of the Tay are owned by various noblemen and corporations, and it has been estimated that the number of salmon and grilse taken from it in a year average from 75,000 to 100,000. A most systematic method of propagating salmon ova is being carried on, thus ensuring the maintenance of a goodly supply of fish.

Agricultural and pastoral seem to have been the principal pursuits of the inhabitants since time immemorial. Of course, there are other occupations, such as mining and quarrying, as well as textile and other industries. Then there are the linen and cotton trades, woolen and tweed manufactories, bleach fields and print works, paper mills, tanneries, factories for the manufacture of glass, floor cloths, ropes and twines, bricks and chemicals. Numerous grain mills also afford employment to a great many of the inhabitants. There are also many breweries and distilleries throughout the county, but as Newfoundland is now a dry "spot" on the globe,[105] perhaps the mere mention of malt may cause the lips of some of your readers to perspire.

The roads of the county, which are well constructed and well kept, have been systematically laid out, and the network of good highways is an evidence of the foresight and thoughtfulness on the part of those who planned them. Cycles and motor cars traverse the shire in all directions, as these excellent roads afford an easy means of communication. The tired traveller is enabled by means of numerous signposts to learn the distance between the various towns and to get the correct direction to follow. The great Highland Road, which starts at Perth, running along the valley of the Tay, passing through Dunkeld and the Pass of Killicrankie, was planned and carried out in the nineteenth century, and is still in a perfect state of repair.

The universal educational system in Scotland compels the attendance at school of all children between the ages of five and fourteen.[106] This primary education is free. The management of education is entrusted to School Boards, which are elected every three years by the rate-payers. These Boards are established in every parish throughout the country, and are responsible for the management of the schools and the appointment of teachers.

For picturesqueness of architectural designing one would have to search the whole of Scotland and then not find anything to excel that of the ecclesiastical and baronial buildings of this county. Some of the styles date back to the tenth century. The mansions and castles of the Scottish nobility afford numerous fine examples of the strongholds of feudal times. Some of them are still in a good state of preservation. Their massive square

---

105 A reference to prohibition, which was introduced in Newfoundland on January 1, 1917.

106 Compulsory school attendance was legislated in Newfoundland in 1943.

towers, turrets and high embattled walls tell of the habits of a people who, inured to war, had little care for their ordinary dwelling so long as their cattle and movable possessions could be placed beyond the ravages of the invader.

Dunkeld, Perthshire, Scotland

LUMBERMEN'S SPORTS IN SCOTLAND[107]
Newfoundlanders Among the Prize winners

October 22, 1917

Dear Sir,

The most notable event of the past week was the Lumberman's Sports, which took place at Stanley, on Saturday, October 20th. It was under the auspices of the Stanley War Relief Funds Committee, whose funds were augmented by some $300. The occasion was observed by us as a half-holiday, and quite a number of our men went thither by rail.

Many notables from various parts of Scotland were present to witness the unique aquatic and other sports put on by members of the Canadian and Newfoundland Forestry Companies. Amongst them were the Duke and Duchess of Atholl, Colonel and Mrs. Fotheringham,[108] of Murthly Castle, Madame Tempest, Commandant of Dalguise V.A.D. Auxiliary Hospital, William Cox, Managing Director of Highland Railway, Sir John Stirling Maxwell, Timber Controller for Scottish District, Lady Maxwell, Sir Joseph Outerbridge,[109] Lieutenant and Mrs. Herbert Outerbridge,[110] and Mrs. Campbell.[111]

---

107 *The Western Star*, November 21, 1917, p 1. Also published in *The Evening Herald*, November 27, 1917; *The Evening Telegram*, November 24, 1917; and *The Twillingate Sun*, December 8, 1917.
108 Colonel Walter Steuart-Fotheringham (or Fothringham) and Elizabeth Nicholson Fotheringham.
109 Sir Joseph Outerbridge was the vice-president of the Newfoundland Patriotic Association, which oversaw the recruitment of the Newfoundland Regiment until August 1917, at which time the NPA was replaced by a Department of Militia formed by the new coalition government of Prime Minister Edward Morris.
110 Herbert Outerbridge, RNR #0–141, was a son of Joseph and Maria Outerbridge. A member of the Regiment, he was wounded at Sailly-Saillisel in early 1917.
111 Lillian Outerbridge was the daughter of Joseph and Maria and brother of Herbert; she married Captain J.D. Campbell of the Royal Navy.

A band from the Scottish Horse[112] was in attendance, and rendered some very interesting overtures during the afternoon. The event was under the direction of Captain McDougall,[113] Officer Commanding, Canadian Forestry Corps, and Lieutenant H. Cole of the Newfoundland Forestry Companies. The Duke of Atholl, Sir J.S. Maxwell, Major Ferguson[114] (of the Canadian Forestry Corps), and Major Sullivan were judges of the various contests.

But it must be said to the credit of our tug-of-war team, they maintained the reputation gained on September 1st as being the champion team of the district. The Canadian team, made up of big husky chaps from the Western Provinces, one of them weighing over 15 stone, boasted of what they were going to do. Yet our lads had a clean walk over with them every time. When our team got up against a team of Scotchmen, selected from within a radius of forty miles, the tussle waged long and furious. In the final heat, they were thirty-three minutes on the rope, struggling with might and main, while the excited spectators kept vociferously cheering our men. Eventually our team got the brawny Scots across the line, both sides having scored a point; and thus the prize of sixty shillings was equally divided amongst them.

Our tug-of-war team consisted of Lieutenant K. Goodyear (a jolly good sort of anchor-man), Sergeant E. Moore,[115] Corporal

112 The Scottish Horse was a yeomanry unit with origins in the Territorial Army of the British Army that was raised in 1900 in South Africa for the Boer War. In 1902, the Duke of Atholl rebuilt the unit with headquarters at Dunkeld. Its records are housed at the Dunkeld Community Archive.

113 General Officer Commanding (GOC) Brigadier General Alexander Lorne McDougall.

114 Major P.G. Ferguson.

115 Sergeant Edward Moore, NFC #8149, Badger.

J.A. Campbell, Lance Corporal J. Langdon,[116] and Privates E. Hull,[117] C. King,[118] J. Oldford[119] and H. Stockley.[120]

There were a number of entries for the log sawing and log chopping contests, which displayed the marvellous skill and rapidity with which the lumbermen use the axe and the saw. The blocks provided were uniform both in length and diameter, and for a while there were chips flying in all directions. The prize for sawing went to the Canadians, but the chopping prize was won by Sergeant Ball.

The log race on the pond was an interesting event, two Canadians and two Newfoundlanders entering therefor. Each man occupied a single log, and their object was for each man to propel a log with a pike pole from one end of the pond to the other, the person doing it in the quickest time was to receive a prize of 1 pound. This honour fell to Sergeant W. Beaton[121] of Ours.

The log rolling exhibition, which took place in the water, was an intensely exciting sport, the contestants, wearing spiked boots, acquitting themselves creditably, which elicited rounds of applause from the large gathering. Some remarkable feats of skill, daring and agility were performed by these lumberjacks, who appeared to be as much at home on a whirling, twirling single log as Captain Kean would be on the good ship "Prospero."[122]

---

116 Lance Corporal John H. Langdon, NFC #8231, Northern Arm.

117 Private Ephraim Hull, NFC #8191, Springdale.

118 Private Charles King, NFC #8139, Catalina.

119 Private John Oldford, NFC #8222, Salvage.

120 Private Henry Stockley, NFC #8282, Greenspond.

121 Sergeant William Beaton, NFC #8248, Badger.

122 Captain Abram Kean was a renowned sealing captain who commanded the SS *Prospero* from 1915 to 1920. He was Captain of the SS *Newfoundland*, from which 78 sealers died in 1914 when they were caught on the ice in a storm while hunting. For an account of this tragedy, see Brown (1972). Another Newfoundland sealing ship, the SS *Southern Cross*, disappeared in the same storm; all 174

Stanley is only fifteen miles from the nearest station to our Camp, and the return ticket cost each man but thirty-six cents. We left here at 1 p.m., and returned at 9.30. The Canadians have finished operations there, and are about to move to a new scene of labour nearer Perth.

Major Sullivan was highly complimented by quite a number of people over the smart appearance and good behaviour of our men whilst on their vacation last Saturday; it was the first time some of them had seen any of the lads from the Tenth Island.[123]

Sir Joseph Outerbridge visited our Camp last week. He expressed himself as being greatly charmed with the country, and said the two days spent here were the pleasantest of any spent on this side of the "herring pond." A visit was paid A and B Companies, where he inspected the operations of the men, congratulating the officers upon the success already attained. He was accompanied by Lieutenant Herbert Outerbridge and Mrs. Outerbridge.

The new Draft of 43 men arrived safely on the 17th, and the men are now established among us, performing the same tricks as all the other men are doing.

There was a cessation of hostilities between our men and the trees from Oct. 8th to 18th, to enable our forces to remove the dead "bodies," which in their thousands strewed the hillsides. But now they have again renewed the engagement. Every day the battle rages long and furious, and at eventide the Camp is astir with tales of the thousands of giants slain with axes and saws.

The construction of our log chute has been improved upon by the addition of an inclined curve at the lower end, and the

---

aboard were lost. The two tragedies became known as the 1914 Newfoundland Sealing Disaster.

123 This is a reference to a book by Beckles Wilson: *The Tenth Island, Being Some Account of Newfoundland, Its People, Its Politics, Its Problems, and Its Peculiarities.* Wilson contended that a list of the ten largest islands in the world would place Australia first and Newfoundland as "the tenth island" (Wilson, 1897, pp. 1–2).

construction of another chute which leads off from the main in the shape of a broken Y. This was done in order to check the speed of the logs, which go thundering down the long chute with lightning rapidity. Now they come to a halt at the top of the in-clined curve, and, reversing into the short chute, are carried down to the jack-ladder at the mill.

The new building for the second mill is about ready for the installation of the machinery, which has already arrived. With this mill in operation it is expected to turn out daily a cut of 40,000 feet of lumber. It was estimated that some 7,000,000 feet of lum-ber was on this section when we came here. By felling a million feet per month, it will take to the end of February before it is all down; and with the mills each cutting 500,000 ft. per month, the sawing operations would not be completed before next June. So, you see, there is every probability of our lads spending quite a little while yet with bonnie folk of this part of Scotland.

Dunkeld, Perthshire, Scotland

A group of Newfoundland foresters, Craigvinean, Dunkeld, 1917.
(Courtesy of Ean Parsons)

Praise from Outerbridge

Sir Joseph Outerbridge ("NFLD Foresters," 1917) sent the following telegram to Governor Davidson about his visit to the foresters; it was printed in *The Evening Telegram* on October 20, 1917:

> Have visited Foresters. Am charmed with work already accomplished under excellent arrangements by Major Sullivan and other officers. Men appear very comfortable and satisfied. Lovely country and climate very similar to Newfoundland. More skilled mill hands and lumbermen urgently required. (p. 4)

DOINGS OF OUR FORESTRY COMPANIES[124]

October 29, 1917

Sir,

The autumn season is now upon us, bringing with it shorter days and longer nights and quite a change in atmospheric conditions. A short while ago we could take breakfast and tea[125] without the aid of artificial light, and we could do with very little fire in the huts. Today, all this is changed, and we have not more than ten hours of clear daylight on a fine bright day, and soon it will be shortening down to eight hours. The weather is very unsettled, as it usually is at this time of the year—raining or snowing most every day. This makes it rather unpleasant for our work; but the men, being equipped with oil jackets, long rubber leggings and knee boots, do not seem to mind the change very much, and are daily engaged at their various occupations.

Log felling, browing, transportation, sawing and piling are being pursued with unabated vigor. Machinery is being installed in the second new mill, and it is hoped to have it ready by the middle of November. The little mill we first used on the hill has been removed to the foot of the hill, where it is to be given a place between its two big alien brothers, and will be used for the purpose of cross-cutting refuse for fuel, etc.

The recreation building is about completed, and awaits the installation of the necessary furniture. It is quite a roomy building, being about 60 x 30 feet. It was intended to have a room in it set apart for a library and to be used by our men as a place where they could go and transact their correspondence. Such a room is very necessary, as the men find it rather difficult to write

---

124 *The Western Star*, November 28, 1917, p. 1. Also published in *The Evening Herald*, December 1, 1917.

125 For many in the UK, "tea" was and still is a name for the evening meal.

letters in the huts, which are not very brilliantly lighted at night.

Speaking of lights reminds me of the installation of an electric light plant in the saw mills and the various buildings at the foot of the hill. It is not quite completed as yet; but when it is, it will be quite an improvement and a valuable addition to the Camp, and will enable the men to do better work when the mills start operating on night shift, which is being planned for the near future.

A fine motor car has lately been furnished us by the War Office. Its service will be very essential for our work, especially when we start operations at Kenmore, as we shall then be several miles away from a railroad.

A very interesting concert was given in town a few nights since. It was very largely patronized by our men, who spent a most pleasant evening. The vocalists displayed talent of no mean order, their renditions being so interesting and entertaining as to elicit frequent encores. A similar treat is booked for some night soon.

Last night the citizens of Nottingham presented an aeroplane to New Zealand. The affair was witnessed by a gathering of over one hundred thousand people, many of whom had travelled a considerable distance specially for the occasion. Major Sullivan, who was present, informs me of Sir Edward Morris[126] being there, and making the speech of the day. With his customary volubility, Sir Edward told the gathering of the wonderful doings of the Americans in their continued preparations for the mighty struggle now going on in the theatres of war. Being fresh from the American continent, Sir Edward delivered his address with telling effect, as he pointed out the thousands of men under arms, the numerous fast craft of war being rushed to completion,

---

126 Prime Minister of Newfoundland from 1909 to 1917. Morris tendered his resignation in a letter from England only two weeks after Barrett's letter was written (on November 19, 1917) and effective December 31 (Hiller, 2015).

and the many aeroplanes about to be put in commission for the great European conflict.

Some of our men have been sadly disappointed over the non-receipt of parcels sent from their friends at home. In some cases, these parcels are said to have been forwarded as long ago as two months. Perhaps the delay may be due to their being wrongly addressed, or there may be negligence on the part of postal authorities. Whatever the cause may be, it is really too bad for our men to be deprived of the comforts mailed them, as they do not get a surfeit of any over here.

The price of food commodities in this country has gone exceptionally high; in fact, in some instances it has gone beyond the reach of the ordinary individual. Today in some towns the price of tea is said to be five shillings per pound (and English people are such tea-drinkers); sugar cannot be purchased without a food ticket, and even then, it can only be had in limited quantity. Butter, flour and meats are proportionately high, whilst many articles of fish are looked upon as a luxury. These high prices are not caused by any scarcity of food stuffs, but are said to be largely due to profiteering.[127] It was only a few days since I was informed of a large consignment of food stuff having lain so long in an English warehouse that the article became tainted, and had to be condemned as an article of food.

There has been an abundant yield of all root crops throughout the British Isles this year. But in many parts, there were large quantities of wheat ungarnered last week when a cold spurt of weather set in, greatly damaging the crop. Potatoes and turnips are also said to have been affected by the frosts.

Dunkeld, Perthshire, Scotland

---

127 Similar accusations were levelled at the merchant class of Newfoundland. See O'Brien (2011).

Parcel Lifters

The non-delivery of parcels was an aggravation for those at home and over-seas. *The Western Star* addressed the issue pointedly in an article ("The Non-receipt of Parcels," 1917) that appeared in the same issue as Barrett's letter of October 29 and also offered a solution:

> There appears to be a general complaint regarding parcels ad-dressed to lads over-seas not reaching their destination. While there might be some excuse for long delays in the delivery of par-cels to lads in the trenches, we fail to see any logical reason why those addressed to members of the Forestry Companies and the lads at Ayr should not be delivered within reasonable time. It takes a letter about two weeks to come from Scotland, and we would presume it takes, or should take, a similar time for mail matter to go. We are therefore of the opinion that parcels by mail should be delivered within a month at most; but we know of parcels mailed in August, and correctly addressed, which have not yet been re-ceived by parties they were intended for. So general has this non-delivery of parcels become that expressions of "lifting" are being heard. We know of one case in particular where a woman sending chocolates, tobacco, etc., to her husband, and stating the correct contents upon the packages, the articles were never re-ceived; but where she sent similar articles and marked them "soap," etc., they were received within reasonable time, and not one of them was mislaid. Evidently everybody had "soap" enough. We know of another party who never states the contents of the parcels they send to their friends Overseas, and the parcels are received without exception. In view of this, we would suggest that senders of parcels to members of the Regiment, Navy or Forestry Companies place nothing upon the wrapper to indicate the con-tents, or else mark it "soap." (p. 2)

The Time of My Life

If parcels were important for those serving overseas, letters were important to those at home—and some were shared with local newspapers. While only a small number of letters published were from foresters, those that were from NFC members carried snippets of insight into their life in Scotland. Officials encouraged the foresters, when writing home, to mention the dire need for more recruits. The men complied, often writing enthusiastic, untroubled accounts of life in Scotland.

John R. Martin, NFC #8232, a carpenter from Manuels, was 50 when he enlisted on June 9, 1917. His son, Corporal Robert B. Martin, RNR #499, was a Blue Puttee. In a letter to a friend in St. John's, the elder Martin ("Our Soldier Lads," 1917) was effusive about life in Scotland:

I am having the time of my life. I only wish this thing had happened when I was younger, but as it is I am enjoying myself. All the boys are well and in the pink of health.

I have seen a few of the cities. I had one weekend since I came over and I was in Perth and Glasgow and in Ayr. I was over to see my boy and he is fine, also his wife,[128] and they send regards to you. I visited the home of the famous Scotch poet, Bobbie Burns, and saw his monument and the Banks and Brays of Bonnie Dundee. It is a romantic looking spot.

We have a little city of our own here. Lots of the boys have bicycles and the Major has his motorcar, so you see we are a jolly crowd. Our Major is just as jolly as ever, God bless him, and there is not a man in the bunch but would say that as well as I. There is Captain Ross, he is jolly and fine and as good a man as ever lived, and that's saying a lot. Sergeant-Major James is fine and when he gets

---

128 Isabelle Juner, from Gorebridge, Scotland.

around with his whistle I tell you there is something doing among the boys. It is "Fall in," "Number up," "Form fours," "Get to it," and we all enjoy it fine. Military is alright. All our officers are as fine a bunch as you could get. Everything that can be done to make life happy for our boys is done.

We have one mill running for three weeks or more and will have another in two weeks' time, when we will be turning out about forty-thousand feet a day. So you can see we are doing a little bit to help along the cause.

I am hoping you are doing all you can in the way of recruiting and tell everyone you meet that are able to enlist to come over here and help us put an end to the war.

As ever yours,
John R. Martin (p. 4)

CHILDREN OF DUNKELD
ENTERTAIN FORESTRY CORPS[129]

November 5, 1917

Dear Sir,

Those who have travelled through the Humber Valley or the country surrounding Codroy or George's Ponds in the early part of October can picture on a small scale what the countryside hereabout is like at this season. For the past week or two the trees have been resplendent in their autumn dress. The sere and yellow leaves of beech, chestnut, elm, laburnum, and oak have vied with each other in richness of colour, and show up in marked contrast to the deep green of the spruces and firs. But "Leaves have their time to fall, / And flowers to wither at the north wind's breath;"[130] and now the streets and hedges are strewn with them, making a vast difference in the appearance of the surroundings.

No doubt many of your readers have seen the picture, "Over the Hills and Far Away." If I am correctly informed, it was painted by Sir John Millais. The setting was the valley of the Tay, hemmed in on either side by lofty mountains, with towering Ben Vrackie[131] away in the distance. The tower of the building where the noted painter transferred this beautiful scene to canvas is still standing, and is visible from our Camp, being only about two miles distant.[132]

Yesterday when I went out over the country, which has lately been cut over by our men, and saw the great quantities of large limbs of trees strewn over the hillside, I thought of the numerous

---

129 _The Western Star_, December 5, 1917, p. 3. Also published in _The Evening Herald_, December 5, 1917.

130 Barrett quotes from "The Hour of Death" by Felicia Dorothea Hemans (1907).

131 North of Pitlochry, Ben Vrackie summits at 841 metres.

132 Millais actually painted the picture from the fields near Tomgarrow between Rumbling Ridge Cottage, where he vacationed, and Dundonnachie Cottage (J. Anderson, personal communication, June 21, 2019).

families in Conception Bay who would be gladdened at the prospect of having such in their wood piles. Whilst these sticks are green, yet they are far from being "Starrigans,"[133] because they can be readily ignited by the aid of very little kindlings. It is with such wood that our huts are heated and all our cooking is done.

The gathering of all this fuel and the cutting of it into stove lengths keeps several men constantly employed. Although it is not laborious work, yet it becomes monotonous to those engaged at it. But I expect that this will shortly be changed, as a 5-horsepower oil engine, with saws, is likely to be furnished for this work.

Our men are beginning to go farther afield in the carrying on of their operations, and to-day some of them took out luncheon with them for the first time. They are doing splendid work these days, and are working in a section that is not quite so steep as where they were at first.

Work on the building of another log chute has been undertaken. This chute will be used for the conveyance of logs from the top of the hill down into the lower chute, with which it will be connected, a tunnel being cut underneath the road for that purpose. When completed, the upper end will be about five hundred feet above the roadway where the lower chute begins. It will be very interesting to watch the big logs tumbling down all that stretch of chute right to the mills.

A short while ago a director of the Timber Committee, together with a representative of the Highland Railway Company, visited Camp for the express purpose of learning the feasibility of running a railway siding into the yard where the sawn timber is stacked. I have since heard of their approval of the scheme, and no doubt the work will soon be undertaken.

---

133 In Newfoundland and Labrador English, a starrigan is a small evergreen, good for neither firewood nor lumber.

On Saturday, our men were treated to a free entertainment in town. The performers were mostly children of Dunkeld, who gave several very interesting vocal and instrumental renditions, and performed very creditably some very difficult drills and physical exercises. Upon invitation, we are to attend another concert and tea in the Town Hall next Saturday afternoon, furnished by the ladies of Dunkeld. Newfoundlanders at home have good reason to be grateful to the women of this country who are steadfast and enthusiastic workers on behalf of our men, wherever they may be stationed. The men of our overseas Regiment pay tribute to the kindly women who cheer and encourage them. This may also be said of the men of our Companies. To those patient women workers who do their bit in brightening the lives of the soldiers who come from distant lands, it must be encouraging to learn that their work is appreciated by us.

Dunkeld, Perthshire, Scotland

Foresters and visitors at a mill at Craigvinean, Dunkeld, 1917.
(Courtesy of the Dunkeld Community Archive)

DALGUISE CASTLE, V.A.D. AUXILIARY HOSPITAL[134]

November 7, 1917

Dear Sir,

Dalguise, from the Gaelic word, meaning "Valley of the Fir Trees," is picturesquely situated on an undulating woodland at the base of the Craigvinean, about a mile and a half from the Camp of the Newfoundland Forestry Companies. It is there the above-named Hospital is located. The earliest part of the existing house was built in 1715, and is of Scottish baronial style.

The Hospital, which contains 18 beds, is on the first floor of the Tower, a section of the building standing about 75 feet high, overlooking the magnificent River Tay, which meanders close by. There is also a large ward, a mess-room, and recreation room furnished with billiard table, piano, gramophones, and a great variety of games. All the rooms are large, bright, and airy. In attendance, there is a staff of four very efficient nurses, who are very painstaking and who evince a great interest in the welfare of our boys.

The Hospital is under the control of the British Red Cross Society, and is presided over by Madame Tempest, a very amiable person. This lady is a descendant of the Stewarts, who were at one time the reigning monarchs of Scotland. This Hospital was opened in June, 1915. Since then it has accommodated nearly 700 patients. Some 30 members of the Newfoundland Forestry Companies have been inmates of this institution, besides several out-patients, all of whom speak in highest praise of the treatment received at the hands of the Sisters.[135]

---

134 *The Western Star*, December 24, 1917, p. 4. Also published in *The Evening Herald*, December 5, 1917.

135 Nursing Sisters were professional nurses who provided wartime medical services; civilian women with little formal training volunteered as part of the Red Cross VAD. Francis Cluett of Belleoram, Newfoundland, was one such VAD nurse. For Cluett's story, see Rompkey and Riggs (2006). For a general

The approach to the grounds is through a natural archway of elm and lime trees, some of which rise to a height of 100 feet. In the grounds are beautiful variegated beech trees, larch, yew, oak, and other trees. Several ancient statues adorn the embankment in front of the building. Quite near are the croquet grounds and the bowling green, where the charming nurses frequently indulge in friendly games with the convalescent soldiers. The sun dial is a cozy nook and is much frequented by the patients. A number of walks are made of huge flag-stones, thus enabling one to pass over dry shod immediately after a rainstorm. The great mass of ivy and honeysuckle clinging to the walls of the building adds to its dignified appearance.

Dunkeld, Perthshire, Scotland

Dalguise Castle, Dalguise, Scotland, ca. 1915.
(Courtesy of the Dunkeld Community Archive)

discussion of Newfoundland women in nursing service during the First World War, see Bishop-Stirling (2012).

HUNTING GAME[136]
Other Weekly Doings of Forestry Companies

November 11, 1917

Dear Sir,

Whilst the Caribou hunting season is now on in Newfoundland, the boys of the Forestry Companies are having similar sport in this part of Scotland. Long railway and canoe trips are unnecessary, as deer may be found within a few minutes' walk of our Camp. So, also, is there an abundance of smaller game, such as hares, rabbits, and various species of wild birds, and quite frequently some of them are brought in to supplement our rations.

A few days ago, two large tanks, capable of containing over eight hundred gallons of water, were supplied us. These are to be used by the men for bathing purposes, and will be put up on the grounds of B Company, thus ensuring a means whereby the men can get a good bath, either hot or cold, at least once a week.

Our recreation building has been opened, and men go there nightly to amuse themselves and do their letter writing. A goodly supply of literature, including daily papers and latest magazines, is furnished from various sources. A refreshment room is to be conducted in connection with the recreation building, where teas may be obtained any evening.

Arrangements are about finalized for the maintenance of a Medical Hut in our Camp. One of the roomly section huts is to be used for the purpose, which will accommodate a number of beds where those suffering from minor ailments may be attended to without having to go to Hospital. Madam Tempest, the Commandant of Dalguise V.A.D. Hospital, has very generously

---

136 *The Western Star*, December 12, 1917, p. 1. Also published in *The Evening Herald*, December 18, 1917.

promised to furnish this building and put a nurse in attendance. A medical practitioner will also be in attendance daily.

A V.A.D. Hospital or Home has been opened at Birnam,[137] about four miles from Camp. This is to be used principally by convalescent soldiers, and already some twenty-five persons, from various English and Scottish regiments, are being accommodated there, and there is room for about twenty more. It is run under the auspices of the Red Cross Society. A number of ladies belonging to Birnam and Dunkeld are taking a lively interest in the institution, and are rendering every assistance to help brighten the lives of those brave, wounded boys.

Yesterday afternoon was the occasion of a free concert and tea, tendered us by a number of prominent ladies of Dunkeld. The men of both Companies were at first paraded on the ground of the mill, and after going through various manoeuvers, were photographed in groups. Then we all marched in to town, presenting quite a military appearance with Captain Baird and Captain Ross, on chargers,[138] heading the parade.

The concert consisted of songs, dances, piano duets, violin selections, sketches, etc. Mr. Crombie, headmaster of Dunkeld Academy, was the chairman, and in his opening remarks extended to us a hearty welcome, and a Scottish welcome at that. He hoped that the Newfoundland boys while in this country would find that there were warm hearts in Scotland for them. For over two hours we were entertained by the vocal and instrumental members, which renditions were so creditably given that they were frequently encored. At the close of the performance, Captain Ross, on behalf of the men of the Forestry Companies and

---

137 St. Mary's Tower Auxiliary Hospital, Birnam, was a British Red Cross-run convalescence home for less seriously wounded soldiers. The more seriously wounded were tended at military hospitals. There were over 3,000 such convalescent hospitals in the UK during the war (British Red Cross, n.d.).

138 A charger is a horse ridden by a soldier.

the men of St. Mary's Home, thanked the ladies for the very interesting and enjoyable entertainment. He spoke of the true Scottish hospitality extended to Newfoundlanders in different parts of Scotland, claiming that our boys were being as well received and entertained as they would be at home. Three cheers were called for the ladies who helped towards the afternoon's entertainment, and they were given with such a gusto that they still ring in my ears.

While the concert was in progress a number of ladies were busy behind the scenes, making preparations for the supplying of the wants of the inner man, and soon we were served with tea, sandwiches, scones, tarts, cakes, etc. This treat brought forth more rounds of cheers for the ladies for their untiring efforts on our behalf.

There is not much to report concerning the past weeks' lumbering operations, except to say that everything has been going along smoothly, with all the men engaged at their customary branches of the work.

Last week I spoke of the construction of another log chute above the tramline. When completed it will connect with the present chute, thus making one of a total length of 3,080 feet, with a drop of about 800 feet, or 1 in 25.[139] All the logs used in this work will be taken to the mill and converted into sawn lumber after all the timber on the hill has first been sent down.

Altogether there is over a mile and a half of railway track laid on the hillside and in the yard. On the lineup on the mountain, the log trolleys are drawn by horses; but for a considerable distance the track has such a gradient that the loaded cars can be operated without the assistance of the animals.

139 This measure is the slope (gradient) of the chute as expressed in the ratio of rise to run.

We have our own forges, where Privates A. Squarey[140] and W. Wyatt[141] do all our iron and farriers work. The harnesses and saddlery are kept in a state of good repair by Private M. Glynn, whilst our boots and shoes are attended to without unnecessary cost by Private J. Griffin.

The following lines, written forty years ago by the noted Scottish writer, the late James Smith, have been adapted by his daughter so that they have an application to the present time. I pass them on to you for the benefit of your readers:

THE RALE RIC-MA-TICK[142]
James Smith

Come listen, freens an' neebours, to this rantin' screed o'
rhyme
Concerning twa three bits o' things anent this present
time.
I'll tell ye naething but the truth, an' to the truth I'll stick;
For an honest word in season is the rale Ric-ma-tick.

'Tis said on Dorking's battlefield auld Britain's doom'd to
dee,
But by my faith there never was a bigger thumpin' lee.
She'll strike wi' vigour when she strikes, right siccar, sharp,
an' quick,
And she'll show the rash invader she's the auld Ric-ma-tick.

---

140 Private Arthur Squarey, RNR #3841, Channel.
141 Private William Wyatt, NFC #8185, St. John's.
142 For the full poem, see Smith (1872, pp. 69–70). This excerpt excludes the verses and chorus, leaving only war-related content.

There's a pious German Emperor wha' kills an' prays by
turns,
An' magnifies his glory while a gallant nation mourns;
But France shall rise with strength renewed, an' gie him
lick for lick,
An' she'll prove to Holy Willie she's the rale Ric-ma-tick.

But joyfu' days are comin' yet to Europe's troubled shore,
Sae cheer ye up, my trusty freens, there's better times in
store.
For England. France, an' Belgium shall yet be unco thick,
An' unity an' love shall be the rale Ric-ma-tick.

Dunkeld, Perthshire, Scotland

A log rollaway from a tramline near B Company Camp, Craigvinean, Dunkeld, 1917.
(Courtesy of The Rooms Provincial Archives Division, A 103-96)

PROMOTIONS IN THE FORESTRY[143]
Other Interesting Features

November 18, 1917

Dear Sir,

It scarcely seems possible that we have been in this country a little over five months. What with change of working conditions, and the earnestness with which we have all employed ourselves, the time has slipped by rather pleasantly. None has been idle, as may be gathered from the fact that twenty-one houses (ranging in length from twenty to sixty feet), two large barns, over a mile and a half of railway, three thousand feet of a log-chute, and two mills have been constructed in this incredibly short period.

While all this construction work has been going on, the work of log felling, cross-cutting, browing and transportation to mills has occupied the attention of quite a few men, whose efforts have given satisfactory results.

Starting in at first with a strength of one hundred men, our ranks have been increased by fresh drafts from home until our strength has reached over three hundred. It must not be inferred from this that all these men work at lumbering, because there are a number employed as pioneers,[144] orderlies, cooks, and in other regimental and garrison duties.

Our stabling accommodation is nearly overtaxed with forty-two heavy draught horses. These animals are daily employed, either in the woods or at transportation. Two teams are regularly engaged conveying forage, rations, and supplies from the railway station to Camp, and it would surprise your readers if they were to see the total figures of the various articles brought in by our transports.

---

143 *The Western Star*, December 24, 1917, p. 3. Also published in *The Evening Herald*, December 19, 1917.

144 Members of a military unit who prepare roads and other terrain for use.

A report is being circulated to the effect that Lieutenant Cole and Lieutenant Crowe are about to be promoted to the rank of Captain; and Command Sergeant Major James is to receive a 2nd Lieutenancy. Their promotions will likely be issued before this appears in print.[145] The men have had practical experience in the work at which they are engaged, and during the time we have been here, both Lieutenants Cole and Crowe have very efficiently performed the work allotted them. To them all are extended the congratulations of the Companies.

Now that the Separation Allowance is being granted to married men and those with an aged father or mother dependent on them for support, there should be no reasonable excuse for anyone withholding from enlisting for the Forestry Companies, and we look for a goodly increase in our numbers pretty soon.

The recreation hall is pretty freely patronized these evenings, and the men are greatly pleased over the opening of this institution. Mrs. Fotheringham, of Murthly Castle, has very generously donated towards the enjoyment of the men by giving a splendid piano, gramophone, books, magazines, etc., which the men highly appreciate. Besides these beautiful gifts, the following donations have been made for the purchase of music, writing materials, games, furniture, etc.: Fifty pounds collected by Mr. Beeton from amongst his friends; Sir Joseph Outerbridge, ten pounds; Job Brothers, Liverpool, ten guineas;[146] Mr. Henry Bowring, Liverpool, two guineas; Sir E.P. Morris, a number of good books. A number of other gifts have been promised.

Our supply of Newfoundland dried codfish is being maintained, and a few days since ten quintals of this article arrived in

---

145 All three promotions were granted, effective October 1, 1917.

146 The guinea coin was obsolete by 1813, but it remained in common use as a money value. The value of a guinea was a little more than a pound—one pound, one shilling. Barrett used both coinage references, probably to maintain the currency language in which the respective donations were made.

Camp as a free gift from Messrs. Bowring Brothers, of Liverpool. It is quite a treat to have some of our own codfish served up to us once or twice a week, and it being such a palatable article, is much enjoyed in the mess.[147]

While I am writing this the men of the various religious denominations are on parade for Church services. This takes place regularly every Sunday. Services are held in one or more of the huts by clergymen coming to Camp on Sunday mornings for that purpose. Thus, you will see that the spiritual welfare of our men is being zealously attended to.

The "Indian summer" days of the past week could not be finer under Western skies. Quite frequently there have been some remarkably fine sky effects up here in the Highlands at sunrise and sunset.

Major Sullivan leaves for Newfoundland in a day or two. No doubt he will be able to give the people a more glowing and descriptive account of our operations than my feeble pen can convey and I have no doubt he will be able to bring home to Newfoundlanders the urgency of the need for keeping up the Forestry Companies to full strength. We could do with twice our present numbers.

Dunkeld, Perthshire, Scotland

---

147 Letters of thanks for the gifts of dried codfish from Newfoundland fish merchants to the NFC were published in St. John's newspapers. See, for example, "Fish Donations" (1918).

3,000,000 FEET OF TIMBER CUT
BY FORESTRY COMPANIES[148]

November 26, 1917

Dear Sir,

The field wherein the mills are erected is fast assuming the appearance of a large timber yard. For several hundred feet between the mills and the public road, there are piled numerous stacks of sawn timber, the various grades and sizes being put up separately. Tramlines converging from the mills have been laid in different directions, and over these the lumber is conveyed on trolleys to the piles.

A short distance beyond the other side of the road a railway siding has been built, where cars will be set for loading. It is intended to have our tramline extended to this siding, thus facilitating the work of transportation.

The setting up of our second mill is about completed, except the installation of the boiler, which has not yet been received. The other mill is being operated to its full capacity daily.

A great many visitors continue to come here every week. They find our work very interesting, especially the operations at the mills and the running of logs down the mountain chute. It is all so new to them that they give such descriptive accounts of it to their friends, and then they want to see the novel sights about Camp.

Up to date there have been sufficient trees felled to make nearly three million feet of lumber. Most of these sticks have yet to be taken to the mills. Quite a few men are daily employed transporting the timber over the tramline to the log chute. They work in sections, there being some seven sidings on the tramline,

---

148 *The Western Star*, December 19, 1917, p. 1. Also published in *The Evening Herald*, December 22, 1917.

and two men are teaming on each section, with gangs working at loading points.

The addition to our first log chute is about completed, but has not yet been used. About half a mile from its upper end a number of men are logging and browing, and already there are a goodly number of sticks in that vicinity for the sawyers. Should anything happen to the tramline before the logs along the lower section of the hill are removed, then this timber on the top of the hill could be sent down to the chute with dispatch.

On the hillside, a short distance from our huts, another log chute is being built through the timber belt to the tramline. When completed it will be about fifteen hundred feet in length. It will be used for the purpose of conveying logs to a loading point on the tramline.

This morning there was a crispness in the air like unto Newfoundland. A thin mantle of snow o'erspread the hills and mountains, and the ground was hardened by the frost of last night. It did not continue for long, for as the day wore on a southerly wind brought warmth into the air, and the melting snow softened the earth again.

It is very noticeable that since the recreation building was opened not nearly as many of our men visit the town at nights. This can be attributed to the facilities afforded for enjoyment right here in Camp. It is understood that preparations are being made for the holding of a series of entertainments during the winter season; and probably means may be devised for the instituting of a Debating Club.

Dunkeld, Perthshire, Scotland

BRITISH ADMIRALTY APPROVES OF
WOMEN'S ROYAL NAVAL SERVICE[149]
Doings of Forestry Companies

December 2, 1917

Dear Sir,

When the Newfoundland Forestry Companies came to this part of Scotland, it looked as if we could cut timber from the forest of Craigvinean until the cows come home. But already we have nearly half this section cleared of trees, and the men are daily working farther away from Camp. The cutting down of so many huge trees has so completely changed the appearance of the hillside that it is scarcely recognizable from what it was like when we came here in June. Then it was completely covered with a growth of heavy timber; but to-day all this is changed, and the nakedness of the land is very noticeable by the exposure of crags and barren ground.

Up to date about twelve thousand trees have been felled, making nearly fifty thousand saw-logs, and scaling close upon three million feet b.m.[150] In the construction of the chutes there has been used ninety thousand feet of timber, while the erection of huts, mills, etc., consumed a like quantity.

The log chute nearest the huts was put in use during the week. It is built somewhat after the manner of number one chute. Near the upper end two or three platforms have been built on a level with the chute. The horses draw the logs onto these platforms, from which they are easily rolled into the chute, and then the logs go thundering down the incline to a resting place near the tramline.

---

149 *The Western Star*, January 2, 1918, p. 1. Also published in *The Evening Herald*, January 12, 1918.

150 Board measure, the standard measure in lumbering in North America.

To lovers of the art of lumbering, to those whose hearts are wrapped up in the work, the operations being carried on here are very interesting. It is no ordinary method of labour, because our Camp is being conducted along military lines. In the early morning, the men are awakened by the stentorian voice of the Orderly Sergeant for the customary ablution, after which they are all paraded for breakfast. At 7 a.m. the men are again paraded, and, after roll call, are marched off in squads to work under the care of NCOs.[151] At dinner time and tea time, when the men come in from work, the same routine is performed.

Once the men get into the timber belt they make the forest echo with the hiss of saw, the ringing clang of smiting axe, the crash of falling trees, the harsh voices of the lumberjacks, and the hundred and one sounds of bustling activity which belong to a lumber camp in full work.

All who visit our Camp declare themselves amazed at the amount of work being done. At the mills, they stare and wonder at the creaking machinery. The air is filled with the steady shriek of the saws, and the droning of grinding machinery is broken by the pulsing throb of great shafts and moving log carriages. Men are to be seen hurrying to and fro, full of life and intent upon their labours. The visitors see the great trimmed logs sliding down the chute to the milldam, and watch them being hauled up the jack-ladder into the mill. They keenly follow the process of operations until the huge stick is converted into the required sizes of lumber and taken out on rollers to be carted to the piles in the yard. The newness of it all thrills them, and they extend congratulations for the work we are performing.

You may be interested to know that the British Admiralty have approved of the establishment of a Women's Royal Naval

---

151 Non-commissioned officers, also referred to as "non-coms."

Service,[152] the members of which will be employed on definite duties directly connected with the Royal Navy on shore. In their new vocation, the women of Britain will likely acquit themselves creditably. There are millions of them now toiling for victory. They have given, and are giving, their husband and sons, and their time and energy as workers in accustomed and unaccustomed spheres of activity. In the munition factories, a vast proportion of the ceaseless work required to supply the armies of the Allies with guns and ammunitions is done by women. Women, gentle of birth, as well as the humble, have been tilling the fields and maintaining Britain's agriculture. In the cities, women are working magnificently and are doing their full share of toil. All Britain is bent on triumph for the cause of humanity and the freedom for the nations, the women are as heroically as the men, and with the same inflexible determination.

The Band of the Newfoundland Regiment was in attendance at a concert given at Ayr last Sunday afternoon, and rendered some appropriate music for the occasion. The sum of eighty-five pounds was raised, which was donated to the Wounded Sailor's Fund. At a Whist Drive[153] held there on Tuesday a further sum of thirty pounds was added to the same fund.

On Saturday next a concert is to be given at Dunkeld by members of the Army Pay Corps. The proceeds are to go towards some public undertaking.

A few nights ago, the "Tommies"[154] at St. Mary's Home were treated to an impromptu concert, given by a number of ladies

---

152 The women's branch of the Royal Navy was popularly called "Wrens." The branch was formed in 1917 and disbanded in 1919, with more than 5,000 members having served. It was revived for the Second World War. In 1993, its members became part of the Royal Navy.

153 A fundraising event at which participants played the card game whist.

154 A colloquial term for a British soldier; "Tommy Atkins" was used as a generic name for individual soldiers of the UK.

and gentlemen of Birnam, which was thoroughly enjoyed by the lads. The instituting of this Home for convalescent soldiers may be attributed to the efforts of Mrs. Fotheringham, of Murthly Castle, who has very liberally donated most of the requisites, thereby rendering valuable aid on behalf of the Red Cross Society.

Throughout this country there are many evidences of the noble work being performed by the Red Cross Society. Under its familiar sign, doctors and nurses wage an endless battle against mutilation, sickness and disease. Fleets of swift and comfortable ambulance cars, and specially equipped trains bear the returning sick and wounded from the seaports to the treating stations. Numerous hospitals equipped by the Red Cross Society are nursing our wounded heroes amid surroundings of peace and comfort. This Society, the largest of all Britain's voluntary organizations, is performing a noble, self-sacrificing work that commands the intense admiration of all.

Dunkeld, Perthshire, Scotland

• • •

Trainers for a Military-Style Lumber Camp

As Barrett noted, the woods camps of Scotland were different than those in Newfoundland because the foresters were organized and operated as a military unit, with military routines and expectations. Training for the NFC was conducted at the Catholic Cadet Corps Armoury in St. John's, where recruits were prepared for military life within a lumbering operation. In early December 1917, as the fourth draft completed its training and prepared to head overseas, a contingent presented gifts on behalf of all to their unsung trainers, along with the letter of appreciation ("Presentation," 1917) excerpted here that provides a glimpse of the trainers and the relationships they built with the men they were initiating into service:

In the first place, we have to thank you, Sergeant Hussey,[155] for the patience and care you exercised in our physical development. We feel that the instruction and training we have received from you will be of very great service to us in the hardships we may have to endure in lands beyond the sea.

We must also express our sincere regard for the kindness and assistance we have experienced from Sergeant McKinley.[156] Indeed, we cannot easily forget how much we are indebted to you for the almost paternal care bestowed on us by you since we joined the Forestry Companies.

Finally, we have to express our appreciation for the consideration shown to us by Private Ellis[157] on all occasions. No doubt we may have often caused him some trouble in the discharge of his duties but at the same time we must acknowledge that he has succeeded in discharging an office which is not always popular to the satisfaction of all concerned.

Signed on behalf of the Company,
L.A. Miller, [158] Charles H. Peters,[159]
Ed Driscoll,[160] S.J. Thomey,[161] J.J. Angel[162] (p. 8)

---

155 Sergeant-Instructor and, later, Company Sergeant Major Benjamin Hussey, RNR #4325, St. John's.

156 Company Quartermaster Sergeant Joseph McKinley, RNR #748, St. John's.

157 Private C.H. Ellis, RNR #936, St. John's; Orderly Room Clerk.

158 Private Llewellyn A. Miller, NFC #8305, St. John's.

159 Private Charles H. Peters, NFC #8400, St. John's.

160 Private Edward Driscoll, NFC #8371, St. John's.

161 Private Samuel J. Thomey, NFC #8376, Harbour Grace.

162 Private John J. Angel, NFC #8383, St. John's.

December 9, 1917

Dear Sir,

On the evening of 3rd inst., our Recreation Hall was formally opened by the staging of a very interesting concert, gotten up under the direction of Mrs. (Dr.) Taylor, wife of our acting Medical Officer.[164] Our lads took advantage of this rare treat by filling the building to its utmost capacity. The songs were of a high order and were ably rendered, the musical accompaniments being played by Miss Rutherford.[165] A comic sketch by Captain H. Cole brought out the humorous traits of the jovial Captain, and caused endless merriment for the large gathering. The violin solos were particularly good, and thoroughly enjoyed. Subjoined is the programme:

Violin Duet, by Mrs. Gwyther and Miss Benvie.
Song, by Sergeant T. McGrath.[166]
Song, by Miss Benvie.
Violin Solo, by Mrs. Gwyther.
Sketch, by Miss Underwood and Miss Benvie.
Song, by Sergeant T. McGrath.
Song, by Miss Benvie.
Song, by Private C. Lunnen.[167]
Violin Solo, by Mrs. Gwyther.
Comic Sketch, by Captain H.W. Cole.

163 *The Western Star*, January 16, 1918, p. 1. Also published in *The Evening Herald*, January 14, 1918.

164 Dr. James Anderson Taylor, GP, Dunkeld.

165 The women who participated and who are named in the program were local residents from the Dunkeld-Birnam area.

166 Sergeant Thomas B. McGrath, RNR #128 / #0–222, St. John's.

167 Private Clarence S. Lunnen, NFC #8171, Twillingate.

Sketch, by Miss Underwood and Miss Benvie.

God Save The King.

At the close of the Concert, Major Sullivan kindly extended to the ladies the hearty appreciation of us all for the splendid manner in which we had been entertained.

Last evening the officers and quite a few of our men attended a concert given at Dunkeld Hall by a troupe from the Army Pay Corps.[168] The performance consisted of songs, solos, international dances, sketches, etc., all of which were very interesting and enjoyable to us. The sketches "The Head Waiter" and "The Colonel's Consent" were especially well staged and highly appreciated.

A very pretty military wedding took place at Manchester on Thursday, 6th inst., when our Adjutant, Captain H.H.A. Ross, was united in the bands of holy wedlock to Miss P.B. Reynolds,[169] a charming young lady of Manchester. This is the happy culmination of a romance begun at a hospital where Captain Ross was treated after being wounded at Caribou Hill,[170] in the Gallipoli campaign.[171] The newly married couple have been the recipients of numerous handsome and useful presents, including several from the officers and men of the Newfoundland Forestry

---

168 The Army Pay Corps was responsible for the distribution of pay, allowances, and pensions to all troops. After the war, in recognition of its services, it was designated "Royal."

169 Phyllis Blackmore Reynolds.

170 Barrett refers to a ridge held by Turkish snipers that the Regiment was successful in taking during the Gallipoli Campaign, a minor victory in a larger defeat. Thereafter, the Allied soldiers called it "Caribou Hill."

171 The campaign was an unsuccessful attempt by the Allied Forces to take the Ottoman Empire's (Turkish) stronghold in an effort to control the Dardanelles, which would then open a sea route from Europe to Russia's Black Sea ports. The Regiment casualty rate at Gallipoli was approximately 55 percent, and included 41 fatalities (Baker, 2017).

Companies. Captain Ross returns to Camp tomorrow a member of the great army of Benedicts.

We are expecting to be visited next Thursday by Mr. M.M. Beeton, who is our representative on the Timber Committee, at London. On Friday next, we shall look forward to the promised visit of Governor Sir W.E. Davidson and Prime Minister Sir E.P. Morris both of whom are now on this side of the Atlantic. [172] We hope to be again addressed by His Excellency, and to receive words of encouragement from one who played no small part in the guidance of the affairs of our Island Home during his tenure of office.

We were shocked and grieved yesterday to learn of the recent terrible catastrophe which had befallen the city of Halifax[173] and in which so many precious lives were lost. Having spent some days in that "city by the sea", we have many happy recollections of acquaintances made and of visits to many of its historic places. Today our hearts go out in sincere sympathy to all those, both in Canada and Newfoundland, who have been made to mourn by this dire calamity.

When at Perth last Thursday night, I had the pleasure of meeting one of Britain's sons, who had been wounded whilst mine sweeping in the North Sea. Notwithstanding the injuries when his ship was destroyed, he was very cheerful and related some stirring tales of deeds performed by Britain's mine sweepers and her Royal Naval Reserve craft. Theirs is a very dangerous and arduous work; but, seeking no glory, they go steadfastly on their course, self-denying and self-sacrificing in Old England's name.

Dunkeld, Perthshire, Scotland

---

172 By this time, and unknown to the public, Morris had tendered his resignation, effective at the end of 1917. Davidson's time as Governor was also ending; he would be reassigned to New South Wales.

173 Barrett refers to the Halifax Explosion, which devastated the capital city of Nova Scotia, Canada.

Diversions, Losses, and Coincidences

The Halifax Explosion occurred on December 6, 1917. Two ships, one a fully loaded munitions vessel, collided in the Bedford Basin. The resulting blast killed 2,000 people and injured 9,000 more; 1,500 buildings were destroyed and 12,000 damaged (Kernaghan & Foot, 2011). Just days after the explosion, on December 11, a draft of foresters left Newfoundland for Halifax aboard the SS *Florizel* to join the troop carrier SS *Missanabie* and convoy to the UK.[174] They arrived to a still-smouldering city and were transported by train to Saint John, New Brunswick, the reassigned port of departure. Two foresters, however, did not continue on the journey.

Sergeant John Sheehan, RNR #35, was a 23-year-old labourer from St. John's and a Blue Puttee who had transferred to the NFC after surviving injuries suffered in France that included gassing. Enroute to Halifax that December, he developed respiratory illness and was hospitalized upon arrival. On December 27, he died of pneumonia.

Private Allan Yates, NFC #8362, a 21-year-old lumberer from New Bay, had enlisted at St. John's on October 2. Yates had injured his arm a year earlier at Millertown while working with the ANDCo, but he was considered fit for service in the NFC. Enroute to Halifax, he contracted mumps and was hospitalized at Dartmouth on arrival.

Yates recovered from his illness but was re-hospitalized shortly after with scabies. He made a second recovery and, while awaiting transport overseas, he helped with the cleanup of the Halifax Explosion—likely the only Newfoundland forester to do so. But his efforts ended his service: while participating in cleanup, he reinjured his arm and was deemed medically unfit.

---

174 For an account of this voyage, see Nugent (1938).

GOVERNOR DAVIDSON INSPECTS
FORESTRY CORPS[175]
More Men Needed – Must Double Present Output

December 17, 1917

Dear Sir,

On Friday, 14th inst., we were visited by His Excellency, Sir. W.E. Davidson and Sir E.P. Morris, who had just returned from France, whither they had been visiting the boys of the First Newfoundland Regiment. They were accompanied by Mr. Ball,[176] Timber Controller for the British Government, Mr. M. Beeton, and Major Timewell of the Pay and Record Office. The mills, cook-houses and living quarters of the men were inspected, and a visit paid to the scene of logging operations.

At noon, the officers and men were on parade at Headquarters. Governor Davidson and Prime Minister Morris inspected the ranks; making the acquaintance of all the men. Then we were addressed by His Excellency, who first paid a glowing tribute to the lads of the Regiment, who for smartness and good soldiering, had won an enviable record during the present war; and he expressed the hope that before long the Newfoundland Regiment would receive the prefix "Royal."[177]

Speaking of the Forestry Companies, His Excellency expressed himself as highly pleased to meet us again, and congratulated the men on their smart appearance and splendid turnout. Having gone over the Camp and seen the nature of our work, he

---

175 *The Western Star*, January 30, 1918, p. 1. Also published in *The Evening Herald*, January 16, 1918; *The Evening Advocate*, January 16, 1918; and *The Twillingate Sun*, February 9, 1918.

176 Later, Sir James Ball.

177 At the request of Governor Davidson, this designation was granted by King George V on December 17, 1917, the only occurrence during the First World War of its assignment to a unit (Davidson, 1918a).

was greatly impressed with the methodical manner in which operations were being conducted. As a lasting monument of our labours, he said the barren slopes of Craigvinean would stand out boldly for ages; and the Scotchmen for years to come would point to the mountains as the scene where the Foresters did their bit for the Empire.[178]

Sir E.P. Morris said he was pleased to meet us, and, being a son of the same land,[179] and by the same token its Prime Minister, he congratulated all of us upon the splendid work performed, expressing the desire that we may not only maintain the pace already set, but that we may strive to exceed all past efforts. Whilst our brothers are fighting in France to help maintain the integrity of the British Empire, it behooves us to assist in the same worthy cause by the furnishing of timber necessary for the continuance of the Nation's industries at home. Sir Edward spoke in felicitous terms of our railway, log chutes, etc., pointing with pride to their construction as the outcome of the characteristic ingenuity of Newfoundlanders. At the close of his remarks the Prime Minister asked that three cheers be given for His Excellency; and you may be assured they were given with a will.

Mr. Ball, on behalf of the British Government, congratulated the Forestry Companies upon the excellent work performed in so short a time. He was pleased to see the huge stacks of lumber in the yard and to know of the great quantities of logs awaiting transportation to the mills. So delighted was he over the outcome of our

---

178 At the end of the war, Forestry Commission Scotland was formed and a program of reforestation and afforestation was begun, to ensure Scotland would have a reserve of timber for the sake of national security (Oosthoek, 2013). Barrett (1922) himself, in a piece recalling a visit to Blair Castle after the war, remarked on the success of the tree nurseries of Dunkeld and the reforestation at Craigvinean, noting that "much of the timber in this district was cut by the Newfoundlanders during the war, but the banks are quickly being replanted" (p. 3).

179 Morris was born in St. John's.

effort that he got permission of Major Sullivan to grant us a half holiday in honour of the visit, which was very much appreciated.

But he told us in straight language how urgent was the need for getting out more—and ever more—lumber for the needs of the war, and asked us to point this out to our people when writing home. The output of lumber for the present year for the whole country was about 1,000 Standards[180] a day. Mr. Ball wants this huge quantity to be doubled in 1918. It's up to Newfoundland to send us enough men to double our output, which is now about 20,000 feet or 10 Standards a day.

At the request of Major Sullivan, cheers were called for Sir E.P. Morris and Mr. Ball, and were accorded in real Newfoundland style.

The wedding gift of the officers and men to Captain and Mrs. Ross was presented by Governor Davidson. The gift consisted of a set of Prince's Plate Cutlery, which was enclosed in an oak cabinet bearing the following inscription: "Presented to Capt. and Mrs. H.H.A. Ross, from the officers, noncommissioned officers, and men of the First Newfoundland Regiment, Forestry Companies, on the occasion of their marriage, December 6th, 1917."

Upon the invitation of Madame Tempest, Governor Davidson and party were entertained at Dalguise Castle, after which they were shown over the V.A.D. Hospital and the beautiful grounds surrounding it.

Our electric light plant has been in operation, and was running last night for the first time.

A concert and tea for a number of our lads and the convalescent soldiers was held at Dalguise Castle on Saturday, 22nd inst.

On Wednesday night, we were given a free concert at Dunkeld. It was gotten up by the young ladies of the town, who

---

180 A measure of lumber equalling 165 cubic feet (Haynes, 1921). A standard—or standard hundred—differed by country and changed over time.

spared no effort to make the affair a success. The songs, solos, sketches, etc., were so well rendered that they were frequently encored. At the close of the concert Lieutenant O'Rourke, who acted as Chairman, extended to the performers the hearty appreciation of all for the pleasant evening's amusement furnished us. This appreciation was shown in a marked degree by the hearty cheers accorded the ladies.

At this concert the following tribute to Newfoundland was rendered by Miss Bruce, of the Tea Garden,[181] a favourite resort for our lads:

THE GLORIES OF NEWFOUNDLAND
D.H. Bruce

I'll sing you a song of a far-away land
On the wide Atlantic shore,
Where the rocks rise sheer from the pebbly strand,
And resound to the ocean's roar;
A Land of bays, and the wide lagoon,
Where the scaly codfish feeds,
And the summertime flies but all too soon,
Before the stormking's chariot steeds.

I'll sing you a song of a sturdy race,
'Mong the mist, the snows, and fogs,
At their lumber toll on the rocky face,
Or at sport with the sleigh and dogs;

---

181 One of three daughters—Jean, Hope, and Jessie—of Daniel Hill (D.H.) Bruce and Jane Lamont Bruce, who worked at the Bruce Tea Garden, Dunkeld. The Tea Garden was a family-owned business operated by the Bruces on land leased from the Atholl Estates (J. Anderson, personal communication, September 3, 2019). The poem was included in a posthumous collection of the poems of D.H. Bruce, *Close the Door Softly*, which was published by the Bruce family in 1951.

On the playful crest of the boundful waves,
As the boats out to the sea;
On the fields, gathering in the gifts God gave,
Where Sol smiles benignantly.

I'll sing you a song of their hopes and joys,
When the heart beats a rapturous tune,
And love runs riot 'mongst the girls and boys,
Midst the woodlands in leafy June.
I'll sing you a song of their doubts and fears,
Of a mind now and then depressed,
And I'll tell you of a smile hid behind the tears,
Begot of a soul at rest.

I'll sing you a song of its gallant sons,
Who have sped from the peace of home,
To the hard-fought fields where the bomb and gun,
Go crash, and the hell-fiends roam;
Where the timber cross dots the fields of France,
By the act of a kindly hand,
Is inscribed there for he who scans,
"A Hero from Newfoundland."

Then here's to the mountain, and here's to the moor,
Whereon caribou and ptarmigan's found,
And here's to the rifle, and here's to the spoor,
And the salmon and cod in the sound.
Here's to the matron, and here's to the maid,
The soldier and grandsire bland,
Let the theme of my song swell from hill and glade,
"The glories of Newfoundland."

Before this appears in print, the glad season of Christmastide will have come and gone; and though we are in this far-away land, yet ample provision is being made for our enjoyment of the festive season through the generosity of Mr. Munro, the President of the North of Scotland Timber Suppliers Association, who has collected a handsome cheque among his associates to provide us with a special Christmas dinner. To all our relatives and friends in Newfoundland we extend sincere greetings for a Merry Christmas and a Bright and Prosperous New Year.

Dunkeld, Perthshire, Scotland

• • •

Governor Davidson's Visit to the NFC

Upon his return to Newfoundland, Governor Davidson (1918a) penned an account of his visits to the wounded of the Royal Newfoundland Regiment at the General Hospital, Wandsworth, London, the Newfoundland Forestry Companies at Dunkeld, and the Second (Reserve) Battalion at Ayr. This excerpt covers his visit to the NFC camps at Dunkeld:

> I had the opportunity of inspecting the Forestry Companies on Friday the 14th December 1917 in company with the Right Honourable Sir Edward Morris; Mr. Ball, the controller of Timber in the United Kingdom; Mr. Sinclair, who presented the Scottish interests under the Controller; Mr. Mayson Beeton, who directs the operations of our Foresters; and Major Timewell. Sir John Stirling Maxwell and Colonel Fotheringham who held important positions in the Control of the Timber Supplies from the Scottish forests were unfortunately unable to meet us.

We were met at Dunkeld by Major Sullivan, the Commanding Officer, and we had the pleasure of meeting the other officers and the full Companies at work on Craigvinean (the hill of the goats), a name which I understand is likely to be changed on the maps of the ordinance survey into a name which will associate the name of Newfoundland with their work on this mountain.[182] This forest was originally planted by a Duke of Atholl about the close of the Napoleonic War, and the timber was exactly ripe for felling. The mountainside has been almost denuded and the Companies will shortly be transferred to a portion of the estate of the Marquess of Breadalbane[183] situated in the same valley of the Tay in Perthshire.

The Companies are established in two positions—higher camp being occupied by the felling contingent and the lower by those employed in the sawing operations. I went through all their quarters and found them clean, comfortable, and adequate. The cooking arrangements were good and the rations are good and sufficient for the needs of hardworking men. You can understand that the foresters have done their work thoroughly well; but it is also good to know that they are comfortable and happy in their surroundings and that the whole countryside, in every degree, welcomes the Newfoundlanders and treats them with old fashioned Scottish hospitality. All the famous mansions and castles on Tay side are open to the officers, and a hospital for any who may be disabled by illness is provided at Dalguise Castle through the kindness and generosity of Mrs. Tempest, the owner of that historic house. We all had the pleasure of being the guests of Mrs. Tempest at luncheon on the occasion of our visit

---

182 No such change was made.

183 Gavin Campbell. As do some Scots, Barrett used the French form of the title, Marquis.

The Newfoundlanders have introduced in the course of these logging operations a number of improvements previously unknown in Scotland and looked upon as welcome novelties, and the output (so Mr. Sinclair assured me) was many times as great as the output would have been under normal conditions, if the work had been placed in the hands of local woodsmen (the difference between 1,000 and 6,000).[184]

The special features which are outstanding are the long timber chute 3,600 feet in length by which the logs are shot down from the upper level into the pond which has been dammed to receive them alongside the saw mills; the railway feeder along the hillside carrying the logs to the chute; and the mill installation at the lower camp which is full of ingenious devices which are characteristic of loggers from Newfoundland, and especially those who have had experience of the methods of the A.N.D. Company.

Sir Edward Morris and I inspected the men and addressed them briefly. The men were in good heart and turned out with extraordinary smartness for inspection on parade. I had also the pleasure of presenting, on behalf of the Forestry Companies, a wedding present to Captain and Mrs. Ross on the occasion of their wedding, subscribed to by the officers, N.C.O.'s and men of the Forestry Companies. This in itself is a fair indication that all ranks are working well together, are proud of their output and are maintaining the good reputation of the Royal Newfoundland Regiment. At every turn we realized what an enormous amount of help and kindness has been rendered to the Foresters by Mayson Beeton,

---

184 Presumably this is a ratio (1:6) of trees felled by local foresters and the NFC; by December 1, 1917, the NFC had felled 12,000 trees at Craigvinean.

who has been as kind to the Foresters as Mr. E.R. Morris[185] is to the sick and wounded at No. 3 General Hospital, Wandsworth.

The proceedings were closed by an excellent speech by Mr. Ball, the Controller of Timber Supplies, whose heart was gladdened by the sight of the immense and orderly piles of sawn timber. He highly praised the work of the Newfoundlanders and closed the proceedings by granting the Companies a half-holiday for the rest of the day.

P.S. I cannot imagine how it is that every forester or sawyer should not seize the opportunity of a life time to see the world. The pay is big, the work pleasant and the country delightful. (p. 2)

• • •

Volunteerism and Conscription

By the fall of 1917, the debate over conscription was intensifying in Newfoundland. Recruitment to maintain strength for the Regiment and to build the Forestry Companies was not met with the enthusiasm hoped for by officials. The need for troops was emphasized at every opportunity in both the United Kingdom and Newfoundland. Regular calls to serve were published in local newspapers and officers of the NFC, including Major Sullivan, made trips to various parts of Newfoundland to inspire enlistment. Soldiers and foresters also expressed their feelings on the subject to family and friends and in local newspapers—and were encouraged to do so by those in command.

---

185 E.R. Morris was a member of the Newfoundland War Contingent Association in London, an organization of businesspeople with connections to Newfoundland who oversaw the care of Newfoundland troops in Europe and the United Kingdom. Elsewhere in this same account, Governor Davidson (1918a) described Mr. and Mrs. Morris, who were very active in the organization, as "the guardian angels of the Newfoundland Regiment" (p. 2).

Arthur Case King, NFC #8387, of Grand Falls, enlisted on October 13, 1917, at the age of 24. He arrived in Scotland on January 1, 1918, but his stay was short-lived due to a flare-up of an old muscular injury that made him medically unfit to work. While enlisted, he composed "A Soldier's Farewell," set to the tune of "Just Before the Battle, Mother."[186] In it, he emphasized that, in times of war, duty to "King and Country" trumped the comforts of home and family. The song was published in *The Evening Telegram* (King, 1917) and addressed those men who had not yet heeded the call to serve.

A SOLDIER'S FAREWELL
Private Arthur C. King, Newfoundland Forestry Companies
(Tune: "Just Before The Battle, Mother")

Just before I leave you, mother
I must bid a fond farewell
Where I'm going I cannot tell you
But I hope 'twill all be well
'Tis a call from King and Country
And my duty is to go
Though it breaks my heart to leave you
For I find it hard you know.

Chorus
Good-bye, mother; farewell, father
I must say good-bye to you
When away from home and loved ones
I will always think of you.

When my training here is over
And my duty here is done

---

186 This song was composed by George F. Root and popularized during the American Civil War.

I must leave the dear old homestead
For to battle with the Hun[187]
When the bugle sounds the "Fall in"
I'll be ready for to go
When my King and Country call me
Across to Flanders[188] then to go.

When we sail across the ocean
And are tossed about the sea
And I know my mother's praying
For her boy upon the sea
When on Foreign Fields I'm roaming
Far across the ocean foam
With my eyes towards the Heavens
Leave, ah leave me not alone.

Now my friends are left behind me
Oh get ready now and come
Yes! Your King and Country call you
Men of War to face the Hun
Come on, boys, and don't be cowards
Join the colours right away
Fill the place of them that's falling
Do it now and don't delay. (p. 11)

Private Leo P. O'Brien, NFC #8261, was an 18-year-old clerk from St. John's
who enlisted on July 9, 1917. O'Brien ("A Soldierly Letter," 1917) raised the

---

187 A pejorative name for Germans used in Allied war propaganda. The original
Huns were skilled warriors who moved from eastern Asia westward across
Europe and into the Roman Empire in the fourth and fifth centuries.

188 Flanders Fields; these were First World War battlefields that spanned East and
West Flanders, Belgium, and Nord-Pas-de-Calais (also called "French Flanders").

issue of conscription in a letter to his mother in mid-November, which was later published:

> I have received four or five bundles of newspapers and enjoyed reading the City news. I hear you are going to have conscription at home, and I'm glad of it, as some of the fellows that never offered for anything will now lose their soft jobs and have to come over here. . . . I don't think the war will be over for two years yet, so you need not expect me for some time. (p. 10)

· · ·

Coaker Recruits

The Fishermen's Protective Union (FPU) was Newfoundland's first union of fishers and loggers. Its president, William Ford Coaker, opposed conscription, as did most members of the FPU. Following the losses at Beaumont-Hamel, Coaker felt the need to contribute to the war effort—but the FPU membership insisted Coaker was of greater benefit at home than at the Front.

Coaker had been elected to the House of Assembly in 1913 on an FPU platform of fisheries and social reform. At the Annual Convention of the Supreme Council of the FPU, held at Catalina on December 4, 1916, Coaker expressed his dilemma: whether to stay at the helm of the FPU or enlist to serve, as so many others had done. Coaker (1930) asked that 50 members volunteer in his place. In the end, 78 members of the FPU enlisted. They were dubbed the "Coaker Recruits."[189]

Albert Pelley, NFC #8103, a lumberer from Southwest Arm, Notre Dame Bay, was 21 when he enlisted. The oldest of seven children of Jabez and Mary

---

189 The Coaker Recruits who lost their lives in service were memorialized by the building of the Church of the Holy Martyrs, which opened in Port Union in 1920. A stained-glass window with name plaque honours each fallen soldier. For a discussion of the FPU and the Coaker Recruits, see Coaker (1930).

Knight Pelley, he was in the first NFC draft to go to Scotland. Two of his brothers signed up for the Regiment—Douglas, RNR #3456, and Raymond, RNR #3845. Both Albert and Douglas were Coaker Recruits—Albert the sole forester among them. The boys' father was by this time a widower who worked as a cooper and lumberer. He also enlisted, at age 49, at the end of December 1917. Both Albert and Jabez Pelley, NFC #8459, served in Scotland for the duration.

The NFC motor car parked at camp.
(Courtesy of The Rooms Provincial Archives Division, A 103-108)

OUR PEAVIE AND AXE-MEN RECEIVE PARCELS[190]
Other Doings of Corps

Dear Sir,

Considerable history centres around the ancient town of Dun-keld, which is situated right at the gateway of the Highlands of Scotland. Nestling as it does at the base of Craigiebarns on the northern bank of the Tay, it is thereby sheltered from the sting-ing blasts of Boreas;[191] while on the opposite side of the river, the lofty peak of Birnam silently keeps its vigil.

Prior to the extension of the Highland Railway through the northern part of Scotland, a number of farmers pastured their cattle on the slopes of Craigiebarns, and on market days herded them in the town, where buyers came from many parts of southern Scotland. Some of the stone walls of the pasturage are still standing, but the cottages and pub have long since gone to ruin.

Dunkeld was at one time the principal ecclesiastical and educational centre of the whole of Scotland. Formerly Perth-shire was divided into the bishoprics of Perth, Dunblane, and Dunkeld, over which the Church was the ruling power of both civil and religious life. For miles surrounding the churches, the land was under the guardianship of the ruling clergy. It was the one-time boast of the Bishop of Dunkeld that he could drive for fifteen miles over his own land from the palace to the Cathedral.

History tells us that "shortly before the accession of the Scottish kings to the Pictish throne, Dunkeld was known as a

---

190 *The Western Star*, January 23, 1918, p. 1. Also published in *The Evening Herald*, January 25, 1918.
191 Latin for the north wind.

'Culdee' Church. It was here that MacAlpin[192] had the relics of St. Colomba transferred, and built a church to be the Mother-Church of Celtic Christianity."[193]

The Cathedral, part of which is now in ruins, comprises a seven-bayed nave, a four-bayed, aisleless choir, a rectangular chapterhouse and a massive tower. The doorways are deeply recessed, the arch mouldings being decorated with chevron or zigzag carving. The nave shows many features of the style known as Flamboyant,[194] especially the great west window, which, judging from the remaining fragments of its tracery, must have been of a particularly florid design. After the Reformation, the choir was transformed into the parish church.

Until the erection of a bridge over the Tay, the Cathedral stood in the centre of the town, and the beautiful walk by the side of the river was open to pedestrians at all times. But the town has been so changed as to leave the Cathedral on its western outskirts, and the walk by the riverside, except for a short distance to the west of the bridge, has been closed to the public.

There have been related to me tales of stirring military cavalcades in this very part of Scotland. Battalions of the Scottish Horse, Highland Light Infantry, the "Gallant Greys", Forfar and Fife Imperial Yeomanry, 18th Hussars, and other Scottish army divisions have been engaged in warfare here. Dunkeld has always been accustomed to the spectacle of large bodies of military men within its confines; but to have upwards of ten thousand regulars within its borders at one time was sufficient cause for much excitement.

---

192 The ninth-century Pictish king, Kenneth I.

193 Barrett did not indicate the source he was quoting here. It appears to be an account of Perthshire written by Peter MacNair (1912).

194 A style of French Gothic architecture that is florid and ornate.

The last great military manoeuvre here took place in June, 1907. Great preparations had been made for the event, so much so that everything had a realistic appearance. All the necessary equipment for a long and bloody conflict had been provided, even to the limbering cannon, the field ambulance, and the provisioning for six months.

Guns weighing three and a half tons, with an effective range of 6,500 yards, and extremely quick firing, supported the Royal Field Artillery. These instruments of war were of a new manufacture, and were being tried for the first time. Many notable personages had travelled up from England to witness the experiments; but they were not allowed within certain limits of the guns.

The objective of all this was the capture of Dunkeld by the Southerners from the Northerners. The defending forces were under the command of Lord Tullibardine, now Duke of Atholl. All the rigours of warfare were undertaken. The forced marches were said to have been very trying, especially upon those who covered a distance of 72 miles in 36 hours, over rugged ground, and with the scantiest of rations.

Throughout the conflict not a single human life was lost, although one collar-bone and several limbs were fractured, and many horses sacrificed. The residents of the place tell me of the most stringent conditions under which they existed for a week, and they often shudder when they think of what might have been had the remaining touch of realism been imparted.

In many towns and villages on this side of the Atlantic the praises of Newfoundland, both in prose and poetry, are being sung, the latest composition being that of J. MacDonald,[195] who

---

195 John MacDonald, stationmaster at Dalguise, wrote poetry to sell for the war effort and donated the proceeds to the Red Cross. He was also a violin maker.

resides at Dalguise, a village quite near our Camp. It has been printed on a beautiful post card, bordered with the grand old Union Jack, the fund derived from the sale of which is to be devoted to the Red Cross work. Here is the poem:

ODE TO NEWFOUNDLAND
John MacDonald

Sweet homeland of liberty over the sea,
How sacred and dear are thy precincts to me;
Thy forests of pine and thy prairies of snow,
Are clear to my vision wherever I go.
I've searched o'er the city, the town, and the plain
For treasures like thine, but my quest was in vain;
No scene can I find, though majestic they be,
Compared with grandeur, "Newfoundland," to me.

Afar from the haunts of my youth though I roam
Yet still my heart's true to the dear ones and home,
Which kindle new hopes for to work with a will
The Wrecker of Europe's grim methods to kill.
The peavie, the bob-slide,[196] and keen cutting axe
Keep merrily swinging and each muscle tax,
And stand by the Motherland against the dire foe
Whose rule of "grim piracy" we must o'erthrow.

I long for a cruise in my tiny canoe
And paddle o'er Exploits and Humber anew;
Red Indian Lake waters again for to ply
In search of the silvery salmon so shy.
The buzz of the saw in my ears daily chime

---

196 A bobsled.

As I think of my loved ones and long for the time
To sling on the rifle and track o'er the snow
And furnish the larder with sweet Caribou.

When war's blast is over we'll sail for our homes
To Harbour Grace, Grand Bank, Burin, and St. John's,
Where flags shall be floating, and bells ring with joy
As parents greet sons and each sweetheart her boy.

Preparations are being made for the celebration of Christmas, and already visions of turkey and lager beer rise before us. So far as I can learn, there will be a liberal supply for all, both at the Christmas and New Year festivities, as Mr. Beeton has promised, with his customary good-naturedness, to see that our wants are generously attended. To all the lads desirous of spending Christmas or the New Year away from Camp, leave of several days is being granted. Quite a number will take advantage of it by visiting some of the nearby towns.

So far the weather has kept remarkably mild, which is much appreciated by our men. Should it turn colder, we have a bountiful supply of wood to draw our fuel supply from.

During the past few days quite a number of parcels have been received from Newfoundland. They contain socks, mitts, tobacco, cigarettes, cakes, jam, etc. The favoured ones showed their generosity by sharing their gifts with their less fortunate chums. The receipt of these gifts means much to the men, and are highly treasured by them. The pity is that so many parcels said to have been sent have not yet been received; and it would look as if some postal officials were trading upon the generosity of Newfoundlanders.

Dunkeld, Perthshire, Scotland

Packing Instructions

Private Leo P. O'Brien received a parcel in the weeks before Christmas 1917. In a reply letter home to his mother, Mary, O'Brien ("Hewers of Wood," 1917) offered specific instructions on how to safely ship parcels overseas:

> I received your parcel last Tuesday and I was very thankful for it. It was a little broken when I got it, but the contents were O.K. In it were two pair of socks, three handkerchiefs, some pins, baby box talcum powder, cake, and some soap. It came in very good and myself and my chums had a regular feed on the cake, and it was in perfect condition.

> I have written you two letters and I suppose you will have them when you get this. I received a letter from Tack[197] today and it was written somewhere in France. I guess it was Rouen. He was leaving that night for the firing line, and I suppose he is in the fight now. Rouen is about thirty hours run from the firing line. He wrote you but forgot to tell you to send him some tobacco. I would like you to send him about three pounds every month as this is the only comfort in the trenches. The best way for you to send parcels is to get Mr. Ruby, the tinsmith, to make a round can, put your stuff in and then bring it down to him and get a cover soldered on it,[198] bring it home again, wrap it and sew it well in duck, address it on the outside and then let her go.

---

197 Private John J. O'Brien, RNR #3214, St. John's, was wounded at Rouen on November 20, 1917, and discharged in 1918, after his recovery.

198 Lieutenant Owen Steele provided these same instructions in his letter of November 1, 1915 (Facey-Crowther, 2002, pp. 85–86).

I was down to Stanley Saturday night by train to a dance. Stanley is about twenty miles from us. I had a great time there. This evening I was out in town on a bicycle and got a few little things there.

I think this is all the strange news I have to tell you for the present; have more letters to write. All the boys here are well. We are not downhearted. (p. 12)

Two foresters with swagger sticks at
Craigvinean, Dunkeld, ca. 1917.
(Courtesy of the Dunkeld Community Archive)

GREETINGS FROM OUR FORESTRY CORPS[199]
Scotch Lassies Treat Them Well

December 29, 1917

Dear Sir,

Your readers will be interested to know that the lads of the Newfoundland Forestry Companies spent (under the circumstances) a very enjoyable Christmas season over here. Ample provision had been made for the occasion, and the Christmas dinner was as thoroughly enjoyed by all as if it had been partaken of at home. Turkey was readily overthrown and as quickly divested of its supports by the hearty lads of Newfoundland. There was a supply of fruit, cigarettes, and beer for everybody, even for those who had been away from Camp. It was an unexpected pleasure to be thus treated, and we very much appreciate the kindness and thoughtfulness of Mr. Beeton in securing it for us.

To those desiring a furlough, leave was granted from Saturday evening until Wednesday morning. Quite a number availed of the opportunity to visit various parts of England and Scotland.

My holiday was divided between Stirling, Glasgow, and Ayr. At the latter place I met quite a number of the lads of the Newfoundland Regiment. It is understood that they are shortly to be transferred to the training camp at Winchester, England.

The Race Course at Ayr, where our Regiment used to be stationed, is now occupied by the Royal Flying Corps. It proved very interesting to witness the daily manoeuvres of the aeroplanes. On Christmas morning as I walked along the banks of the River Ayr, the accustomed serenity of the place was disturbed by the buzzing of the machines, there being as many as thirty of them visible at one time.

---

199 *The Western Star*, February 6, 1918, p. 1. Also published in *The Evening Herald*, February 2, 1918.

In the southern part of Scotland it was a "green" Christmas. But up here in the Highlands the weather was seasonable, there being a sprinkling of snow on the ground, adding a Christmassy touch to all.

When on my way back to Camp I never had a finer awakening in my life than at Perth railway station. This is the converging point for the Highland, Caledonian, G. & S.W., and other railways in northern Scotland. There was an awful crowd of troops entraining and detraining for various places, amongst whom were a great many who had been home on furlough and were returning to France. I can assure you it was a busy scene.

There were the trains hurrying into the station with soldiers and sailors, some looking lonely, others weary, and nearly all needing refreshment. Then there was the patriotic "barrow,"[200] heaping high with sandwiches, scones, buns, biscuits, and cake, being wheeled to vantage points where the hungry lads could have their appetites appeased, and their thirst quenched with hot steaming tea, cocoa, coffee. This provision for the troops is a patriotic work that is very highly appreciated. The attention shown and the generous arrangements made for refreshment are consequently of the greatest value.

I was amused by a party of Jack Tars[201] who had just been served with tea and sandwiches, when one of them asked, "Wot's the damage for this little lot?" "Nothing," came the reply from the fair young waitress. Turning to his companions he made the astonished rejoinder, "D'ye hear that, mates? Nothing to pay, and we're in Scotland!"

200 A two-wheeled cart used by street vendors.
201 A term used to describe sailors in the Royal Navy and, later, the American Navy. Barrett's description is in keeping with this meaning. The term is not synonymous with "Jacky Tar," which in Newfoundland and Labrador English is sometimes used to describe a west-coast person of Mi'kmaw and French ancestry and that is widely regarded as pejorative. See Kirwin, Story, and Widdowson (1990).

In this scheme for providing refreshments for soldiers and sailors, the Perthshire Women's Patriotic Committee are warmly to be congratulated upon its success and efficiency. Since its organization in 1914, several hundred thousand troops have been refreshed by a cup of tea or a gift of fruit, and cheered by a kindly word and the friendly interest so evidently shown in them. The "barrow" attends to the needs of soldiers and sailors from 5 a.m. to 1 a.m. next day, and employs in its service nearly 200 voluntary workers. It serves nearly 900 men daily, and during the present year it has furnished refreshments free to about 300,000 troops.

On the afternoon of Saturday, 22nd inst., quite a number of our men attended one of the most enjoyable concerts yet tendered them. It took place in the town hall of Dunkeld, and was also participated in by the convalescent soldiers of St. Mary's. After the concert a very nice tea was served to them, all of which had been freely furnished.

The weather of late has been favourable for our work, and good progress in all branches is being made. Three more large huts are being erected near the mills, where preparations are being made for the reception of another Draft of ninety men soon to arrive.

We can look back over the year now drawing to a close, with thankfulness for the many mercies vouchsafed unto us. Although the strain of the war has been felt in a marked degree by us, yet we have been spared the depredations of the brutal foe, while

Our boys, in the fields of Flanders,
Cheerfully raid the Huns,
Amid the hail of bullets,
And the thunder of the guns.

Amidst all our strange surroundings, it is only natural at this season of the year for our hearts to turn to loved ones at home, and in fancy we see old folk and cheery youth participating in the enjoyments of the festive season; then at eventide we see the brave, loving mother offering at her bedside a fervent prayer for the safety of her absent soldier boy.

To dear old Terra Nova and her sons may the coming year usher in a full measure of peace, happiness and prosperity; and may our gallant boys now fighting on the fields of France and Flanders, and the brave lads in "blue" now sailing the boundless seas be re-united with the cherished ones at home.

Dunkeld, Perthshire, Scotland

An NFC camp at Craigvinean, with the north rail line
to Inverness in the background, Dunkeld, 1917.
(Courtesy of Blair Castle Archive, Pitlochry, Perthshire, Scotland)

FORESTRY CORPS RECEIVE MITTS[202]
Mills Start Night Shift

January 8, 1918

Dear Sir,

The New Year was ushered in by the arrival of another Draft, consisting of eighty men, under the charge of Captains Goodyear and Thistle. Their trip across the Atlantic was not without the customary interesting and exciting events attendant transport ships;[203] but all were pleased when the port of disembarkation[204] was reached.

The arrival of the new Draft was gladly welcomed by those having friends in its ranks, as they were anxiously looking forward to receiving a supply of their favourite tobacco. "Did you bring over any extra tobacco?" "Have you any Mayos?" "Can you spare me a plug or more?" Such were some of the questions that greeted the boys. Of course, some of them had a little to spare, and very generously shared with their friends.

A shipment of 300 pairs of woolen mitts came over with the Draft, and are being distributed amongst the lads.[205] These mitts are very acceptable, and no doubt before the winter is over they will prove very serviceable.

Our strength here is approximately 400. All are comfortably quartered in twenty huts, the walls and roofs of which are covered outside the boards with waterproof felt. In the construction of these buildings the carpenters (intentionally or otherwise)

---

202 *The Western Star*, February 13, 1918, p. 1. Also published in *The Evening Herald*, February 4, 1918.

203 Lieutenant M.J. Nugent, RNR #428 / #0–209, Grand Falls, wrote an account of this voyage. See Nugent (1938).

204 Glasgow.

205 The WPA contributed over 159,000 items of comfort to the overall war effort (Duley, 2012), among them thousands of pairs of mittens and socks.

made ample provision for ventilation, so that the men are at all
times assured of a good current of air passing through the huts.
The furnishing of these huts with fuel entails a great deal of
labour every day, and it is very fortunate that a supply of wood
can be so readily obtained nearby. The edgings and slabs off the
sawn timber supply fuel for the huts at the foot of the hill; but for
the huts of "A" Company the wood has to be brought in by railway from the hillside and sawed by hand. As an oil-burning
engine has been received for this purpose, it is hoped to have it
installed in the course of a few days.

Up to the present there has been very little frost, and except
on the high peaks the ground is entirely free from snow. Yesterday was bright and sunny, somewhat reminding one of a September day at home. Cattle and sheep are grazing in the fields,
just as if it was autumn, instead of winter; it is earnestly hoped
that we may have a continuance of this mild weather.

The mills started night-shift for the first time on the 1st, inst.
The gangs work ten hours, the day-shift beginning at 7 a.m., and
the nightshift at 7 p.m. This means extra work for the transports
on the hill, as there must necessarily be sufficient timber sent
down the chutes by day to keep the mills working both shifts.

The huts at the foot of the hill are lighted by electricity, so
also are the mills and lumber yard. Looking down from the hill
at night the scene is a novel one. The brilliancy of the lights illuminating the surroundings; the steam and smoke issuing from
the tall smokestacks; rhythmic sound of the saws; and the clank-
ing of levers and frictions lend a new spirit to what used to be
practically total darkness and quietness.

With the lengthening of days, it is thought a number of our
men may be going to Kenmore, to make preparations for our
operations in that section when we are finished on Craigvinean,
but we are not going to be through with it here for some time
yet; in fact, it looks as if most of us may be here well into the

summer, as the felling of trees is not being done on the scale at first estimated.

Dunkeld, Perthshire, Scotland

• • •

"Not So Very Far Away, After All"

William J. Woodford, NFC #8211, a machinist, enlisted on May 28, 1917, at the age of 21, a little over a month after his brother Michael, NFC #8030, a 20-year-old boiler maker who had enlisted on April 23. Their older brother Frank, RNR #364, a Blue Puttee, had been killed at Beaumont-Hamel on July 1, 1916. After the war, William Woodford[206] (1930) penned this story about an experience he had one night in the summer of 1918, while tending the machinery at Craigvinean:

> My work consisted of attending to the boiler and dynamo which lighted the camps. As soon as dusk appeared I would take up my duty, and remain on until the men began work in the morning. It was rather weary at times, but as a rule I had a faithful companion in the shape of a book, which whiled away the time. I am afraid that the particular form of literature which it was customary to peruse at that time could hardly be termed "classical," more often than not it was Tit-bits, Answers, or perhaps a light magazine. This night I happened to have an English magazine of the lighter type. After seeing to the oil cups, firebox, water and steam gauges, I laid down on a table or bench and began to read my magazine. The mill was some little distance from the camps, and very little noise penetrated to the boiler-room where I then was.

---

206 In 1949, William J. Woodford was named a Member of the Order of the British Empire (MBE) for his service to veterans through the Great War Veterans' Association.

In fact, about the only noise was the click-clack of the belt as it revolved on the pulley of the dynamo.

It was about 11.30 p.m., and I had then been reading for about an hour and a half. I remember that I had thoroughly enjoyed the jokes, etc., which I had been reading. I was in perfect health, comfortable, and in every way was perfectly normal.

Suddenly, from behind me at a distance which I should judge to be about six or eight feet, a voice sounded. One word was spoken, and it came to me in a friendly pleading voice, casual perhaps, but yet in a manner that vaguely impressed one as not to be ignored. The one word was my own name, and the voice was Frank's. I realized that it was his voice, and that he had been dead about a year. I told myself that there was no such thing as ghosts—"Frank is dead," I told myself. Then I began to wonder, but my materialistic nature came to my aid, and I was on the point of settling down again to my book, determined to banish it from my mind for the rest of the night at least. "Billy" I had always been to Frank, and "Billy" was the name by which I had been called, in the voice which I instantly recognised as his.

Possibly it was a minute, or a minute and a half, after the first call that I again heard the voice. This time it came with vehemence, insistent, dictatorial. One word again, but this time he called me by the name of "Will," sharp and commanding. Gone was the pleading tone, now it was an order, snapped out more in the manner of the Sergeant-Major, but still it was Frank's voice.

Naturally I was upset, but I was not afraid. I determined that I would hold my head—it was only Frank, and Frank wouldn't hurt anyone, he was too good-natured. This thought seemed to exert a calming influence, and with perfect presence of mind, as if it were quite a common occurrence, I sat up and turned towards the voice, at the same time speaking out the words, "Yes, old man, what's the trouble?" There was nothing to be seen, and there was no reply to my question.

That was thirteen years ago. I have neither seen nor heard anything since. I was not ill at the time, neither was I thinking of Frank. As far as I know, I have not been saved from any calamity, so that the old time explanation of its being a warning can hardly apply. It is inexplicable to me—but this much I do know: it has always made me feel that Frank is not so very far away, after all. (pp. 58–59)

• • •

"I Am Lonesome"

The enthusiasm with which those who served seemed to embrace a duty to Empire, oftentimes despite great personal and family losses, did not erase the poignancy of leaving home and the difficulties of separation from loved ones. Those who were away longed to be home as much as those at home longed for their return. John J. Angel, NFC #8383, a baker, was 35 and working in Grand Falls when he enlisted on October 17, 1917. He and his wife, Anastacia Flynn, and family had moved to the new company town just before the war. They joined thousands of others from all over Newfoundland who migrated for work at—or in services related to—the ANDCo pulp and paper mill and its associated woods operations.

Angel left St. John's in mid-December 1917 with the fourth draft of foresters and arrived at Dunkeld on New Year's Day, 1918. Before the NFC operations moved to Kenmore, he was one of many foresters who posed for pictures at the studio of well-known Birnam photographer A.F. MacKenzie. On the back of one such photograph, sent home to Anastacia, he wrote: "I sent you a brooch. I hope you get it. I am lonesome. John xxxxx." The leaf-styled sterling silver brooch, with "EDINBURGH" engraved on its front, arrived safely. John Angel served for the duration and rejoined his family in New-foundland at the end of January 1919. At demobilization, he was classified as permanently unfit for duty.

Some NFC members gathered inside a mill at Craigvinean, Dunkeld, 1918.
(Courtesy of Pat Angel)

FORESTERS SHORT OF WARM CAPS AND
LUMBERMEN'S FOOTWEAR[207]
Wish For What They Left Behind in God's Country

January 14, 1918

Dear Sir,

When I wrote you last week the weather conditions were very promising. But since then a great change has taken place all over Scotland. A cold snap of several days has caused ice to form on all the smaller lochs and rivers in this section, and the whole countryside is covered with a thin layer of snow. The 13th was the coldest, the thermometer registering 22 degrees of frost: that is within 10 degrees of zero. Owing to the absence of warm caps and the lumbermen's customary footwear, some of our men are wishing they had those they left behind in God's country.

At an early hour on Sunday morning the men belonging to the Church of England attended Communion Service. It was the first service of that nature they had an opportunity of participating in since coming across.

On Sunday evenings, quite a few of our men, irrespective of creed, attend Divine service at the United Free Church at Dunkeld, and by their singing help to make the services very enlivening.

Following the example set by the Adjutant, three or four of our lads have taken to themselves wives of Scottish birth. Rumors are rife respecting others who contemplate taking a voyage over the sea of matrimony.

A representative of a Cinematograph Company spent a few days with us last week taking pictures of the various operations. The weather was favourable, thus enabling him to get some fine

---

207 *The Western Star*, February 27, 1918, p. 3. Also published in *The Evening Herald*, February 21, 1918.

views of the men at work felling and cross-cutting the trees, the
horses hauling the timber to the chutes and the trolleys conveying the logs over the railway. Pictures of the work in and about
the mills were taken, as were also the men on parade. It is understood that these pictures have been prepared especially for exhibition in Newfoundland.

Last week quite a large number of parcels were received by
our lads. Evidently these were intended for the Christmas season; nevertheless, though their coming was late, the recipients
were highly pleased to receive them. In this life, more so than in
any other sphere, no man liveth to himself, so it was share and
share alike when these packages came. Some had the disappointment of receiving only the empty wrappings of their parcels, whilst others were doomed not to get the parcels that have
been over three months on the road for them. If the persons who
"lift" the contents of soldiers' parcels were to pass in their
checks[208] at five minutes to nine the following morning, it is likely
there would be a larger roll call in Hades.

Preparations are already being planned for the cultivation of
a much greater acreage throughout Scotland the coming season
than was ever known before. Last year's efforts of the farmers
were the best on record; but these are exceeded this year by the
seeding of at least twenty thousand acres more.

If a farmer of Kelligrews or Codroy Valley had a crop of five
hundred barrels of turnips, it would be counted a large one.
Well, quite near our Camp is a farm that last year yielded a crop
of five hundred tons of turnips, besides large quantities of other
root crops. Potatoes sell at 10½ d.[209] per stone,[210] and turnips at

---

208 A phrase meaning to die; in this usage, in the afterlife, parcel lifters would be
   condemned to hell (Hades).

209 Pennies or pence.

210 One Scottish stone equals 16 pounds (7.26 kilograms); an Imperial stone equals
   14 pounds (6.35 kilograms).

6 ½ d. In consequence of these prices, a goodly supply is regularly furnished our Camp.

Dunkeld, Perthshire, Scotland

• • •

"Some Very Earnest, Warm-Hearted Christians"

The church parade services to which Barrett referred were important events for the foresters, all of whom were Christian. Reverend E. Albert Evans, a Methodist minister from Perth, was responsible for the pastoral care of those among the NFC of his faith. In the *Methodist Recorder*, Evans told the story of the foresters who became part of his congregation and how the Sunday evening services, held at the Free Church of Dunkeld, began. The article ("Newfoundland Foresters," 1918) was reprinted in *The Evening Herald*:

> Some time ago at the close of one of our Sabbath morning parade services, my two leaders there, trusty and godly brethren, spoke to me about having some special service, as there was a spirit of religious inquiry abroad among the men. They told me that one or two of them "wanted to be converted." I promised to do my best in the matter.
>
> The only place that seemed suitable was a little church nearly two miles away from the camp. After some correspondence on the subject, I received the kind permission of the minister and office-bearers to use the church on Saturday and Sunday evenings, April 20th and 21st. Our people at Perth kindly consented to do without their pastor for the Sabbath.
>
> On the Saturday evening, five or six of the praying men came down for a preparatory meeting in the church. They brought two

or three of their unconverted comrades with them, one of whom surrendered to Christ that night. It was a glorious beginning and the sounds of prayer and praise were heard from the little church all around the hamlet.

I had an excellent muster of about 90 Methodists at the parade service in the Camp on Sabbath morning, and announced the evening service in the little church, inviting the men to attend. About 50 came, also a few wounded soldiers from a neighbouring Red Cross Convalescent Home and about 40 or 50 of the villagers so that the little church was well-filled. We had a great time!

After the service I announced a prayer and testimony meeting, to which nearly all present remained. There were five more declarations for Christ, two of them being villagers. We closed with the Doxology. The general inquiry, from foresters and villagers alike, was, "When shall we have another such service?" . . .

So the good work goes on, and our Methodist colonial cousins are happy in it. They have amongst them some very earnest, warm-hearted Christians, and they are well-spoken of amongst the villagers. (p. 4)

DARE-DEVILS FROM "NOO-FOUND-LIN"[211]
Forestry Doings in Auld Scotia

January 21, 1918

Dear Sir,

Notwithstanding the inclemency of the weather of late, we are "carrying on" as usual at the same address, although not meeting with quite as good results as formerly. The past week of weather was the most disagreeable since coming here. Considerable snow fell all over Scotland, whilst in many sections there was sufficient to make good sleighing. The thermometer for a couple of days bordered on the zero mark. People with long memories say that frost so severe as that recently experienced has not been known in Scotland for eight-and-twenty years.

The people of this country do not seem to be inured to the rigours of such winter weather as we get in Newfoundland (pronounced Noo-FOUND-Lin). What is greatly dreaded by the people living in the valleys is the rime, of which there is quite an abundance; but up here on the hillside we did not have it quite as cold as it was in town. Today it is somewhat like our April weather, and nearly all the snow has disappeared. This pleasant change is greatly welcomed throughout the country by the people who are scantily supplied with fuel.

I made a trip to Perth last week, and it was only natural for the train passengers to be discussing the weather, reminded as they were of it on every hand:

> "It was so desperately cold one day on this same line," remarked one man, "that my watch, though fully wound up, was frost-bitten and stopped."

---

211 *The Western Star*, March 6, 1918, p. 1. Also published in *The Evening Herald*, February 22, 1918.

"I could believe it," said another passenger. "D'ye know I remember one morning seeing the steam from the engine falling so thickly in the form of rime that the folk further back on the train were overheard saying, "There's the snow on again."

"Humph, that's nothing," said one who had come from a cold climate. "I was once on an engine from which not a speck of steam came, yet there was a roaring fire. The water in the boiler was frozen hard."

"See here," remarked another, "how could the infernal train move along in that case?"

"That's just where the strange thing came in," was the reply. "So intense was the frost that the continued expansion of the water acted on the valves like steam, and hanged if we didn't go racing on 'til the thaw came."

A little over half the timber estimated to be on our section has been felled, and although the work of transportation to the mills is being carried on with the greatest dispatch possible, yet there are several thousand logs strewn about the hillside. Occasionally slight delays are caused by logs of enormous size damaging the chutes, necessitating the drawing of men from the woods to effect repairs.

Sometimes there are exciting scenes on the railway, as the heavily-laden trolleys go down the grades with great speed when the rails are wet. Occasionally they leave the track, but rarely any great damage is sustained. Today one of the runaway trolleys went as far as the outside terminus where, of its own accord, it deposited its load of logs into the chute and they went safely down to the mill. The brakemen are real daredevils of the true

Newfoundland type, and stick to their trolley to the end. In fine, dry weather a certain amount of sport can be derived therefrom; but when it is slushy and cold no constitution but that of a hardy Newfoundlander could stand up against it. The town folk shrug their shoulders and often wonder how our lads withstand the storms; but a hearty laugh or a cheery joke from them about the Craig of Goats covers up their real feelings.

Throughout England and Scotland they are having "Tank Bank" [212] days, by which means large sums have been raised for the National War Fund. Last week it was Glasgow's turn to be visited by one of these modern machines of warfare, and the amount of money contributed by that city exceeded fourteen million pounds, beating the contribution of any other city by a wide margin.

Queen Alexandra[213] has very graciously sent the following message to the Children's Union through its monthly magazine:

> Let all your thoughts be with the soldiers who are fighting for you. Pray for them, work for them, think of them in all that you do, see in what way you can help those glorious men who are laying down their lives for you. Keep on, and encourage others, so that each one of you, in days to come, may proudly say that when our country called for help, you, her children, gave your all.

---

212 A government fundraising campaign that began in November 1917 in the UK; its purpose was to promote the sale of War Bonds and War Savings Certificates.

213 Queen Alexandra was the widow of King Edward VII and mother of the reigning monarch during the war, King George V. She was the Patroness of the Children's Union, an organization formed in the UK in 1889 to fundraise for homes for children with disabilities. The publication, *Brothers and Sisters*, was sent to every member of the Children's Union. See Cooper (2016).

The speech of Mr. Lloyd George,[214] the British Prime Minister, to the Trades Union Conference last week should act like a series of hammer strokes and ring through the hearts of the nation, and awaken those who are asleep. In almost painful plainness the Prime Minister tells us that if we do not as a nation put our whole strength into the great struggle now raging, there can be but one end. Democracy will be swept like chaff before the armies of the Huns, all that is best in British traditions will vanish, all that British working men have struggled for and suffered for will disappear.

I would like for all your readers to think seriously of the many lads from our native shore who have fought on the fields of France and Flanders, and have given their all for the sake of those at home. Then let your readers take onto themselves the following lines, which are sent specially for their attention:

> We grumble here at the fall of snow
> Or the touch of frost in the air;
> The cold and mud we so little know
> That the boys are having out there.
>
> We feel aggrieved if our quiet's disturbed
> By the bark of the dog next door;
> The boys have more to make them perturbed
> 'Mid the din of the cannon's roar.
>
> We grouse no end if our dinner's late
> Our food is not piping hot;
> But the boys have often hours to wait
> For a bite amidst shell and shot.

---

214 David Lloyd George, a Liberal, was Prime Minister of the wartime coalition government in the UK from December 6, 1916, to October 19, 1922.

We toss and turn in our cosy beds
If sleep comes but slowly our way;
Moans of the maimed don't ring in our heads,
Nor the wounded's cry for the day.

We fret and fume when the day is sped
If affairs are not well in hand;
But think not of our unburied dead,
Stark and stiff over No-Man's-Land.

While we spend our lives in peace and rest
Let us squarely answer this call:
"Is each one doing his level best?"
While the boys are giving their all.

The boys of the Newfoundland Regiment moved away from the town of Ayr on the 14th inst., and have gone into quarters at Winchester, England.

Dunkeld, Perthshire, Scotland

OUR FORESTERS AT SALMON FISHING[215]

February 3, 1918

Last week my work was so congested,
And things to write of were not newsy
So down my pen was laid and rested
From scribbling things sober or boozy.

Dear Sir,

Last Sunday morning the men of the Roman Catholic faith turned out to an early celebration of Mass. After breakfasting at 7:15, they paraded to Birnam, a distance of four miles, where the service was conducted.

In and around the mills everything is going smoothly, there being night and day shifts working regularly; and the stacks of lumber in the yard are increasing in size, notwithstanding the shipments being made as fast as railway cars can be procured.

The closing days of January were very spring-like, the warm southerly winds clearing all the snow from the hillsides and making the ground very soft. A continuance of the same weather ushered in the month of February, and if the old adage respecting Candlemas Day[216] holds good, then the remainder of our winter is likely to be mild.

It is very fortunate that there has not been much snow, otherwise the operation of our railway would be seriously handicapped.

215 *The Western Star*, March 13, 1918, p. 1. Also published in *The Evening Herald*, March 11, 1918, and *The Twillingate Sun*, March 23, 1918.

216 Many people believed that the weather on Candlemas Day, February 2, the halfway point between the winter solstice and the spring equinox, predicted the weather for the season. One Newfoundland saying claimed: "If Candlemas Day is clear and fine, the rest of winter is left behind; if Candlemas Day is rough and glum, there's more of winter left to come." The name is derived from the Christian feast day during which all candles intended for church use were blessed.

So far there has not been enough snow to tie up the trolleys for an hour. There is quite a marked contrast between this weather and what we were accustomed to in our home country; yet after all, clear frosty weather would be far healthier in winter season, and snowballs would be preferable to mud balls.

Those responsible for the issuance of the scale of Army rations did not have any idea as to the capacity of a hard-working Newfoundlander, otherwise they may have granted a larger supply of certain commodities. But as the food situation, not only here, but in many parts of the world, is a serious one at the present day, we have to comply with the order and practice economy. The following economy couplet, composed by a Scottish lady of 76 years, might be profitably applied by many of the younger generation:

> By eating less Bread, and eating less Meat,
> You help the men in our Merchant Fleet.[217]
> By sparing with Butter, and likewise with Bread,
> Remember our Army that has to be fed.
> Every time your belt you tighten,
> The Nation's cares you help to lighten.
> By saving the Bones to boil down for Gravy,
> You are helping the men of the Army and Navy.
> 'Twill help our men the War to win,
> Save scraps of Brass, and Iron and Tin.
> Save Butter, Bread and Margarine,
> Help to defeat the Submarine.
> Help Tommy to give the Huns their gruel,
> By eating less Food, and burning less Fuel.

---

217 One UK wartime poster urged: "Save the Wheat and Help the Fleet—Eat Less Bread."

Since the opening day of the salmon (rod) fishing on the River Tay, some fifty-four fish have been landed. They totalled a weight of 972 pounds, the smallest salmon 17½ lbs. Many of these fish were of clean run, having just come up from the sea.

Golf seems to be a national game in Scotland, and in many parts of the country large tracts of land are reserved for this sport. Now, owing to the agitation for the increased acreage for root and other crops, it is understood that several of the famous golf links are to pass under the Control of the Agricultural Board[218] and will be put under cultivation this year.

London "Opinion" informs us that we are about to have a new General: General Rations. The conservation of the nation's food supply is necessary, and it is claimed that this can only be procured by the rationing of all classes. It is being brought home to the people that the undesirable shortage of food which at present confronts the country is due to three main causes. The first was the world's shortage of crops. The shortage was due almost entirely to the fact that the crops in France were a little more than one-half the normal, and the crop in Italy had fallen short of 15 per cent of the normal. The second cause was the shortage of ships, as one-half of the British merchant Navy was commandeered for purely war purposes, for serving and carrying their fighting men. The third cause was the sinking of food cargoes by submarines.

Whilst the war still drags on its weary way, there is the cry for more men, and still more men. Just a few days ago a large contingent of troops from the United States landed at a nearby seaport town. These men have come overseas for the same worthy cause as our Colonials have come, and are imbued with just as strong a determination to see those aims realized, no matter what the cost, no matter what the sacrifice. It is up to those at

218 Formerly the Board of Agriculture, which was renamed the Board of Agriculture and Fisheries in 1903.

home in all parts of the Empire to emulate the spirit of our fore-fathers, remembering the motto—"Britons never shall be slaves"[219]—least of all to Germany. Remember those words re-cently uttered by the British Prime Minister—"The people must either go on or go under."[220]

Dunkeld, Perthshire, Scotland

• • •

The Real Slackers?

At a recruitment meeting in Harbour Grace in mid-February 1918, Major Sul-livan of the NFC spoke about the desperate need for more foresters to meet the timber demands of the Empire, as well as for recruits to fill the gaps in Regiment strength created by fatalities and injuries. *The Evening Telegram* reported that, during his talk, Sullivan raised questions about who were the real slackers. The article said he suggested that some who were called slack-ers feared losing their lives if they enlisted, but politicians of all stripes who feared losing electoral support, position, or money were the real slackers for failing to invoke conscription ("Slackers in High Places," 1918). His point was quickly picked up and debated in local newspapers.[221]

The comments attributed to Sullivan likely raised eyebrows. Two days later, Sullivan requested a chance to clarify his remarks in *The Evening Her-ald*, which offered his more muted quote that "something more would have to be done [regarding recruitment failure—presumably conscription], and those who threw obstacles in the way were as much to blame as those who were slacking in their duty by failing to enlist" ("Recruiting," 1918, p. 5).

---

219 From "Rule, Britannia," a patriotic song based on a poem by James Thompson and set to music by Thomas Arne in 1740.
220 David Lloyd George.
221 See, for example, "Slackers in High Places" (1918) and "Major Sullivan" (1918).

The topic of slackers was fraught. In the parlance of the war, "doing one's bit" was the honourable response to the needs of the Empire. Those suspected of being slackers were shamed and demonized in public discourse. Local newspapers carried stories of so-called slackers that fed public indignation and resentment of those who were seen to be avoiding service.[222] The meanings of "slacker" were clearly framed around gender.[223] For men, it played on a prevailing notion of masculinity and manhood and its relationship to war service. But the scourge of being labelled a slacker was not reserved just for males. For women, the accusatory label often reiterated restrictive notions of femininity, and women in Newfoundland avoided its taint by participating in patriotic services considered to be within their domain, such as fundraising, knitting, and volunteer nursing.

The white feather campaign aligned that symbol of cowardice and notions of questionable manhood to force perceived slackers into service.[224] Men who were believed to be avoiding service were mailed or pinned with a white feather as a coercive public shaming. The campaign spread from the UK to its colonies, including Newfoundland ("The White Feather," 1916). While not widespread in Newfoundland, the campaign caused consternation and friction within communities and the phrase "showing the white feather" was commonly used to denote cowardice and surrender. In the fall of 1917, young men of St. Mary's who were not enlisted received an envelope containing a white feather and the word "slacker" written on a note. The degree of suspicion aroused in the community prompted police officer Vincent S. Walsh,

---

222 See, for example, "Firemen Wouldn't Sail" (1915), the widely publicized story of a strike aboard the Cunard liner *Saxonia* to protest transporting 600 able-bodied men of the UK to New York.

223 For a glaring example, see a rippling rhyme by Walt Mason (1918) on the subject of women slackers.

224 The so-called Order of the White Feather was begun by Vice-Admiral Charles Penrose Fitzgerald of the UK and then adopted by suffragettes, who saw men's enlistment as an opportunity to promote the value of women's labour and the struggle for the franchise. For a discussion of the impact of the campaign on gender images and understanding, see Hart (2010).

RNR #1958, who had been medically discharged from the Regiment after being wounded at Gueudecourt, to write a denial of responsibility for the letters to *The Evening Telegram* (Walsh, 1918).

Nor did conscription end the tensions. Following its introduction, threats of vigilante justice increased against those perceived to be skirting their war responsibilities ("Will Be Ostracized," 1918). Officials at the Penitentiary in St. John's reported the contempt with which other prisoners held "eligibles" ("Slackers in the Pen," 1918). Less than a week following the passing of conscription legislation, rumours spread from Wesleyville to the capital city of an anti-conscription protest during a patriotic concert, followed by a walkout at a church service when the minister preached a patriotic sermon. Some St. John's newspapers accused the protesters of sedition and treason ("Sedition," 1917).

An NFC member does camp repairs, ca. 1918.
(Courtesy of The Rooms Provincial
Archives Division, A 103-99)

FIRST FATALITY IN THE NEWFOUNDLAND
FORESTRY COMPANY[225]

March 13, 1918

Dear Sir,

Now that the days are getting longer and the weather a little more pleasant, our men are doing better with their operations, and daily large quantities of logs are being taken from the hillside and sent down to the mills. A comparatively small number of men are at present engaged felling trees, owing to the great quantity awaiting transportation to the chutes. It is hoped that by the end of April all the trees already felled shall be cleaned up.

The boiler for the second large mill, which was looked for since last fall, only arrived last week and is now ready for installation. This means that the night shift at the mills is about to be cancelled. Trolley tracks have been laid over a large area of the farm where the mills are operating. The lumber stacks are daily increasing in number and size, and the whole place is growing more and more like a large lumber yard.

The fire engine and pump have been set up near the foot of the jack-ladder, and as the logs are being taken from the dam a stream of water is turned on them, removing the mud and grit collected when being browed. But the logs contain numerous small stones picked up from the hillside when they are rolled or "snigged"[226] to the brows and chutes. These frequently cause a great deal of trouble with the saws, necessitating re-toothing.

Various species of game still continue plentiful in this vicinity, and last week four deer were brought into Camp as a result of the accurate aim of 2nd Lieutenant Gillis.

---

225 *The Western Star*, April 17, 1918, p. 1. Also published in *The Evening Herald*, April 16, 1918.

226 A term for dragging logs.

Corporal B.W. Potts[227] recently applied for and was granted a transfer to the Royal Newfoundland Regiment, and has gone to Winchester to join that unit. We were all sorry to lose him, as he was well liked and proved himself very competent as a scaler,[228] which work was entrusted to him. Several other lads were desirous of obtaining transfers, but, as their services are required here, they have been retained.

Great Britain is continuing her "Tank Bank" days, and meeting with gratifying results. Last week the city of London had its second innings, when over sixty-eight million pounds were contributed. It certainly was a magnificent showing of the patriotic spirit of a people whose latest subscriptions exceeded all previous efforts.

Newfoundland has contributed thousands of her best sons to Britain's infantry, Royal Naval Reserve, and industrial army, all of whom are exerting their brains and muscles and are united in the common cause—for Freedom. When those at home are approached for donations towards any patriotic work, they may be encouraged in their giving by taking to heart the following lines:

Not ours to hear the mad, hoarse shout of battle;
Not ours to see the agonies of strife;
Not ours to feel the grip of death's dread rattle;
Not ours to die for Britain . . . We have life.
We know a peaceful dawn, the sun's soft glowing,
We see the velvet night, and unafraid
Through fields unravaged we may pass, well knowing,
Our land is free because our brothers paid.
They gave their lives, and shall then be inglorious

227 Corporal Brian W. Potts, NFC #8093, Millertown, transferred to the Regiment (RNR #3060) on February 20, 1918.
228 The person whose job it is to measure cut and browed timber.

Close up our purse strings where we gave our sons?
When wealth alone can make our arms victorious
Shall we withhold the gold to feed the guns?
They looked to us in faith that's unafraid,
Let faith in us be met by instant aid.

We were shocked on Saturday, 9th inst., when a fatal accident occurred, causing the death of 8460 Private Selby Taylor.[229] It was the first fatality among the Forestry Companies since enlistment started a year ago. Private Taylor was the son of Pleamon Taylor,[230] St. John's, and arrived here with the Draft on 17th February, being posted to "B" Company. On Saturday, he was engaged in the erection of a landing or platform near the upper end of the larger log chute. At intervals during the day logs were being sent down the chute from the top of the hill, and warnings were given everybody working in that vicinity. But, unfortunately, Private Taylor and two other men remained too long near the chute, they being very anxious to complete the job they had in hand. One log, more erratic in its movements than others, left the chute about one hundred feet above where the men were working, and before they had time to get to a place of safety it hit Private Taylor a terrific blow in the back causing almost instantaneous death. The body was placed upon a stretcher and taken to the medical hut, where Dr. Taylor was quickly in attendance; but his services were not required, as life was then extinct.

The funeral obsequies took place on the afternoon of Tuesday. All the officers and men were in attendance on "B" Company's parade ground, and after they were formed up in a hollow square, the casket bearing the remains of the late Private Taylor, and wrapped in a Union Jack, was placed in the centre. Reverend

229 Private Selby P. Taylor, NFC #8460, St. John's.
230 Private Taylor's parents were Pleamon and Zillah (Pack) Taylor, St. John's.

Gravestone of Private Selby Taylor, Little Dunkeld
Presbyterian Church, Dunkeld.
(Courtesy of Michael Pretty, Trail of the Caribou Research Group)

E.A. Evans, Wesleyan minister at Perth, conducted a short but impressive service, after which the remains were placed on a motor hearse and taken to the graveyard surrounding Little Dunkeld Presbyterian Church,[231] the Forestry Companies marching in slow procession behind the hearse. At the graveside, another solemn requiem was said, then the remains of our departed brother were consigned to Mother Earth, there to await the last great reveille, when soul and body shall again be re-united.

---

231 The grave reference is 636. The gravestone was designed with a stylized timber log motif in the border and base.

A firing squad from the Black Watch Battalion was in attendance as a body guard. The sounding of Last Post terminated the solemn and impressive obsequies.

Those who knew late Private Taylor speak of him as bearing an exemplary character, and was a capable and willing worker. Full of life and vigour, he left his home about a few weeks ago to join his comrades here to loyally make an effort in "freedom's cause." As he went forth to his labour on Saturday morning it was with a light heart and customary jocularity, and little did any of us think that death would so soon overtake him. To the sorrowing young widow[232] and aged parents our sincerest sympathy is extended.

Dunkeld, Perthshire, Scotland

---

232 His widow was Maud Taylor, St. John's.

March 31, 1918

Dear Sir,

The first mail for six weeks arrived yesterday from Newfoundland. From it we gathered the sad particulars of the loss of the ill-fated *Florizel* and the death of so many valuable lives. We were intimately acquainted with quite a number of those who went to their death on that fateful Sunday morning, and the tidings of the catastrophe have saddened our hearts. To those who have been called to pass through the trial of bereavement, our sincerest sympathy is extended.

During the past fortnight, the weather has been beautifully fine and spring-like, something like the weather you get in Newfoundland late in April or early May. This has enabled our men to continue their work uninterruptedly. The greater part of the first tramline on the hillside has been taken up, as the timber in this vicinity has all been sent to the mills. The material used for this line has been removed farther up the hill, where two other tramlines are being constructed. These branch off from the big log chute, running in opposite directions, and will be used for the purpose of conveying logs from the timber belt to the chute. This seems to be the most practicable manner by which to get the logs out of the woods. Owing to the nature of the country and the weather conditions, lumbering operations cannot be conducted as economically here as in Newfoundland. The men do not shrink from work, as evidenced by the large output of timber, and they are daily exerting muscle and sinew to the fullest capacity. Strenuous though the work may be at times, yet it is performed with such a silent determination and so methodically as to cause strangers to wonder at the splendid results achieved.

---

233 *The Western Star*, May 8, 1918, p. 1. Also published in *The Evening Herald*, May 2, 1918.

A week ago the time was advanced an hour. By this means we now have nearly three hours daylight after tea. As the days come on, the evenings will be growing longer until by June it will be practically all daylight. To those of our men who are late comers these long evenings will afford a splendid opportunity for seeing the surrounding country.

The farmer is a busy man these days. With many acres of land already ploughed and harrowed, he is hustling with the seeding. The agricultural implements used are many and varied, some of them being of a make that is rather obsolete. Yet were it not for these machines thousands of valuable acres of fertile land in Scotland would have to remain uncultivated today, as many sections of the country have been practically depopulated of all the able-bodied male help hitherto employed at farm work.

In the spring a young man's fancy to thoughts of love would run,[234]
And with ardent fervour he was wont to woo;
Now he's busily devising fancy ways to strafe the Hun,
And for the nonce[235] love-making is na poo.[236]

In the spring a merry maiden clad herself in colours gay,
And donned a chapeau with bright flower or wing;
Now mostly glack and grimy,[237] with but little time for play,
Overalls are still the fashion in the spring.

To those who live far from the scenes of bustle and activity it would really astonish them if they were to visit some of the larger

234 This line is borrowed from Alfred, Lord Tennyson's "Locksley Hall."
235 For now; for this time.
236 Military slang meaning "no more."
237 This phrase is likely a misprint that should possibly read: "Now, she's in the glack and grimy." In this context, a glack is a ravine or hollow.

towns and cities over here and see the great amount of female help employed at war work. We thought it very interesting recently when visiting a factory where about four hundred women and girls are employed making web[238] equipment for the soldiers; but when we went into an area where munition works are being vigorously operated, in which some seventeen thousand women are engaged, we were greatly amazed at the immensity of it all. There were women of noble birth, clad in overalls, working side by side with women of more lowly birth, all intent on doing their full share of toil, and are ceaselessly working so that the cause of humanity and the freedom of nations may be hastened.

Dunkeld, Perthshire, Scotland

• • •

Major Sullivan Survives

The six-week span during which the Forestry Companies received no mail from Newfoundland coincided with the period following the sinking of the SS *Florizel*. The *Florizel* was the flagship of the Bowring Brothers fleet in Newfoundland and an iconic ship for the Regiment and the Forestry Companies—during the war, the passenger liner and sealing ship was used as a troop carrier. Many members of the Regiment, including the Blue Puttees, embarked for overseas on the *Florizel*. Several drafts of the NFC also left home for Scotland aboard the ship, and many foresters had relatives who were crew members.

On February 23, 1918, the *Florizel* was on its regular run to New York via Halifax carrying 138 passengers and crew. It departed St. John's in the early

---

238 A strong woven cotton introduced before the First World War that replaced leather in the manufacture of belts, ammunitions pouches, and other items used in combat uniforms.

evening with a storm approaching and steamed southward along the coast in gale-force winds and limited visibility. Hours later, erroneously believing he was rounding Cape Race, Captain William J. Martin ran the ship aground on a reef at Horn Head Point near Cappahayden. Over the following hours, the ship slowly broke up, pounding on the offshore rocks and being pummelled by the high seas. Of those aboard, 44 survived.

Among the passengers and crew with whom the foresters were acquainted was their Commanding Officer, Major Michael S. Sullivan. Sullivan had left the UK from Liverpool on December 23, 1917, to meet with the Minister of Militia in Newfoundland. Captain Baird was left in command of the foresters during his absence. Sullivan postponed his departure from Newfoundland to do additional recruiting[239] and, on Sunday, February 23, 1918, boarded the *Florizel* for Halifax. There he was to meet his wife and children, who had been living in Montreal, and they would all travel together overseas.

In his stateroom that night, Sullivan found that sleep was eluding him. He left his cabin and attempted to rest on a sofa in the social room, then visited with John Munn.[240] By that time the ship was rolling heavily and Sullivan left Munn's cabin to investigate. He was halfway down the passageway when the *Florizel* hit the rocks. Thrown by the impact, he eventually found his way back to his stateroom. He collected his coat and a small flashlight and headed for the Captain's cabin to offer assistance. As the ship continued to pound against the rocks, he found shelter with others near the smokehouse. Sullivan watched helplessly as the force of the sea destroyed the ship's superstructure, sweeping away passengers and crew, many of whom were wearing only their nightclothes.

---

239 See a description of the work at Dunkeld provided by Major Sullivan at a recruitment address at St. Bonaventure's College, February 21, 1918, prior to his departure ("Our Foresters," 1918).

240 John S. Munn was the stepson of Sir Edgar Bowring and Managing Director of Bowring Brothers, owners of the *Florizel*. Munn lost his 3-year-old daughter Betty when she was swept from his arms by the force of the sea during the shipwreck. Munn also perished in the disaster. A statue of Peter Pan was commissioned in Betty Munn's memory and erected in Bowring Park, St. John's, by her grandfather.

As Sullivan attempted to reach a safer location at the smokestack he, too, was knocked down by the rushing water—but he managed to grab a wire and stop himself from being swept into the icy sea. He eventually made his way to the fiddley,[241] inside which he and several others huddled in the hope of surviving until they could be rescued. At intervals, Sullivan stepped outside to use his flashlight to signal to residents of Cappahayden that survivors were aboard the ruined ship.

Eventually, boats were able to make their way to the stricken vessel, despite the still threatening conditions. During the rescue, as he was about to step into a dory, Sullivan was thrown into the sea, but he was grabbed by another survivor, Alexander Ledingham. Sullivan clung to the gunwale of the dory and directed his own rescue. He was dragged through the water and away from the wreckage, where he was safely pulled aboard another dory. It was not until about 8:00 in the morning on Tuesday, February 25 that the last survivors, Captain William Martin among them, were taken ashore.

Following his rescue, Major Sullivan remained for several weeks in Newfoundland to recover from his injuries. He testified at the inquiry into the disaster, which began on March 5 and continued into April 1918.[242] Sullivan finally embarked from Halifax for Scotland on April 9 and arrived at Dunkeld on April 21, accompanied by his wife, Kathleen, and two children, Arthur and Vera.[243]

• • •

Captain Perry's Aide

Private John C.M. Hayward, NFC #8470, a photographer from Grand Falls, was 42 when he enlisted at Grand Falls on January 23, 1918. Major Sullivan

---

241 The iron cover or hatch on the deck above the engine room.

242 For an account of Sullivan's testimony, see "The Florizel Inquiry" (1918). For the best-known account of the disaster, see Brown (1976).

243 On August 22, 1919, Lieutenant-Colonel Sullivan (he had been promoted effective January 1, 1919) was deemed unfit for service because of medical conditions resulting from the exposure he had endured during the wreck of the SS *Florizel*.

was his enlisting officer. Hayward was training at the NFC Depot in St. John's when news broke of the wreck of the *Florizel*. He was aboard the SS *Home*, one of four rescue ships sent from St. John's that, along with smaller boats from Cappahayden, participated in the rescue efforts.

Captain Ernest C. Perry of the SS *Gordon C*, the first ship on the scene, made three successful runs through the perilous waters in his dory to collect survivors; on the fourth, he was washed overboard and the dory destroyed. Perry was unconscious when rescued by crew aboard the SS *Home*. It was Private Hayward who, for over three hours, administered medical aid to Captain Perry ("Captain Perry," 1918).

Hayward served with the NFC for the duration. He moved to Halifax following the war, where he again worked as a professional photographer. His gelatin silver prints of the early ANDCo operations in Newfoundland, taken in 1912, are part of the collections of the Art Gallery of Ontario.

The SS *Florizel*, sometime after 1909 and before 1918.
(Courtesy of the Maritime History Archive, PF-001.1-T06b,
Memorial University of Newfoundland)

ANOTHER FORESTRY DRAFT
REACHES SCOTLAND[244]

April 21, 1918

Dear Sir,

Another Draft reached here today, they having left Newfoundland the latter part of March, and came across with a large contingent of Canadians and Americans. The transports were convoyed by a number of torpedo boat destroyers, which are reported to have put out of commission two German submarines.

We are pleased to have Major Sullivan with us again, he having arrived here last night, being accompanied by Mrs. Sullivan.[245]

The fine weather together with the long evenings combine to make life more pleasant for the men, and after tea they can visit the nearby villages, whilst those having bicycles often visit places ten and fifteen miles distant, whither a number of their female friends sometimes accompany them. The roads are in excellent condition, and whether awheel or afoot, one can enjoy a tour of the country.

Our second large mill has been working in conjunction with number one since 8th inst., thus dispensing with the night shift. With these two mills now in operation the daily output of sawn timber is being very largely increased, and busy scenes are to be witnessed in the lumber yard, where there are over two million feet of lumber graded and stacked ready for shipment. The increment to these piles is being kept up faster than cars can be obtained for shipping purposes.

Owing to the felling and transportation of all timber in close proximity to the Camp, number two chute has been abandoned

---

244 *The Western Star*, May 22, 1918, p. 1. Also published in *The Evening Herald*, May 27, 1918.
245 Kathleen E. Thomson Sullivan.

and the logs used in its construction have been taken up and sent down to the mills. Another log chute, much shorter than the others, is now being built about a mile from Camp. It also is to be connected with a trolley tramline, which in turn connects with the main chute leading down to the mills. The two other tramlines have been built, both of which are being used for the purpose of conveying logs from the timber belt to the large chute.

There being no further use for the first tramline built, all the material has been taken up and used on the other roads. This opens up our road once more, enabling the transport wagons to again come right to the Camp on the hill, doing away with a lot of extra handling of rations, forage, and supplies. For nearly eight months the road from the chute to Camp had been closed to traffic, except by trolleys; now it seems good to again have this mile of road open to the wagons.

Daily the hillside is becoming more naked, and the aspect is not nearly as pleasing as a few months since. At the present rate of felling it is likely that all the trees will be down by the early part of June, and a couple of months from then the greater portion will be converted into sawn timber.

Notwithstanding the prediction of Private Sullivan (Uncle Tom),[246] the motor engine installed for saving fuel is being operated under the skillful management of Private Dunn,[247] and is giving good satisfaction in furnishing fuel for the huts and cook-houses of "A" Company.

Dunkeld, Perthshire, Scotland

---

246 Private Thomas F.J. Sullivan, NFC #8125, St. John's, was nicknamed "Uncle Tom." In Newfoundland communities at the time, "Uncle" was used as a sign of respect for an older man, and Private Sullivan was 70. The term did not necessarily denote nor preclude familial relationship.

247 Private John S. Dunn, NFC #8023, Grand Falls.

Conscription (Finally)

Although drafts continued to be sent to Scotland throughout the war, the numbers in each one were small and set against an increasing need for more foresters. In Newfoundland, voluntary enlistment was maintained until only a few months before the end of the war; the debate about conscription intensified over the duration, especially when other dominions, including Canada, moved on adopting some form of forced enlistment. By 1918, Regiment numbers were critically low, with few reserves, and the number of fatalities and injuries continued to grow. The British Army Council estimated the Regiment needed 300 soldiers immediately and a regular enlistment of 60 men per month thereafter. During his recruitment tour of early winter, Major Sullivan emphasized the critical needs of the NFC, hoping to enlist another 500 men ("More Men Wanted," 1918), but the resulting numbers were modest.

On April 4, 1918, another recruitment campaign was launched to "fill the gaps" in the Regiment ranks. Officials hoped to take advantage of the seasonal change then occurring in the outports—it was the time of year when men were leaving the lumber woods after the winter cut and had not yet begun spring fishing. As noted earlier, many people still believed that outport men were not stepping up to serve in sufficient numbers. An appeal from Governor Harris,[248] published in newspapers throughout the country, was directed "to the people of Newfoundland, but especially to those of the Outports." While some of the campaign slogans were subtle ("The fashionable spring suit this year is khaki. Is yours ordered?"), most utilized tactics of shame, dishonour, and failure to perform one's duty. Newspapers ran campaign advertisements that demanded, "Newfoundlanders! Think Imperially," or asked, "Are your folks ashamed of you for not enlisting?" The choice: become a volunteer now, or a conscript later.

In a letter to Adjutant Captain Hector H.A. Ross on April 12, District Officer Commanding (Newfoundland) Major Alexander Montgomerie (1918) expressed his concerns:

---

248 Sir Charles Alexander Harris replaced Sir Walter Davidson as Governor of Newfoundland. His appointment was from 1917 to 1922.

We have had the pleasure of seeing the pictures of the operations at Dunkeld, and they are extremely interesting.

Major Sullivan is here and gone again. I believe at present he is in Halifax awaiting transport. He was very fortunate in escaping with his life when the *Florizel* was lost. He will also be able to tell you of recruiting conditions here. It is almost impossible to get men for the Forestry Companies. They are making so much money at the fishery that they cannot be persuaded that their duty lies across seas. (p. 1)

This campaign to enlist voluntary recruits was the final one. Conscription was introduced on May 11, 1918.

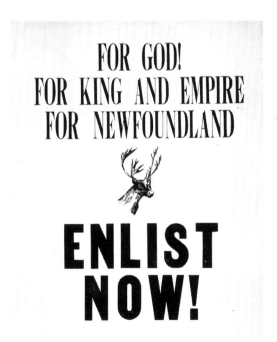

A Newfoundland First World War recruitment poster.
(Courtesy of Toronto Reference Library, Baldwin
Collection, 1914–18, Newfoundland, Item 2.L)

NEWFOUNDLAND FORESTRY CORPS
MOVE TO KENMORE[249]
How Private Gerald Hogan Was Killed
Interesting Letter from Orderly J.A. Barrett

August 23, 1918

Dear Brother,[250]

Our leaving Dunkeld was mingled with regrets, as we had become so well acquainted with its surroundings and with a number of its people. However, as there are many meetings and partings in this life, one has to meekly bow to the Inevitable.

The work of felling trees at Dunkeld finished early in July, and a few weeks later they were all converted into lumber. In the meantime, the tramlines and chutes were taken up and some of the huts removed. At the same time, small drafts of men and quantities of supplies were being sent forward to Kenmore; until now all have been transferred except about seventy men. These are cleaning up pit props at Craigvinean, and will follow in the course of a few weeks.

The Camp of "A" Company is situated on a small field by the side of Loch Tay one mile from Kenmore, and is headquarters for the unit. "C" Company is two miles to the westward of us, while "B" Company is one mile east. Each Company will have a mill, and these are now in course of erection. It is proposed to make

---

249 *The Western Star*, September 18, 1918, p.3 . Also published in *The Evening Herald*, September 20, 1918. The *Herald* appended a note to this letter indicating, "We copy the above descriptive letter from *The Western Star*, as we know it will be read with interest by the relatives and friends of our boys of the Forestry Battalion."

250 The brother addressed is Andrew L. Barrett. This is the only letter in which Barrett uses this salutation. Unlike the other letters published in the *Western Star*, no signature was included with this one. The salutation, absence of signature, and the editorial note included in *The Herald*'s published version all suggest it was a personal letter and not part of Barrett's official correspondence.

the lumber shipments from a pier close by, and have it taken to Killin Station[251] at the head of the Loch (15 miles distant). Large and commodious huts for each Company have been erected. A supply of water for domestic purposes is to come down pipe lines from the mountain, and this system is now being installed. We have ideal camping sites; but yet we seem to be so far removed from the old-world connections, being from six to nine miles from the nearest railway. Yet we are not faring so badly, because we have motor lorries by which easy connection may be made with the trains.

I came here on 7th inst., having ridden by motor lorry from Dunkeld. I was not much interested in the country scenes until after passing through Aberfeldy, but from there to Camp (seven miles) it was glorious. Passing through what appeared to be one long well-wooded avenue, with here and there small openings through which glimpses of cottages, the River Tay and mountain peaks could be obtained. I can assure you it was simply grand. Then as we approached the village of Kenmore, there was the broad expanse of Loch Tay flowing peacefully at the foot of Drummond Hill—a majestic eminence well covered with larch, oak, spruce and pine trees, some of them rearing to a height of 130 feet and measuring up to six feet at the trunk. In the distance were lofty heather-covered mountain peaks, capped with a mist of a colour peculiarly all its own; whilst on the southern side of the Loch, and sloping gradually up from the shore, were numerous fields of ripening corn and oats. It was a sight to inspire and gladden the most despondent. Not much time was given to drink in the beauties of the place, as I had to go into harness[252] immediately upon arrival.

---

251 Killin Station, on the Killin Railway line, was closed in 1965. The arrangement Barrett describes was not completed because of the costly upgrades it required (Maxwell, 1919).

252 Return to work.

Since coming here I have had the pleasure of viewing the magnificent Falls of Acharn on the opposite of the Loch; have looked down onto Kenmore from Black Rock; and have viewed the surrounding country from the top of Drummond Hill. Such picturesqueness of mountain grandeur witnessed from these heights is indescribable, as it has to be seen to be fully appreciated. Ever-changing scenes on the landscape occur as sun beams and shadows o'erspread it, and as the shadowy grey mists roll down the mountains, an awe-thrilling sensation runs through ones veins.

With a sunshiny breeze raising white caps on the waves of the Loch, the water appears in its bluest transparency, presenting a scene only equalled by the blue waters of the Mediterranean. In its highest order is Nature's beauty displayed in this section of Scotland; and to me it is small wonder that so many pilgrimages are annually made by tourists to the Highlands. Why, the rippling of the waves breaking over the pebbly strand of Loch Tay is sufficient music in itself to awaken all dormant feelings of admiration for the beautiful works of a wondrous Creator.

We are to have a visit from Prime Minister Lloyd[253] tomorrow, and on Sunday a Brigadier-General of the Scottish Command is coming to Camp.

On the 15th inst., a fatal accident occurred, by which Private Gerald Hogan,[254] of Conception Bay, met an untimely end. He was engaged with his brother John in cross-cutting a blown down tree, when it suddenly started to roll down hill, and before Hogan could get clear he was caught by the roots of the tree and

---

253 Dr. William F. Lloyd, Prime Minister of Newfoundland from January 5, 1918, to May 20, 1919. Lloyd was in the UK for an extended period from June until October 1918, during which time he attended meetings of the Imperial War Cabinet and dealt with other colonial matters.

254 Private Gerald Hogan, NFC #8111, Northern Bay, son of Richard and Mary Lillie (Tucker) Hogan.

whirled around several times. When picked up it was found that the body was lifeless. The funeral with full military honours took place on Sunday afternoon, when the remains were laid to rest in the Kenmore burial ground.[255]

Kenmore is a rather quaint-looking place, and is said to be the model village of Scotland. When I get better acquainted with its surroundings I shall write you further about it and its surroundings, as well as about our work.

Kenmore, Perthshire, Scotland

• • •

Comrade Killed in Service

The death of Private Hogan was recorded in fuller detail by a fellow Conception Bay forester, Private James A. Power, NFC #8124, a labourer from Harbour Grace who had enlisted on May 11, 1917, at St. John's at the age of 36. Power was present at the Hospital Hut when the body of Private Hogan arrived for examination. In a letter home written August 18, 1918, a portion of which was printed in *The Harbour Grace Standard*, Power ("Comrade Killed," 1918) described the fatality and funeral.

A fatal accident happened in A Company's section of the woods on Friday [August 16th], when Gerald Hogan, a chap from Northern Bay, Bay de Verde, was killed by a tree, or rather the stump of a tree. Himself and his brother Jack were cutting up a windfall, that is, a tree blown down by the wind, and as they cut through the tree, the stump which was held by one root rolled suddenly

---

255 He is buried in grave 374, Kenmore, Aberfeldy. The gravestone was designed in the same fashion as that of Private Taylor, with a stylized timber log motif in the border and base.

over, snapped off the root and turned a double somersault. Hogan tried to get out of the way but the stump was too quick for him and coming down on top of him pinned him to the ground. He was killed instantly and his brother only just escaped as one of the moors[256] of the stump struck him in the back. It took thirty-five men to move the stump off poor Hogan.

They brought him to the Camp and placed him in the Hospital Hut, which I happened to be putting the finishing touches on at the time, and myself and the Medical Orderly (after the doctor had examined him) washed him and dressed him in a new uniform and laid him out. We had the Rosary[257] for him each night, and a crowd stopped up each night. The Officers gave orders to have tea for them at 12 o'clock each night. We had the Rosary for him this morning, and the Priest came from Grandtully this evening and we had a military funeral. The three Companies, A, B and C, paraded and the casket, which was a splendid one, was draped with the flags and placed on a four-wheel lorry and drawn to the cemetery about a mile away accompanied by a firing party and the full battalion and preceded by two pipers.

Though this is only a small place, the people were in from miles around 'til the graveyard was filled to overflowing.

Besides the brother who is here, Hogan has another brother, a prisoner of war,[258] and a brother at home in Northern Bay. (p. 2)

---

256 The lateral and sinker roots of a tree, which anchor or moor it in the ground.
257 Private Hogan refers here to the Holy Rosary, the Roman Catholic prayer arranged in five sets of ten decades. The Rosary is often recited at Catholic wakes.
258 Private Bernard J. Hogan, RNR #2252.

The funeral procession of Private Gerald Hogan,
August 18, 1918, Kenmore, Scotland.
(Courtesy of Ean Parsons)

• • •

1st Viscount Northcliffe Visits the NFC at Kenmore

Alfred Harmsworth, Viscount Northcliffe, was the owner (with his brother, Harold, Viscount Rothermere) of the ANDCo at Grand Falls, from where hundreds of the foresters were recruited. He visited the NFC at Kenmore on September 19, 1918. Northcliffe had been ill with influenza and bronchitis in early 1918 and complained of a growth in his throat that compromised his voice. He was in Scotland to rest and to consult with Major James Walker Downie, an esteemed throat specialist at the University of Glasgow[259] (Pound & Harmsworth, 1959; Bourne, 2015).

Northcliffe was well-known for his oratorical skills and his rousing speeches about the war, so Major Sullivan invited him to address the foresters

---

259 Downie was the author of *Clinical Manual of Diseases of the Throat*, published in 1894 by James MacLehose and Sons, Glasgow.

and, despite his voice limitations, he accepted. The speech is an example of Northcliffe's style as well as of the war rhetoric of the time; it was published in the United Kingdom in *The Daily Mail*, one of his own newspapers, and reprinted in Newfoundland in the November 1, 1918, edition of *The Evening Herald* ("Prussia Must Pay," 1918) and *The St. John's Daily Star* ("Address," 1918), from which this transcript was taken:

Praise of Newfoundland

Many of you have heard my war utterances as far back as the better part of a score of years. But neither you nor I could have realized that the youth of Newfoundland would one day, by some mysterious instinct, and with no selfish object, revisit the lands of their fathers, there to prepare for the crusade in France.

I have often been asked by my own folk as to the origin of the Newfoundlanders. You all know the authentic story of a noble Dane who, when bidding a well-known Prime Minister of Newfoundland to a smart London function, added to her card of invitation the word, "Please come in native dress, if possible" (laughter). The Newfoundland friends around me are mostly the sons of men whose forebearers came from Thomas Hardy's Wessex. They sailed from Poole Harbour and from Bristol, and their descendants today will find their character accurately described by Mr. Hardy in his books "The Woodlanders," "Far From the Madding Crowd," and "Under the Greenwood Tree," and the great array of works of genius in which Mr. Hardy has enshrined the people of the chief state of the ancient heptarchy.

Most Purely British

When these men of Wessex arrived in Newfoundland they found themselves to be contemporaries of Portuguese, Frenchmen, and Basques, who were also making their way to what was then called "the Isle," to fish for cod. More recently came the great migration of Irish to Newfoundland, and so, interwoven in the language of the Isle, are to be found not only ancient Wessex words preserved by Hardy and by Barnes,[260] the Wessex poet, but also many Irish words. Here and there in Newfoundland may be found descendants of the original French who settled there, and also those of some of the Red Indian invaders,[261] but on the whole the claim of Newfoundland to be the most purely British overseas community in the world is probably accurate. None of the King's far-flung island peoples rushed to his standard with greater zeal and rapidity. None have exceeded the valour of the Newfoundland troops who fought at Beaumont-Hamel. None are more determined that foul Prussia[262] shall be deposed from her position as the bully of the world.

The position of the war today is on the whole satisfactory, but there are some who forget the maxim inscribed on our barometers, "Slow come, slow go." That which has been preparing for nigh on 50 years following the gradual development of Prussianism[263] evoked by Frederick the Great is not going to collapse, as certain foolish people think. "Crumble" is the better word. Prussianism is crumbling on the Western Front today, but while the Kaiser's right hand is faltering on the west, his left hand is burgling in the east. While the arch-ventriloquist uses Karl of Austria as his vocal puppet, he is striving to arrange for the withdrawal of more divisions from Russia to face the British, French, and American divisions in France.

260 William Barnes.
261 A reference to the Beothuk, an Indigenous People who inhabited the Island. Northcliffe's description of the Beothuk as "invaders" is indicative of the colonial perspectives of the time.
262 The leading state of Imperial Germany.
263 A system of beliefs associated with Prussia that centred on extreme nationalism, ultra-efficiency, harsh discipline, militarism, and the ruthless pursuit of power and dominance.

False Optimism About U-boats

The question of the duration of the gradual crumbling process comes back to the question of ships. In this matter the Newfoundlanders here around me are assuredly helping to crumble Prussianism by providing timber that would otherwise have to come from Scandinavia or across the Atlantic—to come at a risk that is, in my opinion, too lightly minimized by our officials. You who have crossed the Atlantic know that the submarine is by no means at an end. True, it is being checked, but the U-boat is still steadily sinking valuable tonnage and valuable cargoes. All politicians would like you to believe that the submarine is finished because they like you to hear pleasant things and submarine news is heavily censored. From this results the general optimism which now surrounds that ugly topic. I have often thought that one of the worst evils of censorship is that it lulls or "dopes," as you boys say, the government and the people. Do not, I pray, let this false optimism about the submarine cause you to relax your efforts in getting that timber, which is one of the great necessities of war.

Every stick, as you call them, that is felled is one more plank in the bridge of victory. Few can desire peace more eagerly than those who face the submarine in that long, long journey across the Atlantic. It is this voyage which helps to give to Trans-Atlantic troops that grim and sober look which somewhat surprises those of us who suppose that the Americans, the Canadians, and the New Zealanders would go to war whistling ragtime.

Every tree that is felled by the axes wielded by woodsmen trained for generations in the vast forests of Newfoundland brings those Prussian thieves nearer to the seat of judgement, nearer to the prisoners' dock, where they will assuredly stand to await their sentence. Every tree you cut down brings nearer the day when the world will hold the German railways and the German minds in part payment for the illimitable and horrible destruction of the cities, villages, and churches or France and Belgium.

Town for Town

I have never wavered in my conviction that peace will be dictated by the entente allies in Berlin or thereabouts, but it will not be necessary for the Allied armies to fight their way to the Prussian capital. Remember that Germany is not a homogeneous country but an upstart confederation of peoples who greatly dislike each other. Once the Entente forces enter Germany, as they certainly will, the white flag already hoisted by Austria will be sent up by a score of petty courts. Prussia, which is as much hated in Dresden and Munich as in Great Britain and her proud Dominions, will then stand almost alone. Her satellites and parasites will, like Austria, endeavour to make peace.

We must stand behind our gay and gallant Prime Minister, Mr. Lloyd George (cheers), President Wilson[264] (cheers), Monsieur Clemenceau[265] (cheers) and Signor Orlando[266] (cheers), not forgetting that noble and pathetic pair, the King and Queen of the Belgiums[267] (cheers). We must see to it that Prussia pays town for town, village for village, ship for ship, jewel for jewel, picture for picture, and dollar for dollar. That is, she must pay full compensation for all that she has gorged and stolen, sacked and burned, drunken as she is with lust over her paper victories. (A voice: "And shivering in paper clothes") (laughter). Prussia will be reluctant to yield but yield she must to the will of the civilized peoples of the world fighting for the liberties of mankind (cheers). (p. 3)

264 Woodrow Wilson, President of the United States, 1913 to 1921.
265 Georges Clemenceau, Prime Minister of France, 1906 to 1909 and again from 1917 to 1920.
266 Vittorio Emanuele Orlando, Prime Minister of Italy, 1917 to 1919.
267 King Albert I and Queen Elisabeth.

In a letter to Major Sullivan dated November 9, 1918, Minister of Militia J.R. Bennett (1918) commented that "it was most complimentary to your Corps to have Viscount Northcliffe pay you a visit and express such high praise on the work of the Forestry Companies and such complimentary reference to our Country" (p. 2).

• • •

A Desperate Need for Men, to the Very End

On October 17, 1918, another draft of foresters arrived at Kenmore from Newfoundland. Frustration with the continued small size of the NFC and the many obstacles to the efficient completion of work at Kenmore had propelled Major Sullivan to write to the Minister of Militia on October 3, 1918, to express these concerns. Foreseeing an end to the war, Sullivan recommended to Minister Bennett that recruits for the Regiment in Newfoundland be sent directly to the NFC at Kenmore and that Regiment troops at Winchester awaiting deployment to the Front also be sent to Scotland. The former suggestion was not received well by Bennett, who believed that, in the wake of conscription, such executive changes to troop deployment would be questioned in Newfoundland. Bennett (1918) wrote: "[C]ompelling men to enlist for fighting purposes and finding they are not required for same, and to transfer them to the Forestry, or other work, would, I fear, call forth every opposition" (p. 1). He agreed, however, that 300 troops at Winchester could transfer to the NFC if they so wished, but this proposed voluntary transfer was later vetoed by authorities in London. Two days after Bennett's letter was written, the war ended. The NFC agreed to stay at Kenmore to mill the remaining timber already felled at Drummond Hill, a job that took an additional three months.

THE FORESTRY CORPS[268]

November 27, 1918

Many and varied are the conjectures as to when we may be getting away from here; but it is not likely we shall be long here after the signing of peace. Quite a number of men are being transferred to us from the Royal Newfoundland Regiment, and by next week we expect to have our ranks increased by an addition of 200. Most of these will be men from the last draft from Newfoundland, who had not been over to France.[269]

The men are now working about 8½ hours a day and only half of Saturday. This somewhat lightens their labour. There is not much vantage gained by the half-holiday at this season as men cannot go far to enjoy themselves.

Our new recreation hut has been opened and nightly the sound of violin, guitar, piano and other musical instruments awaken the stillness of the hills. Refreshments and teas are served there nightly, while next door is the wet canteen where one need never go dry though stony broke.

We have been spared the depredations of the "flu"[270] which has been so epidemic all over the continent.

Three mills are now in running order, and are sawing up logs at a rate faster than they can be taken to the mills. Great care

---

268 *The Western Star*, January 15, 1919, p. 2. Also published in *The Evening Advocate*, January 17, 1919.

269 At a November 26, 1918, meeting in London of the Provisional Advisory Committee on Demobilization, this arrangement, earlier approved by Bennett (1918), was deemed unfeasible (Newfoundland Contingent Provisional Advisory Committee, 1918).

270 Barrett refers to the so-called Spanish flu. The 1918 influenza pandemic killed 3 to 5 percent of the world's population. On the Island, less than 1 percent of the population died of the flu. In Labrador, however, 10 percent of the population died (Higgins, 2007). For an account of the 1918 flu in Labrador, see Budgell (2018).

has to be exercised, and an enormous amount of hard labour expended in getting the timber from the hillside. It is not so much in the getting down as in preventing it from coming down too fast. For tricks that are vain these logs have a way of their own, and if not properly checked they are liable to run down the hill and go into the loch or anywhere they are not wanted.

The daily climbing of the hill is beginning to tell upon most of the men who go there, as a constitution equal to the highest tempered steel is unable to bear up under the strain.

Kenmore, Perthshire, Scotland

Loch Tay and a denuded Drummond Hill, with Ben Lawers in the background and Taymouth Castle in the right foreground, ca. 1920.
(Courtesy of Aberfeldy Museum)

NEWFOUNDLAND FORESTERS COMING HOME[271]
Interesting Letter from J.A. Barrett

Early January, 1919

The granting of 12 days leave to all the boys for Christmas has been gladly hailed by all. The first bunch to get away from our Camp left there on the 16th, and I was among the number. It gave me an opportunity to see quite a few places and to spend Christmas with new friends.

My stay at Edinburgh was pleasantly and profitably spent, because I availed of the opportunity of seeing quite a few bonny and historical places. The chief centre of interest was the Castle, which in 1915 was garrisoned by the Newfoundland Regiment.[272] It is a quaint old spot, standing on a hill overlooking the capital city of Edinburgh. The Esplanade is where the troops are drilled and was once known as "Heading Hill", as it was there that witches and heretics were burned and state prisoners executed. The Castle gateway with moat and drawbridge, above which is the half-moon battery where the time gun is daily fired, Mary Queen of Scots' apartments, the State Prison where the Argyles (father and son) were confined before execution, the Jewel Room, the Reception Room, and the Armoury Room where battle-torn flags of past ages and all styles of ancient Scottish armour are to be seen were some of the most interesting and notable places and things seen there. I may say in passing that the Crown Room contains the crown, sceptre, sword of state, and Lord Treasurer's rod of office. The crown is said to have been worn by

---

271 *The Western Star*, February 2, 1919, p. 1.
272 The Regiment was the first overseas unit—and the only non-Scottish one—to be assigned to guard Edinburgh Castle. To commemorate these honours, the Royal Canadian Legion placed a plaque at the Castle in 1954.

Bruce,[273] but additions were made at later periods. The sword of state was presented to King James IV by Pope Julius II in 1507, and the sceptre was made for James V in Paris. The Regalia was lost sight of for 110 years, they having been locked up in an oak chest in the Crown Room until discovered by Sir Walter Scott. In Queen Mary's little bedroom where her only son, James VI, was born in 1566, part of the original ceiling has been preserved.

To enter the Castle one crosses the drawbridge over the old moat and then passes through the new battlemented gateway, representing the former outer part. The steep winding causeway leads first to the ancient Portcullis Gate underneath the Argyle Tower. This was the Gate Tower constructed by David II. The walls vary from ten to seventeen feet in thickness.

From Castle Hill a most beautiful panoramic view can be obtained on a clear day, as there is a radius of forty miles visible in nearly every direction.

Unfortunately for me, Holyrood Palace was closed to visitors during my stay at Edinburgh. But viewing it from the street, one beholds a handsome castellated building, the oldest part of which was built by James V in 1525. Owing to suffragette outbreaks[274] a strong guard is continually on duty there.

As an educational centre, Edinburgh has been famed for nearly two centuries, and within its confines are to be seen a

---

273 Robert the Bruce reigned from 1306 to 1329; he was known as the father of Scottish independence.

274 Suffragettes adopted a militant approach to gaining the franchise that distinguished them from suffragists. Their campaigns included iconoclasm, window smashing, arson, and bombing. Following suffragette damage at the Tower of London, palaces in London and Holyrood Palace in Edinburgh were closed temporarily and assigned increased security to discourage attacks ("Holyrood Palace Closed," 1913). Although some women in the UK secured the vote in early 1918, full franchise (including parity with male voters) was not legislated until 1928. For a discussion of suffragette iconoclasm, see Scott (2016).

number of schools, colleges and academies and to the Medical School students flock from all parts of the world. In the Old University,[275] there are forty professors distributed over the six faculties of Divinity, Law, Medicine, Music, Arts, Science. Each session there are about 3,000 students enrolled.

The Museum and Art Gallery contain rare gems illustrative of the progress of civilization and culture in Scotland. In the National Portrait Gallery are to be seen several instruments of torture used against the Covenanters,[276] the ancient Scottish, John Knox's pulpit, and other rare antiquities.

The monuments erected to Sir Walter Scott and Lord Nelson occupy prominent positions. By a narrow winding stairway, the top of either may be reached, from where magnificent views can be obtained. The Scott monument is 200 feet high, and is centrally located on Princes Street. On Carlton Hill is Nelson's monument, raised to a height of 102 feet. At its base are three cannons captured in the Crimean war.

The Botanic Garden, twenty-seven acres in extent, is beautifully laid out. In it is a palm-house 100 feet in length and 70 feet in height. During each summer session of the University of Edinburgh, four or five hundred students attend lectures given by the Professor of Botany.

The Zoological Garden is situated on a beautiful estate a few minutes' ride from the heart of the city. It occupies seventy-four acres, and is expertly set out. There is a splendid collection of birds and animals living in natural surroundings. On the premises is a specially constructed building for the acclimatization of birds and animals brought from other countries.

---

275 Barrett refers here to Old College, the original site of the University of Edinburgh. Founded in 1583, the university is among the oldest in the English-speaking world.

276 The Covenanters were Scottish Presbyterians who were part of a 17th-century movement that protested the Stuart belief in Divine Rule and the monarch's spiritual leadership of the church.

St. Giles Cathedral is to Edinburgh what Westminster is to London. It was the first parochial church in Edinburgh, and its history dates from the early part of the twelfth century. Being on several occasions partly destroyed by fire, yet the sacred edifice was quickly restored after each accident. The architectural designs are wonderful, and the carvings in the Thistle Chapel are most beautifully executed.

The largest railway station in the United Kingdom is the Waverly, in Edinburgh. It covers 23 acres of ground, of which 11 acres are under roof. It has eight main lines and fifty-six roads and sidings. The total length of all the platform is 4660 yards, or about 2¾ miles.

One of the greatest triumphs of modern engineering is the Forth Bridge.[277] Its total length is one and a fifth of a mile, and it is the highest bridge in the world, being 450 feet from base to highest point. Fifty thousand tons of steel were used in this gigantic structure. It takes 250 tons of paint and 35,000 gallons of oil to paint the work. Painting goes on continually, and it takes three years to cover the structure from end to end. At St. Margaret's Hope, on the north side of the bridge, is situated the Forth Naval Base, and in this stretch of water are to be seen the guard ships of the Forth, and a large fleet of cruisers, destroyers, and other ships.

Whilst at Leith[278] I visited two of the German submarines. They are somewhat cigar-shaped, the larger one measuring 200 feet in length. The interior of these boats is occupied with such a mass of intricate machinery that there is scarcely room enough for two persons to pass each other.

I would like to speak of other interesting points visited, but time is limited; and as I expect to be back to Newfoundland again

277 A railway bridge that crosses the Firth of Forth. It was designated a UNESCO World Heritage site in 2015.
278 Port of Edinburgh, in the north of the city.

pretty soon, I shall then be able to give you a longer narrative. Word has been received from London that we are to be sent home soon, the first draft probably getting away by the end of January, and perhaps all of us to be out of this by the first of March.

Our lads who were in camp for Christmas had a jolly good time. A great feast was prepared for their dinner; then there was fruit, beer, gifts of tobacco, cigarettes, socks, woolen scarves and caps. In the afternoon, they were treated to a cinema show, and at night there was a concert followed by a dance. Since then there has been an illustrated lecture given free, and on the 6th inst. there will be another free cinema show for all.

Kenmore, Perthshire, Scotland

RQMS John A. Barrett, ca. 1919.
(Courtesy of The Rooms Provincial
Archives Division, VA 125-15)

Commendations . . . and Concerns

As the NFC prepared to leave Scotland in January 1919, letters of commendation to Major Sullivan and Mayson Beeton arrived from various departments that oversaw the work of the Companies during their time in Scotland. At the request of Minister Bennett, these letters, which were included in the Report of the Department of Militia ("Report," 1919, pp. 115–19), were reprinted in full in the March 18, 1919, edition of *The Evening Telegram*. The four letters quoted in this section are from *The Telegram* ("Further Appreciation," 1919).

In his letter of January 15, 1919, Colonel Commanding W.E. Gordon, Number One District, Perthshire, wrote to Mayson Beeton to wish the departing draft farewell, noting:

> I desire to express to one and all my thanks for their loyal support, their exemplary conduct and bearing, and their labours on behalf of the Empire throughout the period during which I have had the Newfoundland Forestry Corps in the District under my command, an honour of which I am and will always remain deeply conscious. (p. 9)

Sir John Stirling Maxwell, Assistant Controller of Timber Supply, wrote Major Sullivan on January 31, 1919, to express thanks on behalf of the Scotland branch of his Department, and included these remarks:

> You have battled two of the most difficult operations which have come within the scope of the Department's work in Scotland. . . . The 3,000-foot chute which you constructed at Craigvinean will long be remembered as marking an epoch in forest utilization in Scotland. If it had not been for the difficulty of arranging matters with the Railway Company at Killin, I have no doubt that the floating of the timber down Loch Tay, as you proposed, would have lent similar distinction to your work at Kenmore. . . . Your work has been of the greatest value to this country at a time when timber

was sorely needed for war purposes and labour impossible to obtain. . . . I am delighted to hear that it is proposed to erect a permanent monument to [the Foresters'] work at Craigvinean. (p. 9)

The Controller of Timber Supply for the United Kingdom, J.B. Ball, wrote to Mayson Beeton on February 16, 1919, to comment on the officers of the NFC, stating:

I give myself the pleasure of putting upon record my very high appreciation of the work of the Corps, and more especially of the services rendered by those responsible for its organization and direction, Major Sullivan, Major Baird, and Captain Ross, in particular. The promptitude with which the Corps was raised, and the concurrence of all concerned to do their utmost to assist the Old Country by developing the production of timber in Britain, deserves to go down into history along with many patriotic achievements of Britain's Oldest Colony. (p. 9)

Finally, on February 21, 1919, Mayson Beeton wrote the following to Major Sullivan:

As godfather, so to speak, of the Corps, I made promises on its behalf to the Controller before its arrival in this country, that it would prove equal to tackling the hardest proposition which might be selected for the operations of the Force. It was certainly given one of the hardest operations undertaken anywhere in the United Kingdom and carried through the first with complete success, and was well on its way with the second with even better prospects of success, when the Armistice came and with it Demobilization. Yours has been the main burden of responsibility, and therefore, the credit of achieving success, and you have been most ably and loyally seconded, by Major Baird, in particular, and by your officers generally, each in their sphere of work and responsibility. (p. 9)

The letters from officials in the United Kingdom offered strong endorsement for the work of the NFC and an appreciation of their wartime service. At home, however, some expressed concern that the foresters were under-appreciated and might not receive fair recognition. Days before the arrival home of a large contingent of the NFC aboard the SS *Corsican*, at which time it remained unclear if foresters would receive the war service gratuity available to members of the Regiment, an editorial appeared in *The Evening Telegram* ("The Responsibilities," 1919) that reminded the public of the Country's obligation to all who served, and drew particular attention to the foresters:

> Their work, though not so spectacular as that of the fighting battalions, has been of no small importance in aiding the decision of victory, and their performance has been of such a nature that it has brought forth the encomiums of those in authority, who have repeatedly stated that there were no men more adaptable to any labour calling for the use of tools than the boys from Newfoundland. We knew this when they went over, but the people of the British Isles did not know that the lads from the oldest Colony were the handymen of the Empire, and capable of turning their hands to any trade or profession without previous training. We owe it to the men of the Forestry, just as much as we do to the combatant units, to make ample provision for their future, or at least to assist them in taking up where they left off. They are part and parcel of the Royal Newfoundland Regiment and, as such, have to be considered. (p. 4)

Following Minister Bennett's announcement that the war service gratuity would be available to foresters, the editor of *The Evening Telegram* wrote again ("The Forestry Battalion," 1919):

> [T]here is another khaki-clad division whose services during the great struggle were of a very high order, but for whom, while they worked, industriously and unostentatiously, there was little, if any,

praise or laudation. Nevertheless, their part in the war game was none the less important and their duties none the less imperative, though their form of service did not oblige them to go into the battle line. . . . They were in reality the hewers of wood. For them the cross cut saw and the broad bitted axe, yet with these tools they kept the armies supplied with the products of the forest, and in so doing contributed in no small measure to the final success of the Allied arms. And now their reward is coming. Recognition of their invaluable services, though somewhat belated, is at length being made. (p. 4)

• • •

The Last NFC Fatality in Scotland

Private Arthur H. Wyatt, NFC #8130, a lumberer and blacksmith, was 42 and a resident of Traytown when he enlisted on May 10, 1917, at Grand Falls. Wyatt's parents, Catherine and William, a blacksmith, and several of their children (including Arthur) had immigrated to Newfoundland from Prince Edward Island in the mid-1870s, just after that colony became a province of Canada. Arthur married Mabel Julia Pike of Harbour Grace at St. John's prior to going overseas to serve with the NFC.

On Tuesday, December 10, 1918, Private Wyatt went missing from his camp at Kenmore. Search parties trawled the River Tay and combed the surrounding hillsides for days, but there was no trace of Wyatt. Months later, on April 4, 1919, workers at the estate of Taymouth Castle spotted a body washed aground on an area of the Tay called The Bulwarks. One of the workers waded to the spot and identified the remains as Private Wyatt ("Kenmore Mystery Solved, 1919).[279]

---

279 See also "Perthshire Mystery Solved," (1919). In both newspaper accounts of the recovery of Wyatt's body, he was incorrectly identified as a member of the Canadian Forestry Corps.

By the time the body was recovered, the camps at Kenmore were closing and most of the Newfoundland foresters had returned home, among them Wyatt's brother William, NFC #8185, who was demobilized at St. John's on March 10, 1919. By the end of March, only 69 men still remained at Kenmore to complete camp closure, including the foresters' scribe, RQMS Barrett; unexpectedly, they also arranged Wyatt's burial. Private Wyatt was interred with Private Gerald Hogan, NFC #8111 of Northern Bay, at Kenmore Parish Churchyard, Kenmore, Perthshire.[280] .

Gravestone of Private Gerald Hogan and Private
Arthur Wyatt, Kenmore Parish Churchyard, Kenmore.
(Courtesy of Michael Pretty, Trail of the Caribou Research Group)

---

280 Grave reference 374, Kenmore, Aberfeldy.

The announcement of Wyatt's death in Newfoundland was published on April 7, 1919, in *The St. John's Daily Star*: "Found drowned in the River Tay, Taymouth Castle, Scotland—8130, Private Arthur H. Wyatt" ("Late List," 1919, p. 7).

• • •

Scottish War Brides

In one of his earliest letters (July 16, 1917), Barrett speculated on the attachments forming between some of the foresters and Scottish women: "Don't be surprised if some of our confirmed bachelors join the Benedicts before they return to the Homeland." These early musings about marriages between Newfoundland foresters and Scottish women were confirmed throughout the time during which the NFC served in Scotland. The "war brides," as the women who married war service personnel were called, often immigrated with the men to their homelands. They were given special note in *The Daily Mail* of London, in an article about the departure of troops from Liverpool in February 1919 ("Scottish War Brides," 1919):

> Vociferous good-byes were shouted from the crowded decks of the Canadian Pacific liner *Corsican* yesterday as she left the Mersey for St. John's with 1,100 officers and men of the Newfoundland Regiment returning home. All were enthusiastic at returning to their work as lumbermen or fishermen and at the pulp and paper mill of the Anglo-Newfoundland Development Company, at Grand Falls, which supplies *The Daily Mail* with paper. In Perthshire, several hundred men were working on forestry, and several soldiers were taking back Scotch brides. None was more elated than the newly married couples at the prospects awaiting them in Newfoundland. (p. 8)

Only one-quarter of the Newfoundland foresters were married at enlistment. There were 30 known marriages[281] of Newfoundland foresters and women of the United Kingdom—most especially, Scotland—during or shortly after the war. In most cases, the women emigrated with their husbands, although all couples did not remain in Newfoundland. Approximately a third of the couples would emigrate again, most settling in Canada or the USA. The stories of these wartime migrations and changes—for the women who sailed to Newfoundland and the men who remained in Scotland—are another little-known aspect of the history of war as it relates to Newfoundland and Labrador.

• • •

Balance of Troops Departs Glasgow

Barrett's final letter to *The Western Star* was published as a summary only on June 25, 1919 ("Balance of Troops," 1919). In it, he detailed that the last of the foresters left Kenmore on May 10 and Captain Ross on May 13. Barrett left on June 2 for London, where he was attached to the staff of the Pay and Record Office. Barrett finally departed the UK from Scotland with the last draft of the Regiment, Naval Reserve, and Forestry Companies, approximately 500 in total, on June 24, 1919, aboard SS *Cassandra*, which took a week to cross the Atlantic to Newfoundland.

On that day, the docks at Glasgow were crowded with appreciative Scots, including the Mayor and Councillors, who came to bid farewell:

> On behalf of the citizens of Glasgow the Mayor addressed the troops and paid high encomiums to the splendid service performed by the Colonials in the Great War. He wished them all God-speed and a safe return to their homes and loved ones. Three rousing cheers were then given by the troops for the Mayor and citizens of

---

281 Marriage-status information was available for 489 foresters.

Newfoundland soldiers board the SS *Cassandra*
at Glasgow, June 24, 1919.
(Courtesy of The Rooms Provincial Archives Division, VA 125-16.1)

Glasgow for their kind wishes and for their liberal donation of 50,000 cigarettes. After the singing of "Auld Lang Syne," and while the Scottish bands played "Britannia Rules the Waves," the SS *Cassandra* moved out of dock into the Clyde on her way to sea with the last draft of the Royal Newfoundland Regiment. ("Glasgow Appreciation," 1919, p. 8)

The *Cassandra* arrived in St. John's on July 1. As the last forester to arrive home, Barrett's return was noted in both *The Evening Telegram* of July 2 and *The Western Star* of July 16, the latter ("Back From Scotland," 1919) also announcing his return to his home of Curling following disembarkation at St. John's:

RQMS Barrett, of the Newfoundland Forestry Companies, returned to Curling on Thursday [July 10th]. Mr. Barrett enlisted in April, 1917, and went Overseas with the first draft of the unit. He was attached to the Quartermaster's department, and for the first few months was doing single handed the work of Quartermaster, Storeman, Ration Corporal, and also Orderly Room work. As a recognition of his efficiency he was promoted to Regimental Quartermaster Sergeant, and performed his duties to the satisfaction of the three companies of the unit. His work and the climate of Old Scotia surely agreed with him, for he is looking the picture of health. All his old friends are pleased to welcome him back again. (p. 2)

3

CONCLUSION

Gilbert Bayes' model for the forester and fisher,
National War Memorial, St. John's, 1923.
(Courtesy of The Rooms Provincial Archives Division, B 20-137)

Official commendations indicated that the Newfoundland foresters distinguished themselves in Scotland through their skills, efficiencies, and creative methods in lumbering. The NFC was a unit of the Regiment; its distinctions added to the reputation of the Regiment, which had won praise for its wartime service. But after the war, grumblings about anticipated, perceived, or real inequities of treatment expressed by members of both the NFC and the Regiment pointed to clearly defined hierarchies of value regarding each service. Parity in support, recognition, and commemoration were ongoing concerns in a country severely burdened by the fiscal impact of war participation.[1]

In the winter of 1919, as drafts of the foresters returned to Newfoundland, *The Evening Telegram* featured two editorials highlighting the contribution of the foresters and the country's responsibility to provide for them to the same extent as the other units. In the first, the editor[2] ("The Responsibilities," 1919) argued that the foresters "should be placed on the same basis with regard to repatriation and other allowances as the men of the Regiment who saw active service on the Continent, and the men of the Naval Reserve, who so gallantly did their part on the Seven Seas" (p. 4). The second editorial

---

1   For a brief overview of wartime and postwar economies in Newfoundland, see Higgins (2009).

2   C.T. James.

("The Forestry Battalion," 1919) celebrated recognition of the foresters following the Colonial Secretary's confirmation of Minister Bennett's recommendation that the foresters be paid the war service gratuity at the same rate as Regiment soldiers, a rescinding of his earlier recommendation to the contrary (Bennett, 1919).

There was also perceived inequity regarding postwar clothing allowances and the awarding of medals. One forester wrote to *The Evening Telegram* using the pseudonym Discharged Forester (1919) and expressed concern about disparities regarding "pay and other items" between the NFC and the Regiment. He cited a three-to-one ratio in clothing allowance amounts for the Regiment and the NFC. He stated, "I don't mean to say [foresters] should get as much, but they are simply forgotten about" (p. 8).

In another instance, an officer of the Regiment complained to Officer of Records Lieutenant H.C. Janes, RNR #109 / #0–308, and threatened to return his medals, citing what he believed were discrepancies between his own qualifications as one who served in a theatre of war and those of the NFC awardees.[3] In his reply, Janes (1921) wrote that "the feelings you express in your letter in regard to the Forestry Corps personnel are felt not only by yourself but also by every individual of the Regiment" (p. 1). Despite the fact that the foresters met the criteria for the service medals they received, some members of the Regiment questioned the awarding of any medals to foresters. Such discontent was likely exacerbated by the issuing of medals to foresters that were marked "Royal Newfoundland Regiment"; the medals were recalled for reissue, with replacements marked "Newfoundland Forestry Companies" (Rendell, 1921).

The Great War Veterans' Association, formed during the war, was the key advocate for the postwar care and advancement of demobilized soldiers, sailors, and foresters who had served overseas. It sought "to perpetuate the close and kindly ties of mutual service in the Great War" (Great War Veterans' Association, 1918, p. 3), to ensure appropriate commemoration, to

---

3   All members of the NFC who served overseas received the British War Medal. Sergeants Andrew Ball, Enos Lane, and Philip Morey were also awarded the Meritorious Service Medal ("Report," 1920, p. 18).

fundraise, and to provide for the wellbeing of its members. Another of its key aims (Great War Veterans' Association, 1918) was

> to ensure that provision is made for the due care of the sick, wounded and needy among those who have served, including reasonable pensions, employment for such as are capable, soldiers' homes, medical care and proper provision for dependent families of enlisted men, and also for such further educational or vocational training as the needs of any returned soldier or sailor may render desirable. (p. 4).

It was not long, however, before the realities of a postwar economic downturn set in for a country that had invested in the war to an extent that was incommensurate with its size or fiscal capacity and whose under-diversified economy left it vulnerable in a competitive postwar trade context (Hiller & O'Brien, 2019). The care and support of veterans became an increasing challenge in a deepening economic crisis. Along with the casualties and costs of waging war, the end of the fighting coincided with the influenza pandemic. Tuberculosis cases were also increasing among the population.

Still, Newfoundland's residents sought to regain a semblance of life beyond the shadow of the war. Many activities that had been suspended during the conflict now resumed. At least two were historically noteworthy, but for very different reasons. A competition to complete the first non-stop trans-Atlantic flight, begun in 1913 that had been put on hold during the war, resumed in spring of 1919; in mid-June, aviators John Alcock and Arthur Whitten Brown successfully flew from St. John's to Galway, Ireland (Higgins, 2012), placing Newfoundland's capital city at the centre of a historic moment in aviation. The St. John's Regatta had also been suspended during the war; it resumed in summer of 1919 with a special Victory Regatta on Quidi Vidi Lake. To mark the celebrations, the Prince of Wales, His Royal Highness Edward Albert, who would later become King Edward VIII, visited the city and attended a morning race. For former NFC members, these victory celebrations turned to tragedy, however. At midday, Sergeant Charles Peters, NFC #8400, of

St. John's, a 41-year-old oarsman on the *Nellie R* of the Reid Newfoundland Company, drowned during the Mercantile race when the boat was swamped at the turn ("Victory Regatta Ends Tragically," 1919).

COMMEMORATING THOSE WHO SERVED

After the war, at both local and national levels, there was much debate about how best to commemorate war sacrifice and service. In Scotland, the renaming of a site near Craigvinean in honour of the NFC, as mentioned by Davidson (1918a) and, later, Maxwell ("Further Appreciation," 1919), never materialized. In December 1918, months after the NFC departed Craigvinean and a few weeks after the war ended, the Duke of Atholl wrote to Mayson Beeton, apparently in response to a suggestion by Beeton himself, to support a proposal for a cairn to honour their work (Atholl, 1918): "I'm all for a Newfoundland cairn. I'll get hold of Sullivan and we'll suggest a spot to you. There ought to be an inscription, I think, on one big block. This sort of thing, the rougher the better" (p. 1). Atholl included a sketch of what he had in mind—a pyramid-shaped cairn and plaque—but the memorial was never built.

In Newfoundland, the NPA and the GWVA endorsed two commemorations, one conventional and one "living" monument. The former was Newfoundland's National[4] War Memorial, which was unveiled on July 1, 1924. The location chosen was King's Beach, close to Furness Withy Wharf, the embarkation and disembarkation site of those who served outside Newfoundland in the First World War.

The National War Memorial monument includes five figures: at the top is a woman, with sword and torch, facing forward (south)—she is the nation in victory and liberty. To her right, facing away and to the west, is a sailor with a spyglass, representing the Royal Naval Reserve; to her left, facing away and

---

4   At the time, Newfoundland was a country, thus the reference to a "national" monument.

to the east, is a soldier with a rifle, the Royal Newfoundland Regiment representative. Below them all and directly beneath a large cross, standing together and facing forward, are a logger with axe and peavie, representing the Newfoundland Forestry Companies, and a fisher, in oilskins, symbolizing those who served in the Merchant Navy. The top three figures were completed by F.V. Blundstone; the fisher and forester by Gilbert Hayes.

The National War Memorial, St. John's, ca. 1924.
(Courtesy of Archives and Special Collections, Geography
Collection 05.05.137, Memorial University of Newfoundland)

Many elements of the monument were contested throughout its design phase, during which English sculptor Captain Basil Gotto, who also designed Newfoundland's Caribou monuments,[5] was influential. But the relationship between Gotto and Lieutenant Colonel Nangle, President of the GWVA and the man who oversaw the process, acrimoniously dissolved on issues of cost

---

5   Battlefield monuments in the form of a caribou were erected at five sites of key engagement for the Regiment: Beaumont-Hamel, Gueudecourt, Masnières, Monchy-le-Preux, and Courtrai. A sixth Caribou monument was erected at Bowring Park, St. John's.

and time overruns. Additionally, Gotto somehow usurped the original designer, W.H. Greene.[6] Nangle contested many of the design elements: he did not like the circular stairs on each side of the monument; he objected to the sailor holding a gun (it was replaced by the spyglass); and neither the forester nor the fisher was part of Nangle's vision for the monument.

Commander Anthony MacDermott of the Royal Naval Reserve was a go-between trying to align Nangle and Gotto. A year before the official unveiling, on July 23, 1923, he wrote Nangle to discuss a fisher figure that Gotto was designing for the monument. Nangle (1923) wrote back: "I have no idea of putting a fisherman on the Memorial" (p. 1). MacDermott (1923) reported that Gotto wanted the fisher to represent "a Newfoundlander engaged in his usual occupation in times of peace, hearing the call to arms" (p. 2). He added that, for his part, regardless of whose idea it was, he was unsure of what the figure was meant to express:

> The Newfoundlanders do not serve in the Mercantile Marine to any very great extent outside the fishing—and fish-carrying—business. During the war, numbers of Newfoundlanders were serving on board merchant ships as gun crews, but as they wore no distinctive costume and were just as other able seamen of the Royal Navy similarly employed, they are already represented by the figure of the blue-jacket.[7] (pp. 2–3)

The unveiling timeline of July 1, 1924, was pressing, however, so both Nangle and MacDermott agreed the fisher figure would remain—but on a lower level of the monument and to represent the Merchant Mariners. Nangle (1923) noted: "I would balance this [fisher figure] on the other side by putting in a statue of a forester" (pp. 1–2). Gotto was fired in September 1923

---

6   Archival records related to this stage of development of the National War Memorial are scant. See Bormanis (2010) for a discussion of the building of the Newfoundland war memorials in Europe, in particular at Beaumont-Hamel, and in Newfoundland.

7   A sailor in the navy.

but his influence over the design remained, as did Nangle's afterthought of a forester figure. As a result, and ironically, the foresters hold a prominent position on the monument, if not in public memory—unlike the Canadian National War Memorial, in which the Canadian Forestry Corps is represented near the back in a series of figures representing several support services.

Simultaneous with the development of the National War Memorial, plans for a living memorial—an institution of higher education, which had been discussed and debated in the country for several decades prior to the war (MacLeod, 1990)—were also emerging. Increased cooperation in the postwar period among Christian clergy, who controlled education in Newfoundland's denominationally based system, created the conditions for the realization of what became a memorial educational building built on Parade Street, St. John's, as a living commemoration of the fallen of the Great War.[8] Memorial University College, as it was initially known, first opened as a Normal School for teacher training in 1924. At this writing almost a century later, Memorial University of Newfoundland is an internationally renowned multi-campus post-secondary institution. Its outstanding research and archival facilities were essential in the development of this project to detail and honour the Newfoundland Forestry Companies.

THE NEWFOUNDLAND FORESTRY COMPANIES AND THE GREAT WAR

Through my research on the forestry sector of Newfoundland and Labrador, I have sought to challenge its tenuous and marginal place in the collective memory of labour and culture in this province. The dominant narrative of the settler fishing culture prevails to the near exclusion of accounts of other ways

---

8   For an account of the establishment of Memorial University College, see MacLeod (1990). For autobiographical accounts of the early University on Elizabeth Avenue, see various essays in Riggins and Buchanan (2019).

of working and living here, and of the cultural legacies that are related to them. Similarly, in historical narratives of war and commemorative practices, here—as elsewhere—combat service eclipses contributions made by other services. In a recruitment essay for the NFC published in *Newfoundland Magazine*, Lieutenant David Thistle (1917), NFC #0–181, predicted:

> The generations unborn will undoubtedly honour and bless the names and memory of the Newfoundland Forestry Companies, as well as those of the Navy and Army, because they will understand better than we do the urgency which excited the greatness of the cause, and the horrors that the free nations and peoples of the earth were delivered from. (p. 33)

In Newfoundland and Labrador, however, war remembrance centres predominantly on the First Battalion of the Newfoundland Regiment and, in particular, those who died at Beaumont-Hamel during the Battle of the Somme. Commemoration of the massive losses incurred there overshadows remembrance of other battles and campaigns, and other forms of service, including that of the foresters.

During the war, the Beaumont-Hamel-focussed character of war remembrance in Newfoundland was a result of the presiding government's desire, supported by the St. John's elite, to maintain the Newfoundland Regiment despite the grievous impact of the losses at that battle. There was an orchestrated effort to reinvent its meaning—from senseless slaughter to "glorious tragedy" (Harding, 2006) and "noble martyrdom" (Cadigan, 2016, para. 1). On July 1, 1917, as the Newfoundland Patriotic Association was holding the first of what would become yearly Memorial Day ceremonies, the initial draft of the NFC, which had arrived in Scotland only three weeks earlier, was building its first camp high on Craigvinean Hill to begin the work of felling and milling timber. If the dominant cultural memory of the Great War in Newfoundland had its roots in those early days of commemoration, so did the marginalization of the cultural memory of the NFC and other wartime services.

The idea of a Newfoundland forestry unit that had been devised by Morris and Beeton in London in the winter of 1917, a year after the first Canadian Forestry Corps recruits had left Canada for the UK, was one more demonstration of government zeal to support the war effort. Against a backdrop of increasing debates about and threats of conscription, recruitment for the NFC began in the spring of 1917 at a time when problems with recruitment for the Regiment had already reached a head. Despite adjusting the physical requirements for the recruits, the number of new enlistments failed to keep up with the ever-increasing casualties. In Canada at the same time, enlistments were also faltering—after the Battle of Vimy Ridge, enlistments were insufficient to maintain the size of the Canadian Expeditionary Force (Sharpe, 2015). Canada quickly introduced conscription in response, a full year earlier than Newfoundland.

The establishment of the NFC was one way to increase enlistment from the outports. Most woods workers lived in coastal and interior communities far from the capital city. They were the very population who, it was believed, were failing to "do their bit" for the war effort. Faced with disappointing recruitment results, leaders blamed Newfoundlanders—labelling them selfish, disloyal, and unattuned to the gravity of the stakes of war. Chris Martin (2009) argues that, in its recruitment efforts, government showed little understanding of the socioeconomic realities of outport life and its basis in household production, and thus it was unable to recruit effectively. The campaigns of fall 1917 and spring 1918 vilified outport residents—despite the fact that most members of the NFC were recruited from locations outside St. John's. The belated introduction of the Military Service Act in May 1918 resulted in only a small handful of NFC conscripts.

The paternalism and near-contempt expressed toward those who did not enlist—which was seen, for example, in the correspondence of Beeton (1917c), Davidson (1917c), and others, including some St. John's elites such as P.T. McGrath ("Recruiting," 1918)—conveyed a thinly veiled attack on the very outport residents at whom the recruitment efforts were largely directed. The debate that accompanied the granting of commissions when the NFC was first formed also played into this division; the public was quick to suspect class-based cronyism was at the heart of the appointments.[9] These divides were further deepened by opportunistic, largely St. John's-based mercantile profiteering during the war. Commemorative debates and practices also became part of a divisive politics in which the symbolic meaning of the war dead and how best to honour them were contested.

Echoing the meanings of Beaumont-Hamel that had been reflected in press coverage throughout the preceding year (Harding, 2001), Prime Minister Morris (1917b) spoke the following words about the fatalities in his public address on the first Memorial Day—July 1, 1917:

> Those who died that day were heroes. They represented the best of Colonial life. . . . They need not have gone. They could have stayed at home and lived, but without glory and [with] dishonour. They chose a glorious death rather than bring dishonour on themselves, their parents, and their country. They are now our most precious assets. Nothing in the country today is as valuable as their memory. (p. 6)

Beaumont-Hamel, he argued, was a defining moment for the country, and commemoration of the country's triumph, he predicted, "will be cherished by Newfoundlanders as the most precious anniversary in their annals" (p. 6). The comments by Morris echoed Governor Davidson's insistence ("Gracious Message," 1916) that "the Glory of it can never fade . . . [and] will stand forever as the proudest day in the history of the Loyal Colony," as well as the assertion by Field Marshall Earl Douglas Haig, a year earlier, that "the heroism and devotion to duty [the Newfoundland Regiment] displayed on 1st July has never been surpassed" (p. 4). The iconic status of Beaumont-Hamel, the framing of its war dead as "better than the best"[10] and their loss as a

---

9   Outport residents also expressed concern that their Regiment soldiers were passed over for promotion (Martin, 2009).

10 According to an account by Captain Sydney Frost, this phrase was first used to describe the Regiment by Lieutenant-General Sir Arthur Hunter-Weston in an address to the survivors of Beaumont-Hamel: "I salute you individually,

generational denudation all took hold, with what some historians argue had both immediate and long-term consequences for the country (Cadigan, 2013; Candow, 2016; Harding, 2001).

A pernicious effect of an almost exclusive focus on combat service and the loss of those cast as "our most precious assets" (Morris, 1917b, p. 6), then, was the reinforcement of social hierarchies and geographic divisions. Those who served in the NFC did not meet the enlistment standards of the Regiment; many were older and, by Regiment standards (and the social standards of the times), some were even seen as impaired in some way. Yet they had a desire to serve, and they enlisted and became part of what was a highly productive, successful, and—in Scotland—a greatly valued unit in an essential area of war supply and service. The number who were deemed medically unfit at discharge suggests their hard work also resulted in hardship that affected their ability to reintegrate into postwar life. A lack of attention to their achievements and experiences, unfortunately—if unintentionally—reproduced the marginalization some may have felt at the time based on their positions within and experiences of the social hierarchies of community life, war service, and postwar commemoration.

The postwar disregard for the contributions of the wartime foresters ultimately became part of a broader pattern of indifference to woods workers more generally. In the pulp and paper industry throughout the first half of the twentieth century, woods work was defined by harsh labour for poor wages combined with dangerous working and appalling camp living conditions. Work stoppages and strikes were frequent but had minimal effect; they culminated in the infamous International Woodworkers of America strike of 1959, a half-century after the birth of the industry in Newfoundland (Sutherland, 1991, 1992, 1995; Kelly & Forsyth, 2018b). Inequities within the industry itself, between those who worked in the woods and were largely

---

you have done better than the best" (Roberts, 2014, p. 203). Frost's account is consistent with that of *The Montreal Daily Star* London correspondent, Percy Hurd (pseudonym "Windermere"), reprinted in Newfoundland on July 21, 1916 ("Windermere's Message," 1916).

rural-based and those who worked in the mills and lived in the company towns, fit within other historic hierarchies that resonated within the country and the story of the NFC.

The NFC, along with other non-Regiment and non-Naval services, was bestowed little public honour and its story was assigned minor significance in the broader account of the war. The social divides such a demarcation supported, established and intact before the war, remained unchallenged by this stratification of memory. The Blue Puttees, or the "First Five Hundred," most of whom were St. John's-based[11] and connected to the city's elite, are venerated in war memory while another five hundred, those who served with the NFC and who were mostly rural-based, are largely forgotten. A holistic and interconnected account of war and service would fairly and evenly credit all contributions, while ensuring that the unique contributions of diverse sectors to the war effort are understood and appreciated. More equitable commemorative practices would aim to support the same approach.

Newfoundland's contribution to the Royal Naval Reserve—a total of 1,966 sailors drawn mostly from the outports, who were scattered throughout the Royal Navy fleet (Sharpe, 1988)—was, until recently, also largely ignored. As well, the stories of the women who volunteered for the VAD and the vast network of women whose volunteer work with the WPA helped to craft an immense circle of care throughout the war have only just begun to emerge from the footnotes of war history.

In addition to the combat casualties and fatalities Newfoundland suffered,[12] there were also those on the home front who endured the war and its attendant separations and losses and who vigorously participated in the system of wartime supports that developed. As Sean Cadigan (2013) points out, along with the several thousands of those who returned—soldiers,

---

11   As the Regiment grew, the numbers from outside St. John's increased greatly, with more than two-thirds of total enlistments coming from communities outside the capital (Sharpe, 1988).

12   Regiment fatalities at the end of the war totalled 1,297, more than 20 percent of enlistments, and injuries were 2,314, or 37 percent. Fatalities for all services totalled 1,570 (Sharpe, 1988, p. 49).

sailors, foresters, nurses—they, too, had to make their way in the context of a post-Beaumont-Hamel Newfoundland. About them he notes: "The myth of the lost generation demeaned, intentionally or not, the people who survived the war and, though often damaged in some way, nevertheless went on building their futures" (p. 7). For most returning foresters, building this future meant reintegrating into home life where, it seems, they spoke little about their service. For approximately one-fifth, or 20 percent, of the NFC,[13] coming home after the war led to leaving Newfoundland to build a life elsewhere—in places such as Sydney, Toronto, Boston, or Brooklyn; a very small percentage of the men also remained in or returned to the United Kingdom. The postwar economy of Newfoundland offered few employment opportunities and those who had served were poorly supported by a self-interested government that did not adequately respond to their needs.

Philosopher Judith Butler (2004) has written extensively about the political potency of unbearable loss and the regulation of affect as a mode of social control. She argues that the disorientation created by loss and grief also delivers a time of reorientation and reconsideration that can be a beginning of change and a revitalized attachment to the worth of what remains. The repression of loss, however, can foreclose this possibility in exchange for a stagnating nostalgia and melancholy. As Robert Harding (2001) notes, remembering Beaumont-Hamel in the years following the war

> had more to do with honouring conjured mythic images of the attack than mourning the losses it had caused. . . . The lack of emphasis on what actually happened to the Newfoundland Regiment on 1 July 1916 prevented Beaumont-Hamel from being recognized as a bloody military failure sooner than it did. (p. 27)

This emphasis also prevented proper mourning, for the meaning of loss was realigned for political purposes. Melancholy can stifle optimism and

---

13   This percentage is based on the 489 foresters for whom information was available.

mute civic participation; it can be an obstacle to social progress. The elevation of an unmourned catastrophic military failure to a defining moment in a country's history raises questions about the ongoing impact of melancholia on a cultural collective and its ability to move forward progressively under its psychic burden.[14] It nudges a broader examination of what our (perhaps habitual) collective relationship to loss—in any instance—tells us about ourselves.

Mourning the casualties and costs of the Great War was a missed opportunity to rethink purposefully a relationship to empire as part of the evolution of a more progressive postcolonial identity.[15] During and after the war, however, the reinvention of the meaning of war loss as "sacrificial honour" muted expressions of righteous grief and foreclosed the legitimacy of critical discussions of Newfoundland's participation in the war. Some historians have linked the long-term impact of a view of Beaumont-Hamel as glorious tragedy and national wound to subsequent relinquishment of responsible government in 1934 (Cadigan, 2013) and, a decade and a half later, the decision to enter the Confederation of Canada in 1949.[16]

Like Newfoundland, other dominions also looked to commemoration to find meaning and purpose in the dreadfulness of loss. Canada, for example, suffered approximately 70,000 deaths in the war (Vance, 2015). The Canadian victory at the Battle of Vimy Ridge in April 1917,[17] for which almost 3,600 soldiers died and 7,000 were wounded, emerged as its commemorative focus, mythologized through the lenses of national unification and sacrifice that spawned the rebirth of a nation (Vance, 2015; Cook, 2018)—a

---

14   For a discussion of cultural melancholia in Newfoundland and Labrador, see Kelly (2009). See also Kennedy (2010).

15   For an excellent analysis of this period and its contested ideological stakes, see Cadigan (2013).

16   See, for example, the radio series "What We Might Have Been" (Brookes, 2007).

17   On April 9 through 12, 1917, the Newfoundland Regiment formed part of the British 3rd Army that attacked the enemy east of Arras, near Vimy, at Monchy-le-Preux. The Regiment's casualties there were second only to those they incurred at Beaumont-Hamel.

myth no less problematic, but framed more as a notion of productive passage than fatal wound.

Those who hold the institutional power to shape the dominant discourse of public remembrance—governments, or the media or clergy—largely control who is remembered and how. The selectivity that is part of the machinery of remembrance, here and elsewhere, shores up what matters, who is of value and why, and what visions of the past hold sway in the present and with what effects. The story of the Newfoundland Forestry Companies provides an opportunity to re-examine the measure and meaning of service and to revisit the politics of remembrance and its effects.[18] Increasingly, commemorative practices prompt questions of partiality, purpose, and effect, questions about *why* and *how* we remember *what* and *whom*, and considerations of the implications of the limited interpretive lenses through which the past is often viewed.

Out of such questions and considerations are emerging new and more diverse stories designed to acknowledge and remember those who served in other units—the Royal Naval Reserve, the Merchant Navy, the Voluntary Aid Detachment, the Forestry Companies, for example—and those who came from cultural communities other than Anglo St. John's, such as Labradorians, Francophones, Indigenous Peoples, newer immigrant communities, and women, all of whom have previously existed in the shadows of dominant remembrance stories. These contributions and experiences are essential chapters in a comprehensive and inclusive account of Newfoundland and Labrador in the First World War. By ensuring that these stories are told and considered, we continue to challenge established hierarchies and habits of

---

18　The Living Memorial Conference of 2019 at Memorial University of Newfoundland, and the funded projects under the WW100 Commemoration Program 2014–2019 on which it was based, featured several such stories. The NFC was not a focus of any of the conference presentations or funded projects. At the Corner Brook-based Grenfell Campus of Memorial University a commemorative bronze bench and plaque honouring the foresters of the First and Second World Wars (and designed and sculpted by Morgan MacDonald) was unveiled in August 2019, the final instalment of The Danger Tree project.

living and remembering, and to reflect on and to contest the often restrictive and problematic dominant meanings of sacrifice and service.

Despite the century and more that now separates the Newfoundland dominion of the Great War period and the contemporary Newfoundland and Labrador province of Canada, commonalities remain that include troubling social divisions and stubborn strains of political fatalism and public cynicism. But there also remain the individual and collective need for recognition and value as well as the capacity for productive critical citizenship. Challenging divisions and hierarchies, and engaging in thoughtful conversations about the meanings of the past and their sometimes harmful legacies, can contribute to a productive optimism that has the potential to displace fatalism and cynicism and to inspire concerted actions for a more just future.

APPENDICES

APPENDIX A

Newfoundland Forestry Companies: A Timeline[1]

1917

February 28	Newfoundland Prime Minister Edward P. Morris writes from London to Governor Walter Davidson about interest there in a Newfoundland wartime forestry unit for the UK.
March 25	Governor Davidson writes to Walter B. Grieve, Secretary of the Recruiting Committee of the NPA, to discuss a third option for military service (in addition to the Newfoundland Regiment and the Royal Naval Reserve)—a forestry unit.
April 2	Viscount Walter Long, Secretary of State for the Colonies, outlines in a telegram to Governor Davidson the proposed terms for a UK-based Newfoundland forestry unit.
April 4	Governor Davidson issues a public call for men to serve as foresters in the UK.
April 8	The NPA passes a resolution confirming the terms of the formation of the unit.
April 16	The name of the unit as proposed by Viscount Long—the Newfoundland Forestry Companies—is confirmed at a meeting of the NPA.
April 17	Enlistment begins.
April/May	Recruits are tested and trained at the Catholic Cadet Corps Armoury in St. John's.
May 19	The first draft of 99 foresters, led by Major G. Carty, departs St. John's for Halifax aboard the SS *Florizel*.
June 2	Recruits of the first draft are among thousands from both Newfoundland and Canada to depart Halifax for Liverpool aboard the troop carrier (former liner) RMS *Olympic*.
June 9	The first NFC draft arrives at Liverpool, England.
June 10	The first draft is transported by rail to Ayr, Ayrshire, Scotland, where the men are quartered for two weeks at the Regimental Depot at the Ayr Racecourse.

---

1   Exact dates could not be confirmed for all events in this timeline.

June 25	The first draft arrives at Dunkeld, Perthshire, and establishes camp on Craigvinean Hill on the estate of the Duke of Atholl.
July 27	The NFC fells its first logs at Craigvinean.
August 1	Wooden huts are completed and foresters move from temporary canvas tents.
August	The second draft of 177 foresters, led by Major Michael Sullivan, departs St. John's.
August 23	The second draft arrives at Dunkeld.
September 1	The tramline to transport logs to the chute is operated for the first time.
September 7	Mayson Beeton and Sir John Stirling Maxwell visit the NFC at Dunkeld.
September 21	Commandant Henrietta Tempest and Matron Susan Recketts of the VAD Hospital, Dalguise, visit the NFC.
September 26	The first sawmill at Doig's Farm, at the base of Craigvinean, begins operation.
October 12	A recruitment campaign begins in Newfoundland.
October 17	A third draft of 43 foresters arrives at Dunkeld.
October 19	Sir Joseph and Mrs. Maria Outerbridge, along with their son Lieutenant Herbert Outerbridge, visit the NFC.
October 20	The NFC excels in competitions with the Canadian Forestry Corps at a Lumbermen's Sports Day at Stanley, Perthshire.
November	The upper portion of the log chute, above the tramline, is completed; the full length now measures 3,080 feet (just under 940 metres), reputed to be the longest log chute in the world.
December 11	An NFC draft leaves Newfoundland under the command of Captains Josiah R. Goodyear and David J. Thistle.
December 14	Governor Davidson, Prime Minister Morris, Sir James Ball, Mayson Beeton, and Major Henry Timewell visit the NFC.
December 16	The electric light plant is completed and operates for the first time.

1918

January 1	To meet the demand for lumber, a night shift is implemented at the mill.
January 1	Draft arrives at camp.
January 29	An NFC draft departs Newfoundland.
February	The NFC extends cutting to Blairgowrie.
February 17	Draft arrives at camp.

February 24	Major Sullivan survives the wreck of the SS *Florizel* near Cappahayden, Newfoundland.
March 9	Private Selby Taylor is killed in an accident at Craigvinean, the NFC's first fatality.
April 4	Another recruitment campaign begins in Newfoundland.
April 8	The second mill begins operation and the night shift at the first mill is discontinued.
April 21	Draft arrives at camp.
April 25	"The Newfoundlanders at Dunkeld," a film featuring the work of the NFC, premieres to a full house at The King's Cinema in Perth.
April	Advance NFC groups are dispatched to Kenmore to prepare for a change of location for NFC operations.
May 11	Conscription is introduced in Newfoundland.
May 27	The advance party led by Captain Goodyear dismantles and transports one mill and several huts by lorry from Craigvinean to Dalerb Farm, Kenmore.
June	The NFC commence operations at Drummond Hill, Kenmore, on the estate of the Marquis of Breadalbane.
June 11	An NFC draft departs Newfoundland.
July 6	NFC members aid in the recovery of the bodies of three members of the Women's Forestry Corps, following a drowning accident at the Rock Pool, River Tay.
July	The transfer of operations continues from Craigvinean to Drummond Hill, Kenmore.
July	Minister of Militia J.R. Bennett visits the NFC.
August	The NFC establishes its three companies at Kenmore.
August 15	Private Gerald Hogan is killed in an accident on Drummond Hill, the NFC's second fatality.
August 24	Newfoundland Prime Minister W.F. Lloyd visits the NFC at Kenmore.
September 19	Lord Northcliffe of the Anglo-Newfoundland Development Company visits the NFC at Kenmore.
October 17	Draft arrives at camp.
November 11	Armistice. The NFC stays at Kenmore to mill the remaining felled timber.
December 10	Private Arthur H. Wyatt is drowned in the River Tay, the NFC's third fatality.

1919

February 1	The first returning draft leaves Aberfeldy by train for Liverpool and the voyage to Newfoundland aboard SS *Corsican*.
February 7	SS *Corsican* arrives St. John's.
April 4	The body of Private Arthur H. Wyatt is recovered from the River Tay.
May 10	The remaining members of the NFC depart Kenmore.
June 24	The remaining NFC members depart Glasgow aboard SS *Cassandra*.
July 1	SS *Cassandra* arrives in St. John's.
August 26	The NFC is disbanded.

A War Office truck at an NFC camp, ca. 1918.
(Courtesy of The Rooms Provincial Archives Division, A 103-106)

APPENDIX B

Newfoundland Forestry Companies: The Nominal Roll

This table lists the 528 men who served in the NFC, including those who transferred from the Newfoundland Regiment.[1] Existing individual NFC files are available online in the Great War Military Service Files database of The Rooms Provincial Archives in St. John's.[2]

Legend

*	Transfer from the Newfoundland Regiment
^	Transfer to the Newfoundland Regiment
o-###	Commissioned Officer
NA	Not available: attestation files missing; limited information from ledger only

Service Number	Last Name	First Name	Occupation at Enlistment	Residence at Enlistment	Age at Enlistment
8216	Abbott	Andrew B.	Labourer	St. John's	19
8414	Abbott	James C.	Scaler	Sandy Point, St. George's	22
8478	Adams	Stephen	Mill worker	Come By Chance	34
8397	Alcock	Pearce	Lumberer	Leading Tickles	18
8140	Allen	Richard J.	Chauffeur	St. John's	18

---

1   Four names are not included here: the three members of the Royal Army Medical Corps who were attached to the NFC—Captains A.C. Court, S.D. Fairweather, and W.T. Paterson—and a civilian appointment, Liaison Officer Lieutenant (Honorary) Albert J. Noble.

2   The following service numbers were not used: 8165, 8202, 8303, 8322–8340, and 8343.

Service Number	Last Name	First Name	Occupation at Enlistment	Residence at Enlistment	Age at Enlistment
8110	Anderson	William	Lumberer	Grand Falls	34
8122	Andrews	Adam	Lumberer	Nipper's Harbour	26
8018	Andrews	Robert Herbert	Draper	St. John's	26
8075	Andrews	Walter W.	NA	Point Leamington	22
8383	Angel	John J.	Baker; cook	St. John's	35
8009 / 1875*	Anthony	Joseph	Fisher	Brigus	24
8067	Ash	Richard	Labourer	St. John's	52
8421	Ashford	William J.	NA	Harbour Breton	18
8486	Atkins	Clementine	Labourer	Manuels	27
8192	Atkins	John R.	Lumberer	Port au Choix	18
8375	Auchinleck	James R.	Labourer	St. John's	19
8070	Avery	Edgar	Lumberer	Random Island	18
8053 / 2862*	Avery	William T.	Fisher	Southport	21
8118	Bailey	Andrew P.	Lumberer	Coachman's Cove	21
8112	Bailey	Harry	Lumberer	George's Brook	20
0–192	Baird	William H.	Lumberer	Norris Arm	43
8229	Baker	Benjamin	Lumberer	Clarenville	18
8230	Ball	Andrew F.	Lumberer	Northern Arm	28
8440	Ball	Douglas	Lumberer	Little Burnt Bay	19
8213	Barnes	Alfred	NA	Burgoyne's Cove	20
8028	Barrett	John A.	Journalist	Curling	43
8476	Barrett	Victor	Labourer	Bay Roberts	20
8042	Bartlett	James	Cooper	St. John's	21
8348	Bartlett	Leslie S.	Lumberer	Bishop's Falls	20
8466	Beaton	Archibald	Lumberer	Norris Arm	26

Service Number	Last Name	First Name	Occupation at Enlistment	Residence at Enlistment	Age at Enlistment
8489	Beaton	Joseph	Lumberer	Badger Brook	24
8248	Beaton	William	Lumber fore-man	Badger Brook	36
4224*	Benoit	Julian	Fisher	Ship's Cove, Cape St. George	26
8255	Benoit	Laurence	NA	Bay d'Espoir	18
8300	Benoit	Paul	Lumberer	Bay d'Espoir	18
8320	Best	Charles	Labourer	Grand Falls	18
8402	Best	George	Carpenter; cooper	St. John's	57
8510	Biles	Daniel	Lumberer	St. Anthony	22
8141	Bishop	Edward C.	Lumberer	Catalina	34
8280	Bishop	George	Miner	Long Pond	37
8063	Boone	James D.	Lumberer	Glovertown	29
8233	Boone	John	Teamster	St. John's	28
8016	Bouzan	James P.	Lumberer	Little Bay	21
8363	Bragg	Miles	Labourer	St. John's	19
2217*	Brazil	Richard	Labourer	St. John's	20
8049	Breen	Edward	NA	Grand Falls	21
8485	Brien	James	Labourer	Manuels	33
8506	Broderick	William J.	Labourer	St. John's	37
8385	Brown	Aubrey A.	NA	Bishop's Falls	47
8032	Brown	Charles P.	Lumberer	Gambo	23
8461	Brown	James	Lumberer	Pacquet	20
8384	Brown	Owen	Lumberer; cook	Port Rexton	29
8014	Brown	Peter	Woods worker	Ferryland	22
8252	Brown	Theodore	Lumberer; fisher	King's Cove	25
8448	Buckley	John	NA	Botwood	50
8152	Budgell	Enos G.	Fisher	New Bay	21
8423	Budgell	George	NA	New Bay	42

Service Number	Last Name	First Name	Occupation at Enlistment	Residence at Enlistment	Age at Enlistment
8011	Bulgin	Hubert	NA	Back Harbour, Twillingate	25
2290*	Bursey	Archibald	Lumberer	Gambo	22
8094	Burt	Edwin G.	NA	Musgrave Harbour	22
8101	Byrne	Richard	NA	St. John's	28
8177	Caines	John	Lumberer	Woody Point	29
8419	Caines	Leslie	Fisher	Lamaline	20
8092	Campbell	John A.	Lumberer	Port au Port	27
8511	Campbell	Roland W.	NA	Little Bay Island	20
8408	Chafe	Archibald H.	Fisher	Goulds	22
8207	Chafe	Henry R.	Lumberer; fisher	Petty Harbour	24
8175	Chafe	Howard	Lumberer	Petty Harbour	21
8012	Chafe	Solomon	Labourer	St. John's	29
8153	Chaffey	James E.	Lumberer	Jeffreys	22
8462	Chalk	Job	Lumberer	Little Catalina	26
8422	Champion	Joseph	Lumberer	Botwood	36
8249	Chaytor	Robert	Lumberer	Botwood	19
8353	Childs	Henry	Labourer	Lark Harbour	20
8238	Chippett	Harry T.	Lumberer	Leading Tickles	18
8474	Chiveraux	Simon	NA	Main Gut, St. George's	54
8346	Churchill	James	Labourer	Portugal Cove	30
8351	Clark	Alexander	NA	Delby's Cove, Trinity Bay	29
8378	Cluney	Leo	NA	St. John's	19
8096 / 775*	Coady	Andrew	Cook	St. John's	23
8427	Coish	Leo	NA	St. John's	18

Service Number	Last Name	First Name	Occupation at Enlistment	Residence at Enlistment	Age at Enlistment
8150	Colbourne	Melville	Lumberer	Purcell's Harbour	19
0–170	Cole	Hugh Henry Wilding	Logging superintendent	Badger Brook	33
8055	Collins	Martin J.	Filer	St. John's	59
8081	Coloumb	David	Lumberer	Shallop Cove	18
8428	Combdon	Silas	Lumberer; fisher	Jackson's Arm	27
8467	Connors	Michael F.	Lumberer	Norris Arm	26
8435	Constable	Thomas	NA	St. John's	19
439*	Cooper	Herbert George	Fisher; engineer	Tilt Cove	25
8166	Cooper	Obediah	Lumberer; fisher	Comfort Cove	30
8483	Coveyduck	William J.	Shoemaker	St. John's	34
8426	Cox	Charles	Lumberer	New Bay	39
8005	Cranford	Walter	Clerk	New Harbour	23
8220	Crickard	William	Labourer	St. John's	18
8228	Crocker	Andrew P.	Lumberer	Port Blandford	18
8386	Cross	William J.	Lumberer	Greenspond	26
0–25	Crowe	Henry S.	Lumberer	Grand Falls	36
8129	Curlow	Henry W.	Lumberer	Northern Arm	33
8488	Curran	Eugene W.	Labourer	Manuels	18
8260	Cusick	James J.	Labourer	St. Lawrence	18
8047 / 2859*	Daniels	Cyril E.	Labourer	St. John's	18
8410	Dawe	Frederick N.	Lumberer	Seldom-Come-By	21
8417	Dawe	Hubert	Farmer	Upper Gullies	18
8411	Dawe	Rowland	Lumberer	Seldom-Come-By	19
8214 / 0–041	Dean	Kenneth W.	Millwright	Botwood	52

Service Number	Last Name	First Name	Occupation at Enlistment	Residence at Enlistment	Age at Enlistment
8512	Decker	James H.	Lumberer; fisher	Cape Onion	24
8304	Dicks	Hubert P.	Labourer; steward	St. John's	27
8244	Dobbin	Bernard J.	Lumberer	Salmonier	20
8146	Dodman	Leslie B.	Lumberer; fisher	Grand Bank	21
8147	Donnelly	Thomas	Labourer	St. John's	18
8371	Driscoll	Edward	NA	St. John's	31
8356	Driscoll	Simeon	Labourer	St. John's	20
8366	Duhart	Joseph V.	Lumberer	St. George's	18
8301	Duke	Peter	Labourer	St. John's	18
8023	Dunn	John S.	Surveyor	Grand Falls	24
8477	Dwyer	James	Labourer	Shearstown	19
811*	Eaton	Duncan M.	Drygoods clerk	St. John's	34
8069	Elliott	Adam	Lumberer	Lewisporte	32
8452	Elliott	Samuel	Lumberer	Botwood	43
8017	Ellis	Nutting F.	Draper	St. John's	21
8041	England	James R.	Mill worker	St. John's	45
8097	Fanning	Augustus F.	Stenographer	St. John's	19
8453	Farnell	Wallace	Millwright	Stephenville Crossing	44
8098	Farrell	Eugene S.	Lumberer	North Bay, LaPoile	23
8217	Felix	Ernest	Lumberer	Flat Bay	35
8480	Fewer	William	Lumberer	Placentia	66
8377	Fisher	William	Labourer	St. John's	24
8438	Fitzpatrick	James J.	Drummer; bugler	St. John's	18
8349	Foley	Edward	Teamster	St. John's	21
8455	Follett	James	Lumberer	Shoal Brook, Bonne Bay	19

Service Number	Last Name	First Name	Occupation at Enlistment	Residence at Enlistment	Age at Enlistment
8120	Foote	John H.	Railway worker	Botwood	44
8246	Forsey	Joseph	Lumberer	Clarke's Head, Gander Bay	43
8006	Freeman	Gerald	Labourer	St. John's	25
8109	Frost	William B.	Lumberer	Hillview	21
8056	Fudge	Ambrose W.	Lumberer	Newstead	25
8031	Furlong	Stephen J.	Lumberer; teamster	Grand Falls	24
8500	Gabriel	Roland O.	Labourer	St. John's	20
8295	Gale	Neil	NA	West Bay, St. George's	18
8313	Garland	William B.	Labourer	St. John's	19
8054	Geary	Alexander	Labourer	St. John's	56
8412	Genge	Abram	Lumberer	Flower's Cove	28
8490	Gillingham	Esau	Lumberer	Glenwood	36
8170	Gillingham	Isaac	Lumberer	Jackson's Arm	22
8060	Gillingham	James Jacob	Lumberer	Bishop's Falls	23
8089 / 1464*	Gillingham	Luke	Fisher; lumberer	Ochre Pit Cove	19
8509	Gillingham	Thomas	Lumberer	Harbour Deep	21
8044	Gillis	Michael J.	Lumberer; farmer	Highlands	39
8151	Gleeson	Joseph J.	Lumberer	Virgin Arm	31
8052	Glynn	Matthew J.	Harness maker	St. John's	31
8437	Goobie	Herbert	NA	St. John's	25
8498	Gooby	Charles	Labourer	St. John's	18
8176 / 219*	Good	Robert J.	Steward	St. John's	39
8119	Goodyear	Aubrey C.	Lumberer	Millertown	21
0–74 / 1193*	Goodyear	Harold Kenneth	Lumberer	Grand Falls	19
0–166 / 573*	Goodyear	Josiah R.	Lumberer	Grand Falls	30

Service Number	Last Name	First Name	Occupation at Enlistment	Residence at Enlistment	Age at Enlistment
8090	Goodyear	Theophilus	Lumberer	Little Catalina	19
8457	Gordon	Thomas B.	Labourer	St. John's	30
8080	Gosse	Richard	Lumberer	Dildo	18
132*	Gough	Frank George	Labourer; cooper	St. John's	19
8123	Gough	Joseph	Fisher	Elliston	18
8179	Gould	Thomas	Lumberer	Bartlett's Harbour	20
8291	Goulding	Thomas	Lumberer	Gambo	34
8121	Granville	John H.	Lumberer	Millertown	38
984*	Green	Cecil	Bank clerk	Trinity	19
8475	Green	Constant	Lumberer	Mainland	23
8274	Greenslade	John W.	Carpenter	Long Pond	43
8040	Griffin	John	Shoemaker	St. John's	39
8469	Gunn	John	Lumberer	Norris Arm	20
8293	Gushue	William	Mill worker; machinist	St. John's	20
8156	Hale	Garland	Fisher	Change Islands	21
8245	Hall	Patrick J.	Lumberer	Port au Port	18
8285	Hall	Reggie	Mill worker	Stephenville Crossing	18
8212	Hall	Thomas	Labourer	St. John's	18
8193	Hallett	John	NA	Port au Bras	18
8073	Hancock	Howard	Lumberer	Norris Arm	18
8065	Hancock	John H.	Lumber fore-man	Norris Arm	40
8450	Hanlon	James	Lumberer	St. John's	54
8406	Hann	Chesley G.	Mill edger	Bay Roberts	26
8025	Harding	George A.	Fisher	Portugal Cove	19
8355	Harris	Frederick	Tailor's cutter	St. John's	22
8102	Hart	Ralph	Lumberer	Champney's East	18

Service Number	Last Name	First Name	Occupation at Enlistment	Residence at Enlistment	Age at Enlistment
8168	Hart	Stewart	Lumberer	Change Islands	20
0–194	Harvey	Guy W.N.	Civil engineer	Grand Falls	30
8270	Harvey	Ralph	Lumberer; fisher	Moreton's Harbour	18
8062	Harvcy	Walter	Lumberer; fisher	Moreton's Harbour	23
8382	Hayse	Pierce	Lumberer	Tilton Harbour	46
8470	Hayward	John C.M.	Labourer; photographer	Grand Falls	42
8493	Head	Dorman	Lumberer	Gander Bay	26
8497	Hewitt	Stephen	Labourer	St. John's	18
8433	Hewitt	Walter	Lumberer	Jackson's Arm	18
8424	Hibbs	William	Labourer	St. John's	42
8262	Hill	Harris	Cooper	St. John's	27
8418	Hillier	Amos G.	Fisher	Point aux Gaul	43
8388	Hillyer	Andrew	Sawyer	Winterton	35
8105	Hinchey	John	Labourer	Northern Bay	21
8091	Hoddinott	Walter J.	Lumberer	Indian Islands	18
8111	Hogan	Gerald	NA	Northern Bay	21
8113	Hogan	John R.	Lumberer	Northern Bay	18
8434	Hogan	Nicholas J.	Labourer	Northern Bay	19
8259	Hollett	John	NA	Port au Bras	18
8035	Horwood	Alexander	Labourer	St. John's	31
8033	Howell	Edmund	Fisher	Catalina	30
8154	Hulan	Edward C.	Lumberer	Jeffreys	18
8191	Hull	Ephraim	Lumberer	Springdale	27
8197	Hull	John S.	NA	St. John's	29
8084	Humby	Edward	Lumberer	St. Leonard's (St. Lunaire-Griquet)	20
8159	Hunt	Kenneth	Lumberer; fisher	Wesleyville	23
8389	Hunt	Victor E.	Lumberer	Bonavista	33

Service Number	Last Name	First Name	Occupation at Enlistment	Residence at Enlistment	Age at Enlistment
8501	Hussey	Thomas B.	Filer	St. John's	33
8039	Hussey	William L.	Steward	St. John's	45
8507	Hutchcroft	William	Lumberer	Point Leamington	25
8370	Hutchings	Albert	Fisher	Charles Brook	23
8137	Hutchings	Alfred W.	Lumberer	Botwood	50
8302	Hutchings	George S.	Clerk	St. John's	20
8058	Hutchings	James	Lumberer	Botwood	19
8108	Hutchings	John	Lumberer	Bay Bulls Arm, Trinity Bay	18
8015	Hynes	Laurence	Fisher	Canada Harbour	27
8294	Ingram	Stanley	Labourer	Harbour Buffett	19
8345	Ivany	Herbert G.	Lumberer	Dark Cove, Gambo	18
8309	Ivany	Jack	Teamster	St. John's	18
8064 / 3105*	Ivany	Solomon	Teamster	St. John's	24
8394	Jackman	Michael J.	Labourer	Renews	23
8241	Jackman	Patrick J.	Clerk	St. John's	24
8104	Jackson	Walter	Mill worker	Cavendish	16
0–171 / 3486*	James	Noel G.	Lumberer	Grand Falls	28
8268	Janes	Archibald A.	Engineer	Alexander Bay	24
8266	Janes	Lewis J.	Lumberer	Phillip's Head, Botwood	17
8272	Jeans	Stanley	Lumberer	Change Islands	43
8100	Jerrett	Elim	Fisher	Cavendish	18
8311	Johnson	James F.	Labourer	St. John's	19
8082	Jones	Elihu M.	Lumberer	Exploits	22
8391	Judge	Joseph	Lumberer	St. John's	44
8416	Kavanagh	James	Labourer	St. John's	45

Service Number	Last Name	First Name	Occupation at Enlistment	Residence at Enlistment	Age at Enlistment
8257	Kearley	Reginald T.	Lumberer	Campbellton	21
8239	Kelly	John Charles	Lumberer	Ireland's Eye	18
8181	Kelly	Michael	Sailmaker	St. John's	18
5571*	Kendell	Nathaniel	Lumberer	Pushthrough	19
8482	Kennedy	William C.	Lumberer	Little Catalina	22
8413	Kent	William	Labourer	St. John's	32
8289	Keough	Leo	Naval engineer	St. John's	21
8387	King	Arthur Case	NA	Grand Falls	24
8399	King	Bertram	Lumberer	Pope's Harbour, Trinity Bay	23
8139	King	Charles	Lumberer	Catalina	27
8227	King	John	Lumberer	Little Harbour, Trinity Bay	26
8409	King	John A.	Lumberer	Sandy Cove, Bonavista Bay	24
8045	King	William Thomas	Woods worker	Broad Cove, Bay de Verde	21
8184 / 2153*	Knight	Elmo	Lumberer; paper cutter	Grand Falls	18
8502	Knight	Fred W.	Surveyor	St. John's	45
8442	Lagatdu	Yves	Lumberer	Cape St. George	18
8439	Laite	Alfred	Lumberer	Lewisporte	37
8115	Lane	Enos	Lumberer	Millertown	37
8128	Langdon	Caleb E.	Lumberer	Northern Arm	38
8231	Langdon	John H.	Lumberer	Northern Arm	51
8271	Layte	Charles	Lumberer	Gander Bay	37
8454	Learning	Robert G.	Lumberer; labourer	St. John's	34
8206	Lee	Thomas	Lumberer	Petty Harbour	22
8288	Lehr	Henry	NA	St. John's	20

Service Number	Last Name	First Name	Occupation at Enlistment	Residence at Enlistment	Age at Enlistment
8443	Lemont	Allen	Lumberer	Cape St. George	18
8431	Leonard	Patrick	Lumberer	Placentia	54
8267	Lewis	Francis	Lumberer	Salmonier	24
8403	Lewis	John	Fisher	Lower Island Cove	18
8215	Lidstone	Walter John	Labourer	St. John's	19
8504	Liscombe	Joseph	Lumberer	Botwood	41
8133	Littlejohn	George	Lumberer	Traytown	55
8401	Locke	Archibald	Labourer	St. John's	18
8200	Locke	Edward	Lumberer	Pilley's Island	24
8236	Luff	Oliver	Lumberer	Exploits, Notre Dame Bay	19
8171	Lunnon	Clarence S.	Lumberer	Twillingate	21
8298	Maher	Peter F.	Labourer	St. John's	18
3648*	Maidment	W. John	Papermaker	Grand Falls	27
8071	Maloney	Michael	Lumberer; fisher	Sweet Bay	20
8275	Mansfield	John	Miner	Bell Island	18
8234	Manuel	Ford	Lumberer; draper	Lewisporte	40
8138	Marshall	Abram	Lumberer	Little Bay	20
8479	Martin	Andrew	Labourer	Harbour Grace	42
8484	Martin	Edward P.	Office clerk	St. John's	18
8232	Martin	John R.	Carpenter	Manuels	50
8221	McAskill	John	Boilermaker	Whitney Pier, NS	33
8027	McCarthy	Thaddeus F.	Carpenter	St. John's	19
8465	McDonald	William	Lumberer	Norris Arm	19
8167	McGinn	John	Lumberer	Change Islands	21
0–222 / 128*	McGrath	Thomas B.	Engineer	St. John's	19
8254	Mead	William	NA	Seal Cove, Hermitage Bay	29

Service Number	Last Name	First Name	Occupation at Enlistment	Residence at Enlistment	Age at Enlistment
8352	Meaney	Basil	Fisher	Caplin Bay	20
8038	Meaney	Frank	NA	Brigus	19
8263	Mercer	Azariah	Lumberer	Bay Roberts	22
8196	Mercer	Harvey	Lumberer	Lushes Bight	22
8296	Merchant	Thomas	Shoemaker	St. John's	18
637*	Michelin	Joseph	Lumberer; trapper	Grand Village (Mud Lake), Labrador	22
2841*	Miller	John	Draper	St. John's	30
8305	Miller	Llewelyn	Clerk	St. John's	25
8407	Miller	Oliver	Fisher	Flat Island	18
8114	Milley	Michael Frank	NA	St. John's	29
8208	Mitchell	Charles F.	Lumberer	John's Beach, Bay of Islands	18
8373	Mitchell	Lawrence	Lumberer	Norris Point	32
8360	Mitchell	Maxwell	Labourer	St. John's	19
8057 / 646*	Moore	Donald L.	Clerk	St. John's	19
8149	Moore	Edward T.	Lumberer	Badger	29
8314	Moore	Patrick W.	NA	St. John's	18
8357	Moore	Victor R.	Lumberer	Dildo	18
8218	Moores	Archibald	Lumberer	Baie Verte	19
8190	Moores	John C.	Lumberer	Pilley's Island	18
8209	Morey	Philip	Lumberer	Millertown	38
8003	Morrissey	James H.	Lumberer	St. John's	25
8390	Moss	John	Lumberer	Grand Falls	49
8447	Moss	Robert	Lumberer	Salvage	33
8264	Mouland	Ronald	Fisher	Musgrave Harbour	20
8169	Moyles	George	Lumberer	Lewisporte	27
8219	Muise	Hubert	Lumberer	South Branch, Bay St. George	20

Service Number	Last Name	First Name	Occupation at Enlistment	Residence at Enlistment	Age at Enlistment
8292	Mullaly	James	NA	St. John's	27
8174	Mullett	Victor	Labourer	St. John's	19
8007	Murphy	James	Teamster	St. John's	28
8312	Murphy	William J.	Blacksmith	Kilbride	19
1896*	Newbury	William	Draper	St. John's	19
8492^	Newell	George H.	Labourer	St. John's	19
8199	Nippard	Charles	Lumberer	Springdale	32
8048	Noftall	Isaiah	Lumberer	Broad Cove, Bay de Verde	18
8022	Noftall	William J.	Carpenter	St. John's	24
8008	Norman	A. Sainsbury	Lumberer	Lewisporte	19
8276	Norman	John	Fisher	Red Island, Placentia Bay	19
8046	Norris	William	Labourer	St. John's	18
8210	Noseworthy	Albert	Teamster	St. John's	18
8404	Noseworthy	Harold	Labourer	St. John's	18
8256	Noseworthy	Jacob	Miner	Long Pond	47
8277	Noseworthy	Samuel	Miner	Long Pond	21
8279	Noseworthy	William	Miner	Long Pond	18
8095	Oakley	Walter H.	NA	Port Blandford	24
8107	O'Brien	Edward	Teamster	St. John's	45
8182	O'Brien	John	Woods worker; fisher	South East Arm, Placentia Bay	42
8318	O'Brien	John William	Lumberer	Grand Falls	20
8261	O'Brien	Leo P.	Clerk	St. John's	18
8344	O'Brien	William	Fisher	Aquaforte	19
8484	O'Driscoll	John D.	Scaler	St. John's	23
8222	Oldford	John	Lumberer	Salvage Bay	39
8358	Oliver	Patrick	Labourer	St. John's	27
0–195	O'Rourke	William T.	Clerk	St. John's	37
8343 / 2471*	Osborne	James William	Machinist	Channel	39

Service Number	Last Name	First Name	Occupation at Enlistment	Residence at Enlistment	Age at Enlistment
8364	Osmond	Oliver	Labourer	Moreton's Harbour	21
8086	Ovens	George	Lumberer	Norris Arm	21
8204	Pardy	Archibald C.	Labourer	Little Harbour, Twillingate	18
8237	Pardy	George	NA	St. John's	24
8473	Pardy	John	Lumberer	Little Burnt Bay	19
8342	Parkinson	William	Carpenter	St. John's	41
8393	Parrell	John Patrick	Carpenter	St. John's	25
8180	Parsons	John N.	Lumberer	Bay Bulls Arm (Sunnyside)	24
8405	Parsons	Richard F.	Labourer	Harbour Breton	19
1876*	Parsons	Wilfred	Lumberer	Bay Roberts	19
438*	Parsons	William J.	Clerk	Parson's Point, Burin	22
8099	Patey	Henry W.	Lumberer	Point Leamington	26
8186	Patey	Isaac	Lumberer	Port Saunders	26
8456	Patey	William	NA	Noddy Bay, Strait of Belle Isle	22
8013	Pearce	Horace	NA	St. John's	34
8019	Pearcey	Ralph	Labourer	St. John's	21
8242	Peckford	Edwin	Lumberer	Charles Brook	43
8243	Peckford	Osmull	Lumberer	Charles Brook	19
8037	Peddle	Archibald	Labourer	St. John's	23
8374	Peddle	William	Shipwright	St. John's	18
8103	Pelley	Albert	Lumberer	South West Arm	21
8458	Pelley	Alpheus	Lumberer	Harry's Harbour	39
8131	Pelley	Edmund	Lumberer; carpenter	Laurencetown	49

Service Number	Last Name	First Name	Occupation at Enlistment	Residence at Enlistment	Age at Enlistment
8459	Pelley	Jabez	Lumberer; cooper	Rattling Brook	46
8223	Pelley	Pierce	Labourer	St. John's	18
8050	Penney	Charles	Mill worker	Hickman's Harbour	29
8194	Perry	Edwin	Lumberer; fisher	Port Saunders	26
8400	Peters	Charles H.	Labourer	St. John's	39
8034	Phillips	Frank	Firefighter	St. John's	21
8163	Picco	John F.	Teamster	St. John's	20
8155	Piercey	Jacob	Lumberer; carpenter	Bay Bulls Arm, Trinity Bay	46
8188	Pike	Alfred E.	Lumberer	Springdale	24
8445	Pike	Joseph	Lumberer	St. Lawrence	19
8051	Pike	Ralph C.	NA	Grand Falls	19
8066	Pike	Robert	Lumberer	Lewisporte	45
8036	Pittman	Kenneth	Machinist	St. John's	31
8043	Pittman	William	Mill worker	Brickyard, Smith's Sound	28
8024	Pollett	George	Lumberer	Little Harbour	23
8068	Pope	John	Labourer	St. John's	30
8093 / 3060^	Potts	Bryan W.	Lumberer; scaler	Millertown	21
8074	Powell	Baxter	Lumberer	Happy Adventure	18
8160 / 2188*	Powell	David	Lumberer	Happy Adventure	19
8124	Power	James A.	Labourer	Harbour Grace	36
8076	Prasuyon	Wallace	Lumberer	St. George's	21
8226	Pretty	Cyril C.	Labourer	Port-aux-Basques	18
8116	Pretty	Edward	Lumberer	Chapel Arm	18
8026	Pynn	William H.	Lumberer	Silverdale	18

Service Number	Last Name	First Name	Occupation at Enlistment	Residence at Enlistment	Age at Enlistment
8468	Quirk	William	Lumberer	Fortune Harbour	22
8430	Ralph	Lambert	Lumberer	Coney Arm	27
94*	Randall	Hubert J.	Paper finisher; lumberer	Grand Falls	24
8251	Read	Charles A.	NA	Woody Point	18
8505	Reardon	Stanley	Lumberer	St. John's	22
8162	Redmond	Thomas J.	Clerk; labourer	St. John's	18
8464	Reid	Caleb	Lumberer	Little Catalina	17
8308	Reid	Josiah	Fisher	Harbour Buffett	19
8240	Rendell	William J.	Lumberer	Change Islands	22
8491	Revellon	Adolphus	Lumberer	Mainland, Port au Port	48
8317	Rideout	Abel J.	Lumberer	King's Point	18
8203	Rideout	Bertie	NA	Crow Head	19
8247	Rideout	Caywood	Lumberer	Moreton's Harbour	19
8087	Rideout	Charles	Lumberer	Moreton's Harbour	22
8187^	Rideout	Dorman C.	Lumberer	Pilley's Island	21
8449	Rideout	Elijah	Lumberer	Botwood	30
8432	Rideout	George	Farmer	Goulds	20
8368	Roberts	Frank	Lumberer	Main River, Bay St. George	20
8381	Rodgers	Edward	Labourer	St. John's	20
8487	Rogers	William P.	Rigger	St. John's	44
8436	Rose	Joshua	NA	St. John's	43
2542*	Rose	R. Clayton	Sales clerk	St. John's	22
0–96 / 768*	Ross	Hector H.A.	NA	St. John's	22
8350	Rowe	Nelson J.	Lumberer	Green's Harbour	17

Service Number	Last Name	First Name	Occupation at Enlistment	Residence at Enlistment	Age at Enlistment
8061	Rowsell	Archibald H.	Lumberer	Leading Tickles	24
8020	Ryall	Thomas J.	Carpenter	St. John's	45
8178	Ryan	John	Lumberer	Port Saunders	25
8396	Ryan	Thomas	Labourer	St. John's	20
8085	Samson	Martin R.	Lumberer	Seal Cove, Twillingate	29
8316	Samuelson	Chesley	Mechanic	St. John's	19
8319	Saunders	Benjamin	Lumberer	Gambo	18
1215*	Saunders	Henry J.	Trucker	St. John's	29
8392	Sawers	David E.	Baker; labourer	St. John's	20
8495	Scott	Ernest	Lumberer	Upper Gullies	18
2410*	Sears	James	Labourer	St. John's	19
8290	Seaward	John	NA	Cupids	18
8354	Sellars	Edward	Labourer	St. John's	39
8001	Sellars	Eldon	Draper	St. John's	25
8059	Seymour	John	Lumberer	Leading Tickles	20
8321	Sharman	Victor Lionel	Clerk	London, UK	22
1750*	Shea	Michael J.	Fisher	Pouch Cove	19
8341	Shears	Howard	Labourer	Jeffries	19
35*	Sheehan	John Joseph	Labourer	St. John's	23
8224	Sheppard	Harold	Labourer	St. John's	19
8310	Sheppard	Kenneth	Teamster	Harbour Grace	18
8136	Sheppard	William A.	Lumberer	Northern Arm	33
8021	Sheppard	William F.	Electrician	Grand Falls	19
8508	Sibley	Gilbert	Teacher; labourer	Fogo	21
8205	Simmons	William J.	NA	Green's Harbour	21
8425	Simms	Alfred	Lumberer	Long Island, Twillingate	42

Service Number	Last Name	First Name	Occupation at Enlistment	Residence at Enlistment	Age at Enlistment
8367	Simms	Edgar	Lumberer	Fogo	20
8198	Simms	Frederick W.	Lumberer; fisher	Pilley's Island	18
3277*	Skeanes	Edward	Shoemaker	Kilbride	25
8446	Skinner	George H.	Cook	Grand Falls	31
8079	Slade	John	Lumberer	Millertown	27
8258	Smith	Clifford	Labourer	Loon's Cove, Burin	19
8144	Smith	Jacob	NA	Norman's Cove	25
8481	Snow	William	Labourer	Harbour Grace	45
8161	Somerton	Solomon	Mechanic	Portugal Cove	27
8164	Sparkes	George	Lumberer	Glovertown	26
8029	Spencer	Archibald	Lumberer	Springdale	22
3841*	Squarey	Arthur	Blacksmith; mechanic	Channel	40
8347	Squires	Alexander	Fisher	Manuels	48
8496	Squires	Alexander G.	Lumberer	Topsail	18
8359	Squires	Benjamin	Mechanic	St. John's	24
8297	Squires	Charles	Labourer	Manuels	19
8004	Squires	Reuben	Woods worker	St. Philip's	20
8463	Stagg	Fred	Lumberer	Little Catalina	20
1449*	Stares	Frank W.	Sawyer	Port Blandford	19
8265	Stares	Harry	NA	Port Blandford	14
8157 / 2941*	Steed	Solomon	Fisher	Alexander Bay	18
8088	Steel	Nathan	Lumberer	Musgrave Harbour	20
618*	Stewart	Henry	Tinsmith	Paisley, Renfrewshire, Scotland	26
8183	Stickland	Meshach	Lumberer	Birchy Head, Bonne Bay	17

Service Number	Last Name	First Name	Occupation at Enlistment	Residence at Enlistment	Age at Enlistment
8282	Stockley	Henry	Lumberer	Greenspond	35
8380	Stone	John	NA	St. John's	19
8225	Stowe	James	Machinist	St. John's	19
8315	Street	John	NA	St. John's	24
2568*	Strickland	James	Lumberer	Botwood	25
8083 / 1325*	Stroude	Frederick William	Lumberer	Alexander Bay	21
0–191	Sullivan	Michael S.	NA	St. John's	41
8125	Sullivan	Thomas F.J.	NA	St. John's	70
8307	Taylor	Dewey	Labourer	St. John's	18
8250	Taylor	Hayward	Labourer	St. John's	19
8499	Taylor	Ronald C.	NA	St. John's	18
8460	Taylor	Selby P.	NA	St. John's	25
0–181	Thistle	David	Lumberer	St. John's	52
8283	Thistle	Frederick	Teamster	St. John's	19
8376	Thomey	Samuel J.	Labourer	Harbour Grace	47
8135	Thompson	James J.	Lumberer; mill worker	Point Leamington	57
8134	Thompson	Leonard E.	Lumberer	Point Leamington	52
8132	Thompson	Thomas G.	Lumberer; mill worker	Point Leamington	23
8299	Tilley	Frank	NA	Chamberlains	18
1224*	Tilley	William	Bookkeeper	Kelligrews	22
8379	Tizzard	Samuel	NA	St. John's	19
8278	Tobin	John	Lumberer; fisher	Red Island, Placentia Bay	18
8273	Torraville	Sidney	NA	Fogo	22
8253	Tracey	Martin	Firefighter	St. John's	42
8106	Tremblett	Thomas	Lumberer	Bonavista	22
8010	Vinnicombe	John J.	Labourer	St. John's	32
8472	Viquers	Clifford	Labourer	Bay Bulls	18

Service Number	Last Name	First Name	Occupation at Enlistment	Residence at Enlistment	Age at Enlistment
8269	Vivian	Alfred R.	Lumberer	Friday's Bay, Notre Dame Bay	18
8281	Vivian	Willis	Lumberer	Friday's Bay, Notre Dame Bay	22
8195	Walkins	Martin J.	NA	St. John's	19
8072	Walsh	John F.	NA	St. John's	18
8126	Walsh	Luke	NA	St. John's	35
8158	Walsh	Michael	NA	St. John's	20
8306^	Walsh	Michael J.	NA	NA	19
8503	Walsh	Patrick	Labourer	St. John's	18
8415	Walters	John	Lumberer	Bank Head, Bay St. George	18
8395	Walters	William	Labourer	Goulds	19
8077	Warford	Azariah	NA	South West Arm, Point Leamington	22
8078	Warr	Charles T.	Lumberer	Little Harbour, Twillingate	37
8127	Weir	Harold	NA	Petty Harbour	20
8444	Weir	William H.	Lumberer	Petty Harbour	23
8172	Wells	Archibald Thomas	NA	Tickle Point, Twillingate	20
8451	Wells	Elias J.	Lumberer	Horwood	23
8471	Whalen	Walter	Lumberer	Chapel's Cove	27
8148	Wheaton	Edwin	Lumberer	Millertown	30
8201	Whelan	Baxter G.	Lumberer	Millertown	26
8143	White	Charles	Lumberer	Norman's Cove	22
8235	White	Dorman	Lumberer	Cottle's Cove	22
8441	White	Frederick	NA	Flat Bay	21
8145	White	George	NA	Grand Bank	25
8142	White	Jacob	Lumberer	Norman's Cove	24

Service Number	Last Name	First Name	Occupation at Enlistment	Residence at Enlistment	Age at Enlistment
8117	White	James	Lumberer	Norman's Cove	18
8002	White	John	Blacksmith	St. John's	23
8173	White	William	Lumberer	Goulds	20
8429	Wicks	William T.	Lumberer; fisher	Jackson's Arm	44
8284	Wight	George	Labourer	St. John's	23
8420	Willar	Henry F.	Wharf operator	St. John's	24
8372	Williams	Allen T.	Labourer	Goulds	20
8398	Williams	Walter	Carpenter	St. John's	21
8189	Winsor	Bertram G.	Lumberer	Triton West	19
8030	Woodford	Michael	Boilermaker	St. John's	20
8211	Woodford	William J.	Machinist	St. John's	21
8130	Wyatt	Arthur Helroyd	Blacksmith; lumberer	Traytown	42
8185	Wyatt	William D.H.	Blacksmith; mill worker	St. John's	47
8362	Yates	Allen	Lumberer	New Bay	21
8365	Young	Herbert G.	NA	Twillingate	19
8369	Young	John	NA	Bank Head, St. George's	37
8287	Young	Michael	Lumberer	Clambank Brook, St. George's	17
8361	Young	Roland	Lumberer	North West Arm, Green Bay	21
8286	Young	William	Lumberer	Clambank Brook, St. George's	20

APPENDIX C

Thirty-five years after he enlisted with the Newfoundland Forestry Companies, John A. Barrett wrote a five-part series for *The Western Star*[1] entitled "The Part Played In World War One By The Newfoundland Forestry Corps," in which he recounted the experiences of the unit in Scotland.[2] This essay is a retitled and abridged version of the original publication, with minor editing.

The Newfoundland Forestry Companies of the First World War
John A. Barrett

Thirty-five years ago (1917) when World War One was utilizing so much of Great Britain's man-power for the Navy, Army and Air Force, it was planned to organize, in Newfoundland, a corps of Foresters, which would be of great service to the Imperial government. At that time a large percentage of our men who were "fit" had already found places in either the Navy, the Regiment or Air Force.

However, there were a number of men over the military age, quite a few who had been rejected for service in the fighting units for medical reasons, and there were many others who had not quite reached the military age. From these, recruits to the number of 778 enlisted, of whom 278 were rejected for various reasons.

King's Khaki
Before going overseas, the men were given a course of training in military discipline under instructor Captain J.J. O'Grady. All ranks were issued with the customary khaki uniforms, and by the time a transport was available,

---

1   A segment of Barrett's memoir was published in *The Western Star* in 1952 on each of these five dates: February 5, March 7, April 11, May 9, and June 13.

2   The use of "Corps" in the original title and throughout Barrett's essay is consistent with the published version and may have been an editorial change to reflect popular usage.

a draft of 100 men had practically completed its "physical jerks".

This draft sailed out from St. John's on board the SS *Florizel*, for the port of Halifax, where, after a further brief period of training, embarkment was made on the liner RMS *Olympic*, which had been transformed into a troopship. Lieutenant-Colonel George Carty was transport officer for the Newfoundlanders, and your scribe did orderly room duty while on the voyage. The *Olympic* was a ship of 45,000 tons, and had a speed of 24 knots. She had about 6,000 on board when we put out to sea, all of whom were comfortably quartered on the great liner.

A smooth sea and perfect weather favoured us all the way across the Atlantic; and a fortunate thing it was, as many of the Canadians who had come from mid-west provinces had never seen salt water before, much less having been on it. Physical exercises and route marching were indulged in every day, and thus the time passed pleasantly for all.

From "reveille" to "lights out" great precautions were taken for saving of life. All the troops (officers included) wore lifebelts all day. At a certain hour of the day the ship's whistle sounded an alarm. Immediately the troops took up their appointed stations, the water-tight compartments were closed and guarded, and the boats' crews stood at their respective stations until the commander and O.C.'s had completed an inspection.

Close Lookout

A strict lookout for enemy ships was kept, as it was understood a reward of $50,000 had been offered the commander of the submarine that would sink us. When about 200 miles off the Irish coast, we were met by an escort of four torpedo boat destroyers. This patrol accompanied us to the entrance of the Mersey, and shortly afterwards we were tied up at Prince's in Liverpool.[3]

Whilst necessary preparations for railway transportation were being arranged, the troops, much to their regret, were kept aboard ship all day. During that period, thousands of people visited the dock and probably 30,000 more crossed on the ferry boats from various landings to bid a hearty

---

3   Prince's Dock, on the River Mersey at Liverpool, England.

welcome to the boys in khaki, who had come so far that they may be of assistance to the Mother Country in her hour of need.

Time at Ayr

It was a glorious Sunday morning when the Newfoundland Forestry Corps moved out from Liverpool, bound for the land of the heather and thistle. Men, women and children enthusiastically greeted us as we passed through city, town, and village. Officers and men of the Royal Newfoundland Regiment were at the station to meet us when we arrived at Ayr, and accompanied us to quarters at the Race Course, where we were given over to the care of Lieutenant Ken Goodyear, who had been transferred from the Regiment to our unit.

We spent a very pleasant fortnight at Ayr, before going north to Dunkeld, at which place we went under canvas on Craigvinean, known as Craig of Goats. Arrangements were made for transporting some portable huts from Kirkconnell, and within six weeks we were comfortably housed in wooden buildings. The location was in a beautifully wooded section of the country, where the timber was of fair growth and very accessible. A good road led right from the county road to where we were to operate.

At the Duke's Estate

The estate upon which we were located belonged to the Duke of Atholl. There was an abundance of wild life on the property, such as deer, rabbits, ptarmigan, hares, pheasants, etc., and having been given permission to help ourselves, it was not a common sight to see carcasses of fresh meat hung up in shady places, to replenish our larder.

Our ranks gradually kept increasing by additional drafts from home, until we had a full complement.

During our first month-and-a-half on Craigvinean, the time was spent chiefly in making preparations for the great undertaking. Thirty railroad cars of supplies, lumber, etc., were transported over the three-mile road from the railway station; a large barn, Quartermaster's store, cookhouse, mess-hall, and living quarters for officers and men were set up, and a pipeline was laid from a newly-erected dam to the various buildings, in order to assure a goodly supply of water for all purposes.

Sites Selected

While these preparations were being undertaken, a survey of the timber and hillside was made, and sites selected for the construction of log chutes and the laying of tramlines to tap the main chute. At the same time the work of constructing a sawmill on Doig's farm, at the foot of the hill, was going ahead under the supervision of Captain Baird and Sergeant Dean,[4] who later received a commission as Lieutenant.

The log chutes previously referred to were constructed of round timber, laid down on V-shaped blocks, and securely fastened together. The main chute extended from the milldam up the mountain side for a distance of 1,800 feet. The smaller, or shorter, chutes were arranged at various points along the side of the hill. Horses would "snig" the timber to the smaller chutes, over which it would be sent down to vantage points for loading on the tramlines, and then taken to the main chute for conveyance to the milldam beside the sawmill. In all, there were over 3,000 feet of log chutes, and a mile-and-a-half of tramline used in these operations.

The first big sawmill on the Doig farm was put into operation on Sept. 26, 1917, less than three weeks after its erection had begun. Up to that time, there had been such a quantity of logs felled, it was found necessary to keep this mill operating day and night until a second mill had been erected.

With the two sawmills operating to full capacity, they were turning out timber faster than railway wagons could be found for transportation; and at one time there were over two million feet, board measure, stacked on the camp grounds.

Tree-Cutting Method

When the Newfoundland Forestry Corps first went into the camp at Craigvinean, in Scotland, the men were astonished over the size of the giants of the

---

4   Lieutenant Kenneth W. Dean, NFC #8214 / #0–041, Botwood.

forests in that area, and many were the conjectures put forward as to how and by what means the felling and transportation of those huge trees could be best handled, as many trees reached a height of over 100 feet, and measured from five to six feet in diameter at the cutting point.

To begin with, all the trees were notched with an axe by a special man in each gang who worked under the supervision of a sergeant. Those men planned which way the trees were to fall, and notched accordingly, so that the sawyers could start as near the notch as possible. If there was any doubt as to which way a tree may fall, the notcher always consulted with his sergeant. As the saw cut through the tree increased, a steel wedge was driven, thus relieving the saw from the pressure of the wood. Great care was taken in every instance to see that the axe cuts were not too deep or broad, thereby avoiding the spoiling of any of the merchantable timber.

Seven Million FBM

It was estimated that the stand of timber on Craigvinean contained some 7,000,000 feet, board measure. So earnestly did the men engage with axe and saw, that an average of practically a million feet was felled per month and sent to the mills. Those two sawmills were equipped with machinery of the latest design and each capable of turning out 500,000 ft. b.m. per month. With the shortening autumn and winter days, it was found that the installation of an electric light plant was a valuable addition to the whole camp, and enabled sawing operations to be continued by night shifts.

There were quite a number of heavy draught horses on the strength of the unit; in fact, for a period there were over 40 of those animals daily employed, either in the woods or at transportation. Every day they conveyed large quantities of materials, rations, and forage from the railway. Privates Dicky Byrne,[5] J.A. Campbell and Charlie King worked long hours on those transports, because it so happened that rations usually arrived at the station by evening trains. This necessitated a separate trip for the transports.

Not infrequently did some of the men suffer from minor injuries, so one

5   Private Richard Byrne, NFC #8101, St. John's.

of the rooms in the sectional huts was converted to a Medical Hut. Provision was made for ten beds, where those suffering from minor ailments were attended to without having to go to hospital. Madame Tempest, the commandant of Dalguise V.A.D., very generously furnished this building and put a nurse in attendance. Daily visits to the Hut were made by Dr. Taylor, of Dunkeld.

Slab Stockade

A well-appointed recreation hut, measuring 60 x 30 feet, was gifted by the Duke of Atholl, and thither the men would nightly gather in large number to enjoy various games and read the goodly supply of literature gratuitously provided by friends of the unit. And those who habitually had a long thirst could get it quenched at the canteen, which was operated by two stalwarts whose individual avoirdupois exceeded that of the Quartermaster's by five stone.

Despite all the attractions placed in the way of the men, to tempt them from the paths of rectitude, it was seldom any of them were found about camp in an unbecoming condition. Yet, one night there were a couple of inebriates, whose voices grew strong and their knees were weak; but Lieutenant Goodyear[6] had them tied up in strong chaff sacks and laid under the trees, where they spent the night. That ruse served as a means in keeping in check their future behaviour.

All military units usually have good substantial structures as guard rooms in which to place those deserving punishment. But the Newfoundland Forestry Corps had what looked like a stockade, built of slabs, to serve as a "clink".[7] To my knowledge, there was but one individual confined within its walls. Owing to the weakness of the structure, his stay herein did not last overnight.

On the Move

We find that by January, 1918, most of the trees had been felled and some 4,000,000 ft. b.m. had passed through the mills. Some of the tramlines at

---

6   Lieutenant Harold Kenneth Goodyear, RNR #1193 / #0–74, Grand Falls.

7   A prison.

far-away points were taken up and the smaller log chutes were dismantled, the timber going to the mills to be saved.

Towards the end of April, advance gangs were dispatched to Kenmore, to look over the prospects for operations at Drummond Hill, by the shores of Loch Tay. This territory, which was part of the estate of the Marquis of Breadalbane, was well wooded, chiefly with larch. But there was one draw-back with the location—it was seven miles from the nearest railway.

It was at first proposed to erect the sawmills at Killin, a railhead, and have the logs towed there from Kenmore. But this idea was eventually can-celled, as it would have necessitated the operation and maintenance of an extra camp for all purposes.

However, in May, 1918, one of the mills and several huts were disman-tled and transported by motor lorries over the county road to Kenmore, where they were set up on Dalerb farm, a beautiful location by the side of the lake,[8] a body of water somewhat resembling our Deer Lake, stretching away to Killin, a distance of 15 miles.

At Kenmore

By June all huts and necessary equipment were moved away to Kenmore, where lumbering operations were soon in full swing. The nearness of the timber to the mills dispensed with the necessity of log chutes, and the logs were taken to the mills by horses. Each of the three companies had its own individual mill, and worked independently. Rations were issued to each camp on the strength of its "parade state". Forage for the horses was dealt with similarly.

All this gave the Quartermaster's department a busy time; and for practi-cally a year I had been attending to it alone. Then Eldon Sellars was appointed store clerk, and Lance Corporal Billy Tilley[9] ration clerk. This afforded a little leisure for your scribe and enabled me to devote more time to my weekly press correspondence, which has been assigned by the Timber Control Board.

---

8   Loch Tay.
9   Lance Corporal William Tilley, RNR #1224, Kelligrews.

Headquarters camp site by the side of Loch Tay was a very desirable one, being on a level stretch of land once used as a farm. There was a bountiful supply of good water for all purposes, and sanitary arrangements were well planned. The village of Kenmore lay at the foot of the lake, about a mile distant from camp. Taymouth Castle, with the beautiful park of Breadalbane, adjoined the village.

Captains Hugh Cole, Harry Crowe and Joe Goodyear had charge of Company operations; Lieutenant Guy Harvey supervised the engineering work; and Lieutenant Mike Gillis had charge of a squad operating about A Company's mill. The transport officer—Ken Goodyear—was a busy man. With sometimes over 40 horses under his care and the daily operations of the motor lorries conveying rations and can supplies from the railway taxed Goodyear's capabilities to the utmost.

Although there were three sawmills operating, the daily production of sawn timber was much below that produced at Craigvinean. The side of Drummond Hill had a steep gradient, rising up from the county road, which ran close by the camp. When the trees were felled they had to be taken to the mills by horses. This often necessitated the services of two or three men with peavies, to accompany a team of horses to the mill. Yet, notwithstanding the many difficulties encountered in this area, they were readily overcome, and during the summer of 1918 about 4,000,000 feet of dressed timber came off the sawmills.

Large trucks were daily employed by the Timber Control Board conveying the timber to the railway at Aberfeldy. But, even so, the production was so great that large quantities had to be stacked in the yards every week. And this accumulation kept increasing up to the end of October.

Armistice

All through the summer and right up to the 11th of November 1918, the Newfoundland Forestry Corps had done an excellent job in felling timber on Drummond Hill, Kenmore. As this work was carried on in close proximity to the sawmills, more timber was felled daily than could be taken care of by the three mills. In consequence thereof, when Armistice was declared, there were thousands of logs awaiting transportation to the mills.

Loading lumber for transport to Aberfeldy railway, Drummond Hill, Kenmore.
(Courtesy of The Rooms Provincial Archives Division, A 103-93)

Notwithstanding the cheering news of cessation of hostilities and the prospect of an early repatriation, yet, when our men were put on parade and the situation explained to them, it was definitely agreed to continue operations until all felled timber was taken to the yards and processed at the mills. This work occupied three months, and in February, 1919, the first big draft of men entrained at the Aberfeldy station, on the first leg of the long journey to Newfoundland. From then onward to May, several small drafts went out to embark on ships as they were available either at Glasgow or Liverpool.

Your scribe and Teddy Driscoll, as cook, were left behind for a month to prepare inventories of equipment and materials, and to return to the various supply depots such articles as clothing, iron rations, etc. For our convenience, the Timber Board placed a motor car and driver at our disposal, which greatly facilitated in the cleaning up process.

Work Commended

The work of the Newfoundland Forestry Corps in Scotland during World War I was declared by competent foresters and lumbermen as being highly satisfactory. Working as they did amidst strange surroundings and under new methods and conditions, it was considered a splendid feat to lay out and construct both camps at Craigvinean and Drummond Hill, and in such a short period to have manufactured over seven million feet, board measure, all being good merchantable stock, and sawn according to specifications.

REFERENCES

Address to the men of Newfoundland. (1918, November 5). *The St. John's Daily Star*, p. 3.

A forestry policy necessary. (1919, August 23). *The Western Star*, p. 2.

A lumber camp in the Highlands. (1917, October 27). *The Evening Herald*, p. 3.

A pathetic letter. (1917, June 6). *The Twillingate Sun*, p. 2.

A soldierly letter. (1917, December 21). *The St. John's Daily Star*, p. 10.

Act the man. (1917, April 17). *The Daily News*, p. 7.

Alas! The poor native! (1917, May 16). *The St. John's Daily Star*, p. 1.

Alexander, D. (1980). Literacy and economic development in nineteenth century Newfoundland. *Acadiensis, 10*(1), 3–34. https://journals.lib.unb.ca/index.php/Acadiensis/article/view/11538

An appeal. (1918, April 9). *The Evening Telegram*, p. 3.

An appeal to the people of Newfoundland. (1917, October 12). *The Evening Telegram*, pp. 4–5.

An outstanding figure. (1932, July 6). *The Western Star*, p. 1.

Anderson, H.A. (1918a, June 7). [Letter to Sir Patrick G. McGrath]. The Great War Military Service Files Database. The Rooms Provincial Archives, St. John's, NL, Canada. https://www.therooms.ca/sites/default/files/anderson_hugh_m_0-179_or_2120.pdf

Anderson, H.A. (1918b, July 8). The Newfoundland Forestry Companies' new camp. *The Evening Herald*, p. 3.

Ashton, J. (1986). The lumbercamp song tradition in Newfoundland. *Newfoundland Studies, 2*(2), 213–31. https://journals.lib.unb.ca/index.php/NFLDS/article/view/580

Atholl. (1918, December 15). [Letter to Mayson Beeton]. Board of Trade Records (BT 71 4 77699). The National Archives, London, UK. https://blog.nationalarchives.gov.uk/keepers-gallery-newfoundland/

Ayre, C.R. (1917, April 14). [Letter to Governor W.E. Davidson]. The Great War Military Service Files Database. The Rooms Provincial Archives, St. John's, NL, Canada. https://www.therooms.ca/sites/default/files/hussey_benjamin_4325.pdf

Back from Scotland. (1919, July 16). *The Western Star*, p. 2.

Baehre, R. (2011). Whose pine-clad hills: Forest rights and access in New-foundland and Labrador's history. *Newfoundland Quarterly, 103*(4), 42–47.

Baker, M. (2005). Crowe, Harry Judson. In D.A. Wilson (Ed.), *Dictionary of Canadian biography*. University of Toronto / Université Laval. http://www.biographi.ca/en/bio/crowe_harry_judson_15E.html

Baker, M. (2017). Warfare 1914–1918. In U. Daniel, P. Gatrell, O. Janz, H. Jones, J. Keene, A. Kramer, & B. Nasson (Eds.), *1914–1918 online: International encyclopedia of the First World War*. Free University. 10.15463/ie1418.10804/1.1

Baker, M. & Miller Pitt, J. (1984). *A discussion of health services in Newfoundland and Labrador to 1982.* http://www.ucs.mun.ca/~melbaker/PublicHealthNL.pdf

Baker, M. & Neary, P. (2012). "A real record for all time": Newfoundland and Great War official history. *Newfoundland and Labrador Studies, 27*(1). https://journals.lib.unb.ca/index.php/nflds/article/view/21044/24281#no57

Balance of troops sailed yesterday. (1919, June 25). *The Western Star*. p. 2.

Barrett, D.G. (1989). The David Barrett family: Our Newfoundland heritage. *The Newfoundland Ancestor, 5*(2), 4–52.

Barrett, J.A. (1917, November 18). [Draft of Letter to Editor, *The Evening Herald*]. Copy in possession of the Barrett family.

Barrett, J.A. (1922, December 20). A visit to Blair Castle. *The Western Star*, p. 3.

Barrett, J.A. (1945, April 21). By the way: Reindeer in Newfoundland. *The Western Star*, p. 2.

Bates, A.C. (1994). Michael S. Sullivan. In C.F. Poole (Ed.), *The encyclopedia of Newfoundland and Labrador* (Vol. 5, p. 322). Harry Cuff Publications.

Beeton, M.M. (1917a, April 21). [Letter to Governor W.E. Davidson]. Newfoundland First World War Correspondence—Forestry Company, General (RG38-D-9, 437, M-6). Library and Archives Canada, Ottawa, ON, Canada.

Beeton, M.M. (1917b, June 10). [Telegram to Governor W.E. Davidson]. World War One Records—Office of the Colonial Secretary Fonds (GN 2.14.217). The Rooms Provincial Archives, St. John's, NL, Canada.

Beeton, M.M. (1917c, June 22). [Letter to Governor W.E. Davidson]. Newfoundland First World War Correspondence—Forestry Company, General (RG38-D-9, 437, M-6). Library and Archives Canada, Ottawa, ON, Canada.

Beeton, M.M. (1917d, July 24). [Telegram to Governor W.E. Davidson]. The Great War Military Service Files Database. The Rooms Provincial Archives, St. John's, NL, Canada. https://www.therooms.ca/sites/default/files/crowe_henry_s_o-25.pdf

Beeton, M.M. (1917e, July 31). Forestry Corps—the need for men: Letter to Governor Davidson. *The Evening Herald*, p. 4.

Beeton, M.M. (1917f, August 18). [Extract of Letter to Governor W.E. Davidson]. The Great War Military Service Files Database. The Rooms Provincial Archives, St. John's, NL, Canada. https://www.therooms.ca/sites/default/files/crowe_henry_s_o-25.pdf

Bennett, J.R. (1917, October 18). An appeal to the people of Newfoundland. *The Evening Telegram*, pp. 3–4.

Bennett, J.R. (1918, November 9). [Letter to Major M. Sullivan]. The Great War Military Service Files Database. The Rooms Provincial Archives, St. John's, NL, Canada. https://www.therooms.ca/sites/default/files/sullivan_michael_s_o-191_o.pdf

Bennett, J.R. (1919, March 18). [Letter to Colonial Secretary Long]. World War One Records—Office of the Colonial Secretary Fonds (GN 2.14.217). The Rooms Provincial Archives, St. John's, NL, Canada.

Bird, C.W. & Davies, J.H. (1919), *The Canadian Forestry Corps: Its inception, development and achievements*. Board of Trade and His Majesty's Stationery Office.

Bishop-Stirling, T. (2012). "Such sights one will never forget": Newfoundland women and overseas nursing in the First World War. In S. Glassford & A. Shaw (Eds.), *A sisterhood of suffering and service: Women and girls of Canada and Newfoundland during the First World War* (pp. 126–47). UBC Press.

Bishop-Stirling, T. (2015). Women's mobilization for war (Newfoundland). In U. Daniel, P. Gatrell, O. Janz, H. Jones, J. Keene, A. Kramer, & B. Nasson (Eds.), *1914–1918 online: International encyclopedia of the First World War*. Free University. 10.15463/ie1418.10736

Bormanis, K. (2010). *The monumental landscape: Canadian, Newfoundland, and Australian Great War capital and battlefield memorials and the topography of national remembrance* [Unpublished doctoral dissertation]. Concordia University, Ottawa, ON.

Bourne, R. (2015). *Lords of Fleet Street: The Harmsworth dynasty*. Routledge.

British Red Cross (n.d.). *List of auxiliary hospitals in the UK during the First World War*. https://tinyurl.com/y6pw6nf6

Brookes, C. (Producer). (2007, June 29). *What we might have been*. [Audio podcast]. Battery Radio. https://www.batteryradio.com/Pages/BHamel.html

Brown, C. (1972). *Death on the ice: The great Newfoundland sealing disaster of 1914*. Doubleday.

Brown, C. (1976). *A winter's tale: The wreck of the Florizel*. Doubleday.

Bruce, D.H. (1951). *Close the door softly*. Family of Author.

Budgell, A. (2018). *We all expected to die: Spanish influenza in Labrador, 1918–1919*. ISER Books.

Butler, J. (2004). *Precarious life: The powers of mourning and violence*. Verso.

Cadigan, S.T. (2009). *Newfoundland and Labrador: A history*. University of Toronto Press.

Cadigan, S.T. (2013). *Death on two fronts: National tragedies and the fate of democracy in Newfoundland 1914–1934*. Allen Lane.

Cadigan, S.T. (2016). Commemoration, cult of the fallen (Newfoundland). In U. Daniel, P. Gatrell, O. Janz, H. Jones, J. Keene, A. Kramer, & B. Nasson (Eds.), *1914–1918 online: International encyclopedia of the First World War*. Free University. 10.15463/ie1418.10955.

Candow, J.E. (2016). Exhibit review: Beaumont-Hamel and the Trail of the Caribou: Newfoundlanders and Labradorians at War and at Home 1914–1949. Permanent Exhibition, The Rooms Provincial Museum, St. John's, NL, 1 July 2016–Ongoing. *Newfoundland and Labrador Studies, 31*(2), 367–72. https://journals.lib.unb.ca/index.php/NFLDS/article/view/25792

Capable, available natives first. (1917, May 22). *The St. John's Daily Star*, pp. 1–2.

Caplan, R. (1983). Cape Bretoners in World War One: Thomas Gillard. *Cape Breton Magazine, 33*, 17–18.

Captain Perry, hero. (1918, March 6). *The Western Star*, p. 1.

Coaker, W.F. (1930). *Twenty years of the Fishermen's Protective Union of Newfoundland from 1909–1939*. Advocate Publishing.

Comrade killed in service (1918, September 20). *The Harbour Grace Standard*, p. 2.

Cook, T. (2018). *Vimy: The battle and the legend*. Penguin.

Cooper, R. (2016, September 1). *The Children's Union; children fundraising on behalf of children (part 1)* [Blog entry]. Hidden Lives Revealed. https://www.hiddenlives.org.uk/blog/2016/09/childrens-union-children-fundraising-behalf-children-part-1/

Cuff, R. (2001). *Railway*. Heritage Newfoundland and Labrador. https://www.heritage.nf.ca/articles/economy/railway.php

Culbard—Barrett marriage. (1920, July 14). *The Western Star*, p. 2.

Curran, T. (1987). *They also served: The Newfoundland Overseas Forestry Unit 1939–1946*. Jesperson Press.

Curtis, B. (1990). Some recent work on the history of literacy in Canada. *History of Education Quarterly, 30*(4), 613–24. 10.2307/368949

Davidson, W.E. (1917a, April 11). H.E. the Governor writes: Letter to Walter B. Grieve. *The Western Star*, p. 3.

Davidson, W.E. (1917b, April 17). [Letter to M.M. Beeton]. Newfoundland First World War Correspondence—Forestry Company, General (RG38-D-9, 437, M-6). Library and Archives Canada, Ottawa, ON, Canada.

Davidson, W.E. (1917c, May 2). [Letter to Minister Bennett]. World War One Records—Office of the Colonial Secretary Fonds (GN 2.14.217). The Rooms Provincial Archives, St. John's, NL, Canada.

Davidson, W.E. (1917d, May 10). [Letter to Prime Minister Morris]. Newfoundland First World War Correspondence—Forestry Company, General (RG38-D-9, 437, M-6). Library and Archives Canada, Ottawa, ON, Canada.

Davidson, W.E. (1917e, May 24). *The report of His Excellency Sir W.E. Davidson, KCMG, Governor, Chair of the Newfoundland Patriotic Association.* http://collections.mun.ca/cdm/compoundobject/ collection/cns2/id/ 32778/rec/51

Davidson, W.E. (1917f, May 27). [Letter to M.M. Beeton]. Newfoundland First World War Correspondence—Forestry Company, General (RG38-D-9, 437, M-6). Library and Archives Canada, Ottawa, ON, Canada.

Davidson, W.E. (1917g, July 23). [Letter to Walter B. Grieve]. The Great War Military Service Files Database. The Rooms Provincial Archives, St. John's, NL, Canada. https://www.therooms.ca/sites/default/files/ goodyear_josiah_robert_o-166_or_573_1.pdf

Davidson, W.E. (1918a, January 16). Royal Newfoundland Regiment. *The Evening Telegram*, p. 2.

Davidson, W.E. (1918b, June). A brief history of the Royal Newfoundland Regiment [Letter to Chief Justice Sir William Horwood]. *The Volunteer*, p. 31.

Discharged Forester (1919, February 4). A square deal. *The Evening Telegram*, p. 8.

Duley, M.I. (2012). The unquiet knitters of Newfoundland: From mothers of the Regiment to mothers of the Nation. In S. Glassford & A. Shaw (Eds.), *A sisterhood of suffering and service: Women and girls of Canada and Newfoundland during the First World War* (pp. 51–74). UBC Press.

Ena Constance Barrett (2018, May). Canada's Early Women Writers. https://cwrc.ca/islandora/object/ceww%3A8af7d620-4173-4ce3-a7c7-856eafbad2d8

Entries related to Notre Dame Bay. (1907–1911). *The Free Press*. http://sites.rootsweb.com/~cannf/nd_freepress1907-1911.htm

Fay, Charles F. (1956). *Life and labour in Newfoundland*. University of Toronto Press.

Facey-Crowther, D.R. (Ed.). (2002). *Lieutenant Owen William Steele of the Newfoundland Regiment: Diary and letters*. McGill-Queens University Press.

Facey-Crowther, D.R. (2003). Home is where the heart is: The correspondence of Newfoundland soldiers in the Great War. *Newfoundland Quarterly*, 96(2), 32–39.

Firemen wouldn't sail until slackers aboard were driven from ship. (1915, November 17). *The St. John's Daily Star*, p. 3.

Fish donations. (1918, March 16). *The St. John's Daily Star*, p. 4.

Fitzgerald, H.F. (1918a, Spring). [Telegram to Walter Grieve]. Newfoundland First World War Correspondence—Forestry Company, Recruiting (RG38-D-9, 437, M-6-17). Library and Archives Canada, Ottawa, ON, Canada.

Fitzgerald, H.F. (1918b, September 23). [Letter to Minister of Militia J.B. Bennett]. The Great War Military Service Files Database. The Rooms Provincial Archives, St. John's, NL, Canada. https://www.therooms.ca/sites/default/files/goodyear_harold_kenneth_o-74_or_1193.pdf

Forestell, N.M. (1989). Times were hard: The pattern of women's paid labour in St. John's between the two World Wars. *Labour/Le Travail, 24*, 147–66.

Foresters are making good. (1917, November 15). *The St. John's Daily Star*, p. 8.

Forestry battalion. (1917, April 13). *The St. John's Daily Star*, p. 8.

Further appreciation—Tribute to the foresters. (1919, March 18). *The Evening Telegram*, p. 9.

Gallishaw, J. (1916). *Trenching at Gallipoli: The personal narrative of a Newfoundlander with the ill-fated Dardanelles expedition*. The Century Company.

Generous donations. (1918, March 21). *The Evening Telegram*, p. 7.

Glasgow appreciation. (1919, July 2). *The Evening Telegram*, p. 8.

Gracious message received by His Excellency the Governor from Field Marshall Sir Douglas Haig. (1916, July 10). *The Evening Telegram*, p. 4.

Great Britain War Office. (1922). *Statistics of the military effort of the British Empire during the Great War, 1914–1920*. His Majesty's Stationery Office.

Great War Veterans' Association of Newfoundland. (1918). *Constitution and bylaws*. http://collections.mun.ca/PDFs/cns/TheGreatWarVeterans AssociationofNewfoundland.pdf

Grieve, W. (1917, July 30). [Letter to Governor W.E. Davidson]. The Great War Military Service Files Database. The Rooms Provincial Archives, St. John's, NL, Canada. https://www.therooms.ca/sites/default/files/ crowe_henry_s_0-25.pdf

Hancock benefit. (1918, April 2). *The St. John's Daily Star*, p. 8.

Haneca, K., van Daalen, S. & Beeckman, H. (2018). Timber for the trenches: A new perspective on archaeological wood from First World War trenches in Flanders Fields. *Antiquity, 92*(366), 1619–1639. https:// doi.org/10.15184/aqy.2018.172

Hanna, M. (2014). War letters: Communication between Front and home front. In U. Daniel, P. Gatrell, O. Janz, H. Jones, J. Keene, A. Kramer, & B. Nasson (Eds.), *1914–1918 online: International encyclopedia of the First World War*. Free University. 10.15463/ie1418.10362

Harding, R.J. (2001). Glorious tragedy: Newfoundland's cultural memory of the attack at Beaumont Hamel, 1916–1925. *Newfoundland and Labrador Studies, 21*(1), 3–40. https://journals.lib.unb.ca/index.php/NFLDS/ article/view/5884

Harris, C.A. (1918, September 2.) [Letter to Nellie Howell]. The Great War Military Service Files Database. The Rooms Provincial Archives, St. John's, NL, Canada. https://www.therooms.ca/sites/default/files/ hogan_bernard_2252.pdf

Hart, P.J. (2010). The white feather campaign: A struggle with masculinity during World War 1. *Inquiries Journal, 2*(2). http://www.inquiriesjournal. com/a?id=151

Haynes, E. (1921). *Timber technicalities*. W. Rider and Son.

Hemans, F.D. (1907). The hour of death. In A.H. Miles (Ed.), *Women poets of the nineteenth century*. George Routledge & Sons. https://www.bartleby.com/293/41.html

Herring, A.D. (2014). Introduction. In A.D. Herring (Ed.), *Damage control: The untold story of venereal disease in Hamilton* (pp. 2–6). McMaster University. https://macsphere.mcmaster.ca/bitstream/11375/14368/2/fulltext.pdf

Hewers of wood doing well. (1917, December 10). *The St. John's Star*, p. 12.

Higgins, J. (2007). *The 1918 Spanish flu*. Heritage Newfoundland and Labrador. https://www.heritage.nf.ca/articles/politics/1918-spanish-flu.php

Higgins, J. (2009). *First World War and the economy*. Heritage Newfoundland and Labrador. https://www.heritage.nf.ca/first-world-war/articles/first-world-war-economy.php

Higgins, J. (2012). *Aviation: The pioneer period*. Heritage Newfoundland and Labrador. https://www.heritage.nf.ca/articles/economy/aviation-pioneer-period.php

Hiller, J.K. (1982). The origins of the pulp and paper industry in Newfoundland. *Acadiensis, 11*(2), 52–64. https://journals.lib.unb.ca/index.php/Acadiensis/article/view/11572

Hiller, J.K. (1990). The politics of newsprint: The Newfoundland pulp and paper industry 1915–1939. *Acadiensis, 19*(2), 3–39. https://journals.lib.unb.ca/index.php/Acadiensis/article/view/11851

Hiller, J.K. (2015). Morris, Edward Patrick, 1st Baron Morris. In D.A. Wilson (Ed.), *Dictionary of Canadian biography*. University of Toronto/Université Laval. http://www.biographi.ca/en/bio/morris_edward_patrick_16E.html

Hiller, J.K & O'Brien, M. (2019). Newfoundland. In U. Daniel, P. Gatrell, O. Janz, H. Jones, J. Keene, A. Kramer, & B. Nasson (Eds.), *1914–1918 online: International encyclopedia of the First World War*. Free University. 10.15463/ie1418.11346

Holyrood Palace closed. (1913, February 3). *Aberdeen Press and Journal*, p. 7.

House, E. (2017). The impact of the First World War on the woods and forests of Scotland. *FCA Today, 60*, 19–26. https://www.forestry-memories.org.uk/pictures/document/3760.pdf?r=4297124

Howell, E. (1918, August 26). [Letter to Governor C.A. Davis]. The Great War Military Service Files Database. The Rooms Provincial Archives, St. John's, NL, Canada. https://www.therooms.ca/sites/default/files/hogan_bernard_2252.pdf

Hull, E. (1923, April 22). [Letter to Lieutenant C.C. Oake]. The Great War Military Service Files Database. The Rooms Provincial Archives, St. John's, NL, Canada. https://www.therooms.ca/sites/default/files/ridout_charles_8087_0.pdf

Hunter, M.C. (2009). *To employ and uplift them: The Newfoundland Naval Reserve, 1899–1926.* ISER Books.

Janes, H.C. (1921, November 2). [Letter to Lieutenant M.C. Nugent]. The Great War Military Service Files Database. The Rooms Provincial Archives, St. John's, NL, Canada. https://www.therooms.ca/sites/default/files/nugent_michael_joseph_0-209_or_428.pdf

Jarratt, M. (2016). *Letters from Beauly: Pat Hennessey and the Canadian Forestry Corps in Scotland 1940–1945.* Goose Lane.

Jeddore, J.N. (2015). *Moccasin tracks: A memoir of Mi'kmaw life in Newfoundland.* ISER Books.

Jolly, M. (2001). War letters. In M. Jolly (Ed.), *Encyclopedia of life writing: Autobiographical and biographical forms.* Routledge. http://qe2a-proxy.mun.ca/login?url=https://search.credoreference.com/content/entry/routlifewrite/war_letters/0?institutionId=379

Kelly, U.A. (2009). *Migration and education in a multicultural world.* Palgrave.

Kelly, U.A. (2014). *Mentioned in song: Song traditions of the loggers of Newfoundland.* [Album]. Centre for Research in Music, Media and Place (MMaP), Memorial University of Newfoundland.

Kelly, U.A. & Forsyth, M.C. (2018a). *Songs and stories of "the forgotten service."* [Travelling exhibit]. Memorial University of Newfoundland.

Kelly, U.A. & Forsyth, M.C. (2018b). *The music of our burnished axes: Songs and stories of the woods workers of Newfoundland and Labrador.* ISER Books.

Kenmore mystery solved—Newfoundland man's fate. (1919, April 12). *The People's Journal*, p. 10.

Kennedy, R.M. (2010). National dreams and inconsolable losses: The burden of melancholia in Newfoundland culture. In U.A. Kelly & E. Yeoman (Eds.), *Despite this loss: Essays on culture, memory, and identity in Newfoundland and Labrador* (pp. 103–16). ISER Books.

Kernaghan, L. & Foot, R. (2011). Halifax explosion. In B. Graves, (Ed.) *The Canadian encyclopedia*. https://www.thecanadianencyclopedia.ca/en/article/halifax-explosion

King, A.C. (1917, December 7). A soldier's farewell. *The Evening Telegram*, p. 11.

Kirwin, W.J, Story, G.A., & Widdowson, J.D.A. (Eds.). (1990). *Dictionary of Newfoundland English* (2nd ed.). University of Toronto Press.

Late list of casualties. (1919, April 7). *The St. John's Daily Star*, p. 7.

Legislative Council. (1918, May 17). *The Evening Herald*, p. 3.

Lind, F.T. (2001). *The letters of Mayo Lind: Newfoundland's unofficial war correspondent, 1914–1916*. Creative Book Publishing.

Long, W. (1917). [Telegram to Governor W.E. Davidson]. In W.E. Davidson, *The report of His Excellency Sir W.E. Davidson, KCMG, Governor, Chair of the Newfoundland Patriotic Association* (pp. 6–7). http://collections.mun.ca/cdm/compoundobject/collection/cns2/id/32778/rec/51

MacDermott, A. (1923, July 12). [Letter to Colonel T. Nangle]. Newfoundland National War Committee Fonds (GN49.2). The Rooms Provincial Archives, St. John's, NL, Canada.

Macfarlane, D. (1991). *The danger tree: Memory, war, and the search for a family's past*. Macfarlane, Walter and Ross.

MacIsaac, D. (2016). Air warfare. In *Encyclopaedia Britannica*. https://www.britannica.com/topic/air-warfare

MacLeod, M. (1990). *A bridge built half-way: A history of Memorial University College 1925–1950*. McGill-Queens University Press.

MacNair, P. (1912). *Perthshire*. Cambridge University Press.

Major Sullivan and his two associates: Editorial. (1918, February 15). *The Harbour Grace Standard*, p. 4.

Mars, P.K. (1924). The all-'round Newfoundlander. *The Veteran, 3*(4), 52–53.

Martin, C. (2009). The right course, the best course, the only course: Voluntary recruitment in the Newfoundland Regiment, 1914–1918. *Newfoundland Studies, 24*(1), 55–89. https://journals.lib.unb.ca/index. php/nflds/article/view/12686/13589

Mason, W. (1918, July 18). Slackers. *The Evening Telegram*, p. 6.

Maxwell, J.S. (1919, February 4). Loch Tay Steamboat Company and Timber Supply [Letter of January 24 from J.S. Maxwell, Timber Supply, to Lord Breadalbane]. *The Scotsman*, p. 3.

McGrath, P.T. (1928, April 7). [Letter to Deputy Colonial Secretary Arthur Mews]. World War One Records—Office of the Colonial Secretary Fonds (GN 2.5.379.2). The Rooms Provincial Archives, St. John's, NL, Canada.

Millais, J.G. (1907). *Newfoundland and its untrodden ways*. Longmans, Green and Company.

Moncrieff, W.F. (1966). *A history of the Presbyterian church in Newfoundland, 1842–1967*. Author.

Montgomerie, A. (1917, December 7). [Memo to Minister of Militia J.B. Bennett Re Lieutenant Thistle]. The Great War Military Service Files Database. The Rooms Provincial Archives, St. John's, NL, Canada. https://www.therooms.ca/sites/default/files/thistle_david_0-181_0.pdf

Montgomerie, A. (1918, April 12). [Letter to Adjutant H.H.A. Ross]. The Great War Military Service Files Database. The Rooms Provincial Archives, St. John's, NL, Canada. https://www.therooms.ca/sites/ default/files/ross_hector_hugh_alexander_0-96_or_768_0.pdf

Montgomerie, A. (1919, January 4). [Letter to Minister of Militia J.B. Bennett]. *Report of the Department of Militia, March 31, 1919* (pp. 30–34). http://collections.mun.ca/PDFs/cns/ ReportoftheDepartmentofMilitiaMarch31st1919.pdf

More men wanted. (1918, January 15). *The Evening Herald*, p. 5.

Morris, E.P. (1917a, March 14). The Prime Minister writes from London. *The Daily News*, p. 2.

Morris, E.P. (1917b, July 2). First anniversary of the Battle of Beaumont Hamel. [Public address]. *The Evening Advocate*, p. 6.

Morry, C.J.A. (Ed.). (2014). *When the great red dawn is shining: Howard L. Morry's memoirs of life in the Newfoundland Regiment.* Breakwater Books.

Nangle, T. (1923, July 23). [Letter to Commander A. MacDermott]. Newfoundland National War Committee Fonds (GN49.2). The Rooms Provincial Archives, St. John's, NL, Canada.

Native officers for Forest battalion. (1917, May 19). *The Evening Herald,* p. 3.

Neary, P. (1998). Venereal disease and public health administration in Newfoundland in the 1930s and 1940s. *Canadian Bulletin of Medical History, 15*(1), 129–151. https://doi.org/10.3138/cbmh.15.1.129

New Lieutenants—Newfoundland Regiment. (1915). *The Newfoundland Quarterly, 15*(3), 3–4.

Newfoundland and the war. (1917). In *The Times history and encyclopaedia of the war* (Vol. 14 (175), pp. 181–216). http://collections.mun.ca/PDFs/cns/TheTimesHistoryandEncyclopaediaoftheWarPart175Vol14Dec241917.pdf

Newfoundland Contingent Provisional Advisory Committee on Demobilization. (1918, November 26). *Minutes of inaugural meeting.* The Great War Military Service Files Database. The Rooms Provincial Archives, St. John's, NL, Canada. https://www.therooms.ca/sites/default/files/anderson_hugh_m_0-179_or_2120.pdf

Newfoundland foresters. (1918, May 2). *The Evening Herald,* p. 4.

NFLD foresters in the Highlands. (1917, October 20). *The Evening Telegram,* p. 4.

Nicholson, G.W.L. (1962). *Canadian Expeditionary Force 1914–1919.* Department of National Defence.

Nicholson, G.W.L. (1964). *The fighting Newfoundlander: A history of the Royal Newfoundland Regiment.* Government of Newfoundland.

Nugent, M.J. (1938). A voyage at Christmas. *The Veteran, 12*(3), 26–27.

O'Brien, M. (2011) Producers versus profiteers: The politics of class in Newfoundland during the First World War. *Acadiensis, 40*(1), 45–69. https://journals.lib.unb.ca/index.php/Acadiensis/article/view/18561

Oosthoek, K.J. (2013). *Conquering the Highlands: A history of the afforestation of the Scottish uplands.* Australian National University E-Press.

Our foresters and their work. (1918, February 22). *The Daily News,* p. 3.

Our soldier lads. (1917, November 28). *The Daily News*, p. 5.

Paddon, H. (1922, May 11). [Letter to Lieutenant Colonel Rendell, Chief Staff Officer]. The Great War Military Service Files Database. The Rooms Provincial Archives, St. John's, NL, Canada. https://www.therooms.ca/sites/default/files/michelin_charles_6102.pdf

Parsons, W.D. & Parsons, E. (2009). *The best small-boat seamen in the Navy: The Newfoundland Division, Royal Naval Reserve, 1900–1922*. DRC.

Paymaster-Commander Goldsmith, RN, obituary. (1935, February 15). *The Times*, p. 19.

Perthshire mystery solved. (1919, April 6). *The Sunday Foot*, p. 5.

Pound, R. & Harmsworth, G. (1959). *Northcliffe*. Cassell.

Presentation to Forestry Officers. (1917, December 5). *The Evening Telegram*, p. 8.

Prussia must pay. (1918, November 1). *The Evening Herald*, p. 3.

Published by authority: Newfoundland Forestry Companies. (1917, May 16). *The Evening Telegram*, p. 5.

Raley, A. (1916). *The Newfoundlanders: The fighters from Britain's oldest colony*. The Great War Military Service Files Database. The Rooms Provincial Archives, St. John's, NL, Canada. https://www.therooms.ca/sites/default/files/anderson_hugh_m_0-179_or_2120.pdf

Recruiting. (1918, February 15). *The Evening Herald*, p. 5.

Rendell, W.F. (1921, October 22). [Letter to Lieutenant N.G. James]. The Great War Military Service Files Database. The Rooms Provincial Archives, St. John's, NL, Canada. https://www.therooms.ca/sites/default/files/james_noel_g_0-171.pdf .

Report of the Department of Militia. (1919, March 31). http://collections.mun.ca/PDFs/cns/ReportoftheDepartmentofMilitiaMarch31st1920.pdf

Report of the Department of Militia. (1920, March 31). http://collections.mun.ca/PDFs/cns/ReportoftheDepartmentofMilitiaMarch31st1920.pdf

Riggins, S.H. & Buchanan, R. (Eds.). (2019). *Creating a university: The Newfoundland experience*. ISER Books.

Riggs, B. (Ed.). (2007). *Grand Bank soldier: The war letters of Lance Corporal Curtis Forsey*. Flanker Press.

Roberts, E. (Ed.). (2014). *A Blue Puttee at war: The memoir of Captain Sydney Frost, MC.* Flanker Press.

Rompkey, B. & Riggs, B. (Eds.). (2006). *Your daughter, Fanny: The war letters of Frances Cluett, VAD.* Flanker Press.

Sandland, T. (1983). *Something about bicycling in Newfoundland.* Dicks and Company.

Scotland and the Newfoundlanders. (1925). *The Veteran*, 4(4), 27–29.

Scott, C. (2017). *Holding the home front: The Women's Land Army in the First World War.* Pen and Sword.

Scott, H.E. (2016). "Their campaign of wonton attacks": Suffragette iconoclasm in British museums and galleries in 1914. *The Museum Review*, 1(1). http://articles.themuseumreview.org/vol1no1scott

Scott, W. (1917, April 16). [Telegram to Governor W.E. Davis]. World War One Records—Office of the Colonial Secretary Fonds (GN 2.14.217). The Rooms Provincial Archives, St. John's, NL, Canada.

Scottish war brides—happy Newfoundland soldiers. (1919, February 27). *The Evening Telegram*, p. 8.

Sedition. (1918, May 16). *The Evening Telegram*, p. 4.

70 year old volunteer. (1917, August 6). *The Evening Telegram*, p. 2.

Sharpe, C.A. (1988). The "race of honour": An analysis of enlistments and casualties in the Armed Forces of Newfoundland: 1914–1918. *Newfoundland and Labrador Studies*, 4(1), 27–55. https://journals.lib.unb.ca/index.php/NFLDS/article/view/616

Sharpe, C.A. (2015). Recruitment and conscription (Canada). In U. Daniel, P. Gatrell, O. Janz, H. Jones, J. Keene, A. Kramer, & B. Nasson (Eds.), *1914–1918 online: International encyclopedia of the First World War.* Free University. 10.15463/ie1418.10670

Simmons, P. & Davies, A.H. (Eds.) (1920). *Twentieth Engineers, France: 1917–1918–1919.* Twentieth Engineers Publishing Association.

Slackers in high places. (1918, February 13). *The Evening Telegram*, p. 4.

Slackers in the pen. (1918, July 16). *The St. John's Daily Star*, p. 8.

Smallwood, J.R.S. (1973). *I chose Canada: Light of day*, Vol.1. Macmillan.

Smith, J. (1872). *Humorous Scottish Stories*, Vol. 3. Oxford University Press.

Some early recollections. (1950, April 4). *The Western Star*, p. 2.

Spare our blushes, friend. (1918, March 9). *The Twillingate Sun*, pp. 1–2.

Splendid spirit of patriotism. (1917, October 25). *The St. John's Daily Star*, p. 2.

Stacey, A.J. & Edwards Stacey, J. (2012). *Memoirs of a Blue Puttee: The Newfoundland Regiment in World War One*. DRC Publishing.

Stanley, L. (2004). The epistolarium: On theorizing letters and correspondence. *Auto/Biography*, 12, 201–235. 10.1191/0967550704ab0140a

Stewart, H. (1917, December 24). [Letter to Major W.F. Rendell, Chief Staff Officer]. The Great War Military Service Files Database. The Rooms Provincial Archives, St. John's, NL, Canada. https://www.therooms.ca/sites/default/files/stewart_henry_618.pdf

Stewart, M. (2016). *Voices of the forest: A social history of Scottish forestry in the twentieth century*. John Donald.

Sutherland, D. (1991). "The men went to work by the stars and came home by them": The experience of work in the Newfoundland woods in the 1930s. *Newfoundland Studies*, 7(2), 143–72. https://journals.lib.unb.ca/index.php/NFLDS/article/view/1030

Sutherland, D. (1992). Newfoundland loggers respond to the Great Depression. *Labour/Le Travail*, 29, 83–115. http://www.lltjournal.ca/index.php/llt/article/view/4836

Sutherland, D. (1995). *We are only loggers: Loggers and the struggle for development in Newfoundland, 1929–1959*. [Unpublished doctoral dissertation]. Simon Fraser University, Burnaby, BC.

Tennyson, B.D. (2013). *The Canadian experience of the Great War: A guide to memoirs*. Scarecrow Press.

The Florizel inquiry. (1918, March 15). *The Evening Telegram*, pp. 3, 7.

The Forestry battalion. (1919, March 19). *The Evening Telegram*, p. 4.

The Forestry Companies: Meeting of Patriotic Association last night. (1917, April 17). *The Evening Telegram*, p. 8.

The King's cinema. (1918, April 27). *Perthshire Advertiser*, p. 4.

The non-receipt of parcels. (1917, November 28). *The Western Star*, p. 2.

The responsibilities of peace. (1919, February 4). *The Evening Telegram*, p. 4.

The white feather. (1916, November 29). *The Evening Telegram*, p. 7.

Thistle, D. (1917). Newfoundland Forestry Companies. *Newfoundland Magazine*, *1*(2), 32–33.

Thoms, J.R. (1967). The sawmill pioneers of Newfoundland. In J.R. Smallwood (Ed.), *The Book of Newfoundland* (Vol. 4, pp. 417–29). Newfoundland Book Publishers.

Thoms, J.R. (1975). Twenty-six notable men: King Cole of Badger. In J.R. Smallwood, *The Book of Newfoundland* (Vol. 6, p. 157). Newfoundland Book Publishers.

Those lieutenants. (1918, July 22). *The Evening Advocate*, p. 6.

Timewell, H.A. (1918). *List of men discharged*. Newfoundland First World War Correspondence—Forestry Company, Drafts General (RG38-D-9, 437, M-6-18-1). Library and Archives Canada, Ottawa, ON, Canada.

Tragedy of the Tay. (1918, July 10). *Perthshire Advertiser*, p. 2.

Vance, J.F. (2015). Commemoration and the cult of the fallen (Canada). In U. Daniel, P. Gatrell, O. Janz, H. Jones, J. Keene, A. Kramer, & B. Nasson (Eds.), *1914–1918 online: International encyclopedia of the First World War*. Free University. 10.15463/ie1418.10617

Victory Regatta ends tragically. (1919, August 14). *The Evening Telegram*, p. 1.

Wallace, A. (1903). *The heather in lore, lyric, and lay*. A.T. De La Mare.

Walsh, V.S. (1918, January 2). A denial. *The Evening Telegram*, p. 6.

Warr, P. (2015). *Sheffield's Great War and beyond, 1916–1918*. Pen and Sword.

Will be ostracized. (1918, July 17). *The Evening Telegram*, p. 5.

Windermere's message. (1916, July 21). *The Evening Telegram*, p. 4.

Wilson, B. (1897). *The tenth island, being some account of Newfoundland, its people, its politics, it problems, and its peculiarities*. Grant Richards.

Woodford, W.J. (1930). A true incident. *The Veteran*, *8*(4), 58–59.

INDEX

ABOUT THE AUTHOR

Photo courtesy of
Patricia Singer

Ursula A. Kelly is John Lewis Paton Distinguished University Professor at Memorial University of Newfoundland, Canada. Her interdisciplinary research is within the areas of cultural studies and critical education.